The Swiss, the Gold, and the Dead

JEAN ZIEGLER

The Swiss,
the Gold,
and the Dead

———

TRANSLATED FROM THE GERMAN
BY JOHN BROWNJOHN

Harcourt Brace & Company

NEW YORK   SAN DIEGO   LONDON

First published in German as *Die Schweiz, das Gold und die Toten*
in 1997 by Bertelsmann Verlag.

Quotation from Bertolt Brecht is reprinted courtesy of Arcade Publishing, New York,
New York. Copyright © 1927 by Universal-Edition A.G., renewed in 1955
by Bertolt Brecht. Translation copyright © 1979 by Stefan S. Brecht.

Library of Congress Cataloging-in-Publication Data
Ziegler, Jean, 1934–
[Schweiz, das Gold und die Toten. English]
The Swiss, the gold, and the dead : how Swiss Bankers helped
finance the Nazi War Machine / Jean Ziegler ; translated from the
German by John Brownjohn.
p.   cm.
Includes bibliographical references and index.
ISBN 0-15-100334-3
1. World War, 1939–1945—Destruction and pillage—Europe.
2. World War, 1939–1945—Confiscations and contributions—Europe.
3. Holocaust, Jewish (1939–1945)   4. Banks and banking—Corrupt
practices—Switzerland.   5. World War, 1939–1945—Economic
aspects—Germany.   6. World War, 1939–1945—Reparations.
7. Germany—Foreign relations—Switzerland.   8. Switzerland—
Foreign relations—Germany.   I. Title.
D810.D6Z5413   1998
940.53'494—dc21   97-36497

Text set in Sabon MT
Designed by Trina Stahl
Printed in the United States of America
First U.S. edition
A C E F D B

This book is dedicated to

my friend Andreas Freund,
painter and journalist, who was born at Breslau in 1925,
interned at Camp Gordola, Canton Ticino, in 1944–45,
and died in Paris on November 17, 1996;

and to

Maurice Bavaud, the Swiss theology student
who made an unsuccessful attempt on Adolf Hitler's life in 1939.
Born in 1916 at Boudry in Canton Neuchâtel, Bavaud was guillotined
in Moabit Penitentiary, Berlin, at 6 A.M. on May 18, 1941.

Contents

Preface

———

Many of Switzerland's so-called world-war generation are still alive. My father belonged to it, and so did my mother. Hundreds of thousands of armed men guarded our frontiers for years, ready to give their lives in battle against the Nazi barbarians. Hundreds of thousands of women assisted them by performing their arduous daily tasks in the home, on the land, and in the auxiliary services.

All of them steadfastly believed that Hitler refrained from invading Switzerland only because he stood in fear of its army's strength and fortitude. The German General Staff had, they believed, been deterred by General Henri Guisan's avowed intention of blowing up the Alpine tunnels. Many members of the wartime generation continue to cherish this misapprehension.

The somber, threatening years 1939–45 live on in my memory. I seldom saw my father in the early days of the war because he was an artillery officer and, like many other Swiss of his age, stationed on the frontier. I recall a Sunday in June 1940. As ever when my father came home on furlough, my mother, my sister, and I went to meet him at the railroad station. He always alighted from the last car, the splendid red epaulets and brass buttons on his officer's uniform glittering in the sunlight. We generally ran to meet him before he got down on the platform, but on this particular day an invisible shadow seemed to hold us back. He came toward us with heavy tread, then halted a few feet away. Making no attempt to embrace us in the usual way, he looked at each of us in turn and said, "Paris has fallen." I detected tears in his eyes. From his tone of voice, he might have been announcing the end of the world.

Still in first grade, I naturally didn't know where Paris was or what role it had played in the history of human liberty. I did, however, grasp that a disaster of unimaginable proportions must have occurred.

Curiously enough, this catastrophe gave me back my father, whom I saw far more often in the future. Switzerland was now completely encircled. On July 25, 1940, the Bundesrat and our mild-mannered, melancholy commander in chief, General Guisan, resolved to pull back our troops from the frontier and establish an impregnable "redoubt" in the Alps.

This was a somewhat brutal decision, because it amounted to leaving two thirds of our territory and almost the whole of our population at the mercy of the Nazi hordes, while planning to defend the Alpine snowfields, glaciers, and crags to the last man.

Since Thun, my birthplace, lay at the foot of the Alps and, thus, at the entrance to the redoubt, my father was often able to come home. By a fortunate coincidence, he commanded the fortress of Beatenberg, an artillery base concealed in some granite mountains overlooking the eastern shores of the Lake of Thun. This fortress was designed to deny the enemy access to the northern route into the redoubt.

My father, whose gentle, expressive eyes contrasted with his powerful physique, was a man of great intellectual ability. He did not feel particularly at home in the society into which he had been born. He loved his family, his books, and his study on the second floor of our home. He seldom went out except to visit the castle, which housed the premises of the district court over which he presided, or to go off on one of his long, solitary mountain treks. He believed in the Swiss Confederation, its army, and the constitution.

Like all his generation, he was disgracefully misled by the rulers of his country.

My book is not an investigative report. When the governments of great powers have failed for fifty years, a lone individual can accomplish nothing. My book is not a wholesale indictment of Swiss bankers, either. To repeat: ours is a land devoid of raw materials, yet we're now the world's second wealthiest country in terms of per capita income. Our raw material is money—foreign money, whatever its source. As a Swiss citizen, I myself benefit from a high standard of living, from the crumbs that fall from the table of the mighty. I have no wish to be ungrateful.

I avow myself a member of the nation of guilty innocents and innocent guilty. I belong to that nation, but the story of the Nazis' looted gold and the proceeds of the Holocaust have tainted it to a degree that I can no longer stomach.

Any theory of collective guilt is profoundly repugnant to me. Collective guilt exists as little in Switzerland as it does in Germany or Austria. Not every gnome acted as a fence for the Nazi executioners, just as not all Swiss industrialists were partners of the SS and not all Swiss border guards accomplices of the Gestapo. Nevertheless, certain Swiss were responsible for what our country did during the period 1939–45—or in the case of Jewish refugees, omitted to do—and I propose to name them.

Let no one come to me and claim that it's easy to criticize with hindsight—that later generations are incapable of understanding or judging their precursors. "Ziegler was still a young child when the war was raging in Europe. What can he know of the fears that haunted Swiss ministers whose job it was to govern a small country encircled by Fascist armies? Doesn't he realize that we would all have starved if the gentlemen in Berlin hadn't kindly allowed us to import wheat from Argentina via the port of Genoa? Does this rabid sociologist have any conception of the Wehrmacht's positively traumatic superiority? Of the cynicism of its high command, which had designs on the Alpine tunnels? Given that Europe was dominated by a madman, how could we have preserved our courage and integrity?"

Unlike my sociological works, this book is clearly subjective, expressive of my great love for my country, the anger and fascination with which I view the aberrations of its mighty, and my hopes for a better Switzerland created by our children. I have no desire to hurt anyone, and that includes the families of those whom I criticize in these pages. My book is an *essai d'intervention* in Sartre's sense: a weapon, a trial intervention.

The gold looted by Adolf Hitler and his henchmen, much of which is still in Switzerland, does not differ in essence from the blood money held by major Swiss banks in the private accounts of the Zairean ex-dictator Joseph Désiré Mobutu. Millions of men, women, and children were driven to their deaths by Hitler's licensed thieves. Hundreds of thousands of children die annually of disease and malnutrition in what was Zaire and elsewhere in Africa, in Asia and Latin America, merely because Mobutu and his fellow tyrants despoiled their countries with the aid of Swiss financial sharks.

I do not wish my grandchildren to feel the same horror, fifty years hence, when they discover that the vast wealth of their native land is being nourished by drug barons' capital and blood money deposited there by rapacious Third World dictators.

This book is intended as a weapon against the inherent guiltlessness of the Swiss and their inability to rue the past. Its purpose is to stimulate awareness and help consciences to rise in revolt: in short, to enlighten.

Introduction

Take note: there are heinous

deeds over which no grass grows.

JOHANN PETER HEBEL

1. Swiss Amnesia

LAKE GENEVA IS BATHED in glorious fall sunlight. The trees are a glowing patchwork of red, yellow, and orange, the sky is clear as crystal, the peaks of the Savoy Alps beyond the southern shore glitter in the sun. The foothills of the Mont Blanc massif have acquired a dusting of fresh snow during the night.

It's Monday, September 30, 1996, and I'm sitting in the Geneva-Bern express as it speeds through the vineyards of Lavaux, high above the lake's northern shore. The vines are gilded with sunlight.

I've spent the weekend preparing my parliamentary speech, answering innumerable phone calls from concerned fellow citizens, and polishing my documentation with two friends from a private bank in Geneva. I'm now endeavoring to marshal my notes, continually distracted by the magnificent scenery.

A big Swiss flag, white cross on a red background, is flying over the Bundeshaus in Bern: the parliament of the Swiss Confederation is in session. The major debate about "dormant Jewish bank accounts" and Nazi gold held in Swiss bank vaults is scheduled to begin at 2:30 P.M.

The atmosphere is unusually agitated—I can see that as soon as I enter the lobby. My parliamentary colleagues are standing around in clusters, whispering together. Of the journalists present, some are talking heatedly into their cellular phones, others protesting loudly, others simply shaking their heads in disbelief. Thomas Reimer, the German TV correspondent in Switzerland, is looking utterly disconcerted. "It can't be true!" I hear him mutter.

The parliamentary usher, Herr Bigler, resplendent in his green uniform and gold chain, comes over to me. Bigler and I are on friendly terms. "I'm sorry," he says sheepishly, "you won't be speaking today. The debate is off."

I can't believe my ears: over the weekend, with the support of the party whips, the speaker has decided to bar a general debate. The only authorized participants will be Foreign Minister Flavio Cotti and one picked spokesman from each parliamentary group. The elected representatives of the people must hold their peace. I go storming up to the rostrum and lodge a vehement protest.

Speaker Jean-François Leuba, a Lausanne lawyer, seems puzzled by my indignation. His rosy face registers profound surprise, his response strikes a reproachful note: "You surely don't want us to make an exhibition of ourselves in front of all these foreigners?"

Yes, there they are, our enemies: foreign journalists.

The Bundeshaus, a palatial edifice dating from the turn of the century, houses a huge, paneled debating chamber built like an amphitheater. The lower tiers are occupied by parliamentary representatives, vote counters, interpreters, secretaries, ushers, and members of the government. Situated high above, and separated from them by protective balustrades, are the seats reserved for the public, the press, and the diplomatic corps.

The two press stands are thronged with American, British, French, and German journalists. High up in the spectators' stand, foreign television companies have set up batteries of cameras, microphones, and lighting equipment directly opposite the speaker's chair.

Seated top right in the diplomats' stand, surrounded by their advisers, are the Israeli and U.S. ambassadors, Gabriel Padon and Madeleine Kunin. Born into a Jewish family from Zurich, Kunin emigrated to the United States after the war.

Jean-François Leuba resembles a cardinal of the Roman Curia as painted by Tiepolo. A roly-poly figure, he moves with a mixture of agility and gravitas. His wrinkled face is illumined by a pair of cheerful, lively eyes. He radiates composure and dignity, believes in the purity of the pure in heart. Doubt is alien to him. Leuba hails from the "Pays de Vaud," the canton that remained under Bernese sovereignty from the middle of the sixteenth century until invaded by Napoleon's troops in 1798. Obedience runs in his blood.

Swiss members of parliament are not subject to any law relating to conflicts of interest. Many of my fellow parliamentarians earn hundreds of thousands of francs a year in their capacity as board members of major banks and the firms dependent on them.

They're looking quietly confident. No criticism will be voiced today; it seldom is.

Speaker Leuba's censorship was fully justified. The journalists themselves were to blame for squelching the debate. Their articles in recent weeks had made anything but pleasant reading.

Der Spiegel of Hamburg (no. 38, 1996): "Hitler's willing fences: in exchange for stolen gold, the Swiss National Bank and the Bank for International Settlements financed the Nazis' wars of aggression."

"Switzerland, the Thieves' Den. . . ." Thus the title of an analysis of Swiss complicity in Nazi war crimes published by the *Frankfurter Allgemeine Zeitung* on September 26, 1996. The same newspaper a week earlier, this time ironically: "When reality surpasses any detective story...." As for *Die Zeit*, it stated on September 13, 1996, that Switzerland had finally been overtaken by "the long shadow of the Holocaust."

The same edition of *Die Zeit* also disclosed, with relish, that Hitler had kept his personal account at the Bern branch of the Union Bank of Switzerland, and that his royalties from *Mein Kampf*, administered on his behalf by SS Lieutenant Colonel Max Amann, had flowed there from 1926 until the end of the war.

American and British newspapers were behaving even worse. The *New York Times* had written of the "Swiss Neutrality Lie," and the London *Evening Standard* of September 13, 1996, trumpeted, "Swiss neutrality: just an excuse to get rich." A Labour member of parliament had risen in the lower house and branded the Swiss Confederation "the pariah of Europe." The *Financial Times* of September 9, 1996, derisively stated that the Swiss government's previous attempts at self-justification were merely a feverish but futile exercise in "damage control."

Even our own press adopted an unwontedly critical stance. *L'Hebdo*, French-speaking Switzerland's leading weekly, stated: "But for Switzerland's assistance, Germany would have been defeated by October 1944.... Switzerland actively assisted Nazi Germany by keeping the Nazis' north-south lines of communication open via the Gotthard [Tunnel], supplying them with large quantities of precision material, optical instruments, etc., and laundering their stolen assets, in particular by changing looted gold into useful foreign exchange."

Indignant voices were also raised in Zurich, the country's financial metropolis. *Die Weltwoche* (no. 40, 1996): "Why the banks are failing to cope with the past: lemmings on the brink of the abyss." The same edition presented another analysis devoted to looted gold and "dormant assets" entitled, "How unique was the gnomes' rapacity?"

Cash (nos. 39 and 40, 1996), Switzerland's foremost financial organ, commented: "Greed knew no bounds. As late as March 1945 the Swiss National Bank was procuring looted gold from

Germany. With the aid of bribery." And again: "The Bundesrat [the government] lied about ... Holocaust funds: [they] deceived Parliament, kowtowed to the banks." Another *Cash* headline story: "Helvetia's war profiteers: But for Switzerland's gold turntable, the war in Europe would have ended much sooner."

Sonntags-Blick, which belongs to the Ringier media group, is Switzerland's biggest newspaper by far. Here is Frank A. Meyer, Ringier's chief executive and star columnist, writing with characteristic trenchancy on September 22, 1996: "Switzerland turned back Jews fleeing from the Nazis at the border, thereby sending them to their deaths. She readily accepted and laundered the gold the Nazis extracted from dead Jews' teeth."

Who is promoting this international flood of revelations? Fanatical anti-Swiss? Veteran ex-Communists with an unbridled hatred of Swiss banks? Young, muddleheaded, left-wing extremists stubbornly entrenched in their opposition to capitalism?

No, the almost exclusive fountainhead of this documentation, which has been gushing continuously ever since the early summer of 1996, is the U.S. government. Investigators working for the Senate Banking Committee, as well as the World Jewish Congress, have unearthed, and continue to unearth, vast amounts of incriminating documentary evidence from Washington's war records, and they are feeding it to the world's press with great regularity.

New York is home not only to the biggest Jewish community in the world but also to many intellectuals of critical disposition and varied origins. These people had long been calling for a full investigation of Nazi crimes, and economic crimes in particular. Foremost among those who espoused this cause were two U.S. legislators from New York, Republican Senator Alfonse D'Amato (chairman of the Senate Banking Committee) and Democratic Representative Carolyn Maloney of the 14th District, Manhattan's Upper East Side. Nothing in the American political system is more effective than a "bipartisan plea," or resolution supported by both the major parties.

On January 3, 1996, the House of Representatives and the Senate unanimously adopted a resolution calling for full disclosure of war crimes. I cite the following extracts:

(1) During the 104th Congress, Americans commemorated the 50th anniversary of the conclusion of the Second World War and the end of the Holocaust, one of the worst tragedies in history;

(2) it is important to learn all that we can about this terrible era so that we can prevent such a catastrophe from ever happening again;

(3) the cold war is over;

(4) numerous nations, including those of the former Soviet Union, are making public their files on Nazi war criminals as well as crimes committed by agencies of their own governments;

[...]

(7) this year marks the 30th anniversary of the passage of the Freedom of Information Act;

(8) agencies of the United States Government possess information on individuals who ordered, incited, assisted, or otherwise participated in Nazi war crimes;

(9) some agencies have routinely denied Freedom of Information Act requests for information about individuals who committed Nazi war crimes;

[...]

(11) it is legitimate not to disclose certain material in Government files if the disclosure would seriously and demonstrably harm current or future national defense, intelligence, or foreign relations activities of the United States, and if protection of these matters from disclosure outweighs the public interest of disclosure;

(12) the disclosure of most Nazi war crimes information should not harm United States national interests.

[...]

It is the sense of Congress that United States Government agencies in possession of records about individuals who are alleged to have committed Nazi war crimes should make these records public.

Under concerted Republican and Democratic pressure, President Bill Clinton signed the War Crimes Disclosure Act. This piece of legislation not only opened up the last secret archives of World War II, but also created an efficient investigative machine, authorized the setting up of agencies, and approved a budget. In short, it provided that hitherto unpublished documents relating to Nazi war criminals and their (willing or unwilling) accomplices could be subject to expert examination and also noted by the public at large.

Peter Bichsel adduces in *Die Zeit* an important and plausible explanation for Clinton's signature on the War Crimes Disclosure Act: "President Clinton is probably the first President of the United States not to have a Zurich bank account."[1]

Where the investigation of Switzerland's gold-laundering and its commercial and financial assistance to Nazi Germany are concerned, paramount importance attaches to two American secret service authorities.

Henry Morgenthau, Jr., was the real driving force behind the worldwide economic blockade against Hitler, which he organized together with Churchill (and London's Ministry of Economic Warfare). It was Morgenthau who set up the Board for Economic Warfare and the Treasury Department's own secret service. In 1943 he organized the Safehaven Program, an intelligence campaign against German commercial "fronts," German businessmen operating abroad, and foreign—mainly Swiss—corporation lawyers, trustees, and bankers in the Nazis' service.

The second source of the American intelligence documents that are now supplying information about the ways and means whereby Switzerland financed Hitler's wars of aggression is the so-called Dulles network.

Notes are on pages 291–303.

In 1942, Allen Welsh Dulles, a wealthy and politically experienced Wall Street lawyer, was assigned to set up an espionage station in Switzerland by William J. Donovan, head of the OSS (Office of Strategic Services), America's foreign intelligence service.

At dawn on November 8, 1942, after an adventurous journey by way of the Bahamas, the Azores, Lisbon, Madrid, Perpignan, and Marseilles, Dulles alighted from a French local train at Annemasse, on the French-Swiss border. It was the day of the Allied landing in North Africa, and Hitler's response was to occupy the South of France. Aside from some bomber pilots shot down and on the run from the Germans, Dulles was the last American to reach Switzerland overland through enemy territory.[2]

The French police and customs officers at the railroad station were already sharing their hut with members of the Gestapo, but a customs officer who belonged to the Resistance helped Dulles to cross the frontier to Geneva.

Dulles established his OSS base at 23 Herrengasse, high above the river Aare in the old quarter of Bern. Officially designated "special assistant" to the U.S. ambassador in Switzerland, he was an unusual kind of spy—one who sought popularity rather than anonymity. His personal contacts with Donovan and President Roosevelt were soon the talk of the town.

Dulles met with all and sundry in the bar of the Hôtel Bellevue, the Du Théâtre restaurant, and his office in Dufourstrasse. A Wall Street lawyer of international repute, he maintained excellent relations with the presidents of the major Swiss banks, the international businessmen who purchased raw materials for Hitler, and the Bern, Basel, and Zurich corporation lawyers who served as straw men for the Nazis worldwide. Inside information was regularly deposited at Herrengasse by numerous Swiss bank employees who disapproved of their bosses' business methods.

The *secret* OSS network, by contrast, was run by Gerry Mayer, Dulles's senior assistant. A sophisticated code that was never cracked, by either the Gestapo or Germany's military intelligence, known as the Abwehr, enabled Dulles to conduct almost nightly telephone conversations with OSS headquarters in Washington.

An important role in the clandestine network was played by two exceptional women, both of whom became (in succession) Dulles's lovers. Mary Bancroft, a Massachusetts intellectual who divided her time between Zurich and Ascona and had studied for her doctorate under the Zurich psychologist Carl Gustav Jung, handled the couriers from the French Resistance organizations. Wally Toscanini, Countess Castelbarco, daughter of the anti-Fascist conductor Arturo Toscanini, supervised communications with, and payments and supplies to, the partisans of northern Italy. Both were women of charm, intelligence, and courage.

Thanks to the two networks—the system of public, social contacts and the secret espionage organization—Dulles very soon obtained extremely accurate and detailed information about almost all the financial, commercial, and arms deals transacted between Switzerland and the Third Reich.

Of the many hundreds of people who served Dulles as informants, one was of special importance: Hans Bernd Gisevius, Abwehr agent and German vice-consul in Zurich. Having been assigned by Admiral Wilhelm Canaris to build up the Abwehr's base in Switzerland, Gisevius possessed highly detailed information about nearly every Swiss banker, lawyer, arms dealer, manufacturer, exporter, trustee, and others in the Nazis' service.

A lanky Prussian, Gisevius was elitist and conservative, snobbish and reactionary, but he was also an efficient spy. Furthermore, he despised Hitler and his cronies, whom he regarded as uncouth, uncivilized boors intent on Germany's destruction.

Gisevius turned up at Herrengasse one night, unannounced but bearing a message from the head of German military intelligence: Canaris requested Dulles to help negotiate a separate peace between the Allies and the German Resistance movement.

Although Roosevelt rejected this proposal, Gisevius continued to supply Dulles with invaluable information until the war ended.

When Dulles transferred his affections from Mary Bancroft to Countess Castelbarco, the former became an intimate friend of his Prussian informant—but continued to work for Dulles. She died in New York on January 19, 1997, at the age of ninety-three.

Thanks to the Clinton Administration's War Crimes Disclosure Act and the congressional resolution, the most secret documents preserved in the archives of the U.S. Treasury Department and the OSS will now be published.

Speaker Leuba perpetrated his act of censorship on September 30, 1996, not only because the public gallery in the Bundeshaus was occupied by "hostile foreigners," but also for another, deeper reason: suppressing the past is a tradition in Switzerland. Free speech, or even mild criticism, has always been taboo, especially when someone threatens to raise the subject of Switzerland's abetment of Nazi war crimes. Here are a few examples from the past:

In April 1946 the U.S. Secret Service published a list of thirty-four Zurich lawyers alleged to have administered and later misappropriated assets and bank accounts stolen from Holocaust victims by the Nazis. Zurich's legislature, the Cantonal Council, appointed a fact-finding committee. This convened in secret under the chairmanship of Hans Pestalozzi, a liberal (Free Democrat). He himself was a corporation lawyer on the American list.

In June 1949, Walther Böckli, a Social Democratic cantonal councilor, called for a public debate on the committee's report and the underhanded dealings of "treasonous, Frontist, and National Socialist lawyers." The Zurich government opposed this and imposed strict censorship: the parliamentary debate was prohibited, and no word of it reached the public, either in Zurich or abroad.

By order of Zurich's Cantonal Court, the Bar Association examined nine cases (out of thirty-four) for possible breaches of "trust and integrity." Three lawyers were disbarred, but this inquiry, too, was held sub rosa.

Early in the 1980s, stories about Swiss financial skullduggery during World War II began to appear in the international press, and the board of the National Bank was compelled to respond. Its archivist, Robert Urs Vogler, drafted a report innocuously entitled, "Gold Transactions Between the Swiss National Bank and the German Reichsbank, 1939–1945." The report was couched in extremely cautious language. The introduction reads as follows: "Between 1939 and 1945 the National Bank acquired billions in gold from the German Reichsbank. These transactions attracted critical crossfire—especially from the Allies—less on account of their magnitude than because there was a suspicion, even during the war, that the German gold came partly from German-occupied territories, and that the Reichsbank had requisitioned it in gross contravention of international law."[3]

Robert Urs Vogler is a respected scholar. His report was technically a matter of public record, yet all public discussion of it, whether in the press or in parliament, was stifled. The board of the National Bank censored it, and Vogler resigned his post as archivist.

A final example of officially prescribed amnesia: Hans Ulrich Jost, who teaches modern history in the philosophico-historical faculty at Lausanne University, has pioneered critical research into the history of Switzerland during the period 1933–45. "Intimidation and Withdrawal 1914–1945" was the innocuous-sounding title of his contribution to a collection of essays published in 1983.[4] This piece, almost a hundred pages long, contained two pages of political dynamite. Jost wrote them after a friend of his, who worked at the Federal Archive, had come across some surprising documents and brought them to his attention. They embodied the following information.

Switzerland was now [in 1940] integrated de facto into the Reichsdeutsch economic area. . . . It is estimated that, in the years

1941–42, 60 percent of the Swiss munitions industry, 50 percent of the optical industry, and 40 percent of the engineering industry were working for the Reich. . . .

Swiss industrial exports to the Reich were not fully offset by German deliveries: the Swiss Confederation granted Berlin loans, or so-called compensating credits. . . . By the war's end these credits amounted to 1,119 billion Swiss francs. . . .

Where the Reich was concerned, Switzerland fulfilled an important function in the gold market. Germany needed foreign currency in order to purchase strategic raw materials, even from allies like Romania. Most countries, including neutrals such as Sweden and Portugal, declined to accept German gold, so the Reich's gold and foreign exchange transactions could be effected with Switzerland alone.

In 1943, gold reserves to the value of 529 million Swiss francs were exchanged for freely disposable foreign currency. All this took place under the supervision of the National Bank and with the express consent of the Bundesrat. . . . A substantial proportion of German gold was looted gold; in particular, gold that had been seized from the victims of the concentration camps. The Swiss authorities were aware of the problem posed by this stolen gold. . . . They took refuge behind the ludicrous argument of Swiss neutrality. They thought themselves obliged to accept this gold without demur. This kind of service was surely a trump card that would guarantee Switzerland's continued existence. . . . Let us leave it an open question whether the preservation of independence—which was much diminished in any case—may be justified by means of actions that are morally so questionable.

Jost was subjected to a hail of abuse, police inquiries, and bureaucratic chicanery. The then federal minister of finance, Georges-André Chevallaz, himself a historian of repute, the *Neue Zürcher Zeitung*—in short, everyone in Switzerland possessed of status, prestige, and influence—cried bloody murder. Jost was branded a shameless, un-Swiss heretic.

His consternation lingers to this day. In October 1996 Jost was interviewed by the editors of *Die Zeit*, the Hamburg weekly, about the ostracism he had endured almost thirteen years earlier. He testified that, although he was a university professor and an air force lieutenant with 2,600 flying hours to his credit, the federal police had kept him under surveillance, tapped his phone, and suspected him of subversion.[5]

And now, in September 1996, the parliamentary debate on Swiss complicity with Hitler had been officially stifled—authoritatively stifled on the ground that our national past could not be discussed in front of foreigners.

2. The Defensive Alliance

WHY THIS INCAPACITY FOR remorse? Why this steadfast, persistent rejection of self-criticism in a fascinating land where four great cultures have coexisted for centuries, where free speech is revered and morality, tolerance, and fidelity to the truth are cherished?

Do all Swiss hate foreigners? Is the entire nation hostile toward outsiders? Are they xenophobic—racist even? Of course not. In Switzerland as elsewhere, there exist a few demented individuals who daub swastikas on cemetery walls and hurl firebombs into buildings occupied by political refugees, but they are a matter for psychiatrists and the police, not a political problem.

For centuries now, one Alemannic and three Romance cultures have coexisted on Switzerland's 16,000 square miles of territory. Their relationship is that of more or less friendly neighbors—so why do the Swiss fear foreigners? Why, in referendums, have they so often reaffirmed their desire for isolation? In 1986 the citizens and cantons of Switzerland rejected UN membership. In 1992 they voted simply on whether to join the European Economic Zone. They refused the European Union. The Swiss want no institutional relations with this European superpower dominated by German Catholics.

Denis de Rougemont states in his *Mémoires d'un Européen:* "Switzerland is not a country—it is a defensive alliance."[6] He is right. Historically, the Swiss Confederation came into being through the slow, gradual, organic amalgamation of regions, valleys, free imperial towns, former subject territories, and insurgent communes. The Swiss tree began to sprout at the end of the twelfth century. It attained its full height six centuries later, in the middle of the nineteenth century.

The Swiss have resisted change at every stage in their history. They have always done the diametrical opposite of the nations around them. The great feudal monarchies of Europe arose at the end of the eleventh century and experienced their heyday in the fourteenth and fifteenth centuries. The Swiss, by contrast, threw out their indigenous or foreign feudal overlords and set up cooperative, self-governing communities—more precisely, peasant states. These grew up first in the Gotthard massif and then in the valleys to the north, east, and west. Later the rebellious communes of the so-called free imperial towns and cities formed an alliance with the regions in the Mittelland. The internal organization of these social formations was often wholly diverse: the peasant states of central Switzerland were governed by the direct democracy of the rural community, whereas the towns were dominated by guilds or patriciates. For six long centuries, the sole purpose of the Confederation has been cooperation against outsiders, reciprocal military assistance against attacks by the powerful feudal monarchies beyond the Jura and the Rhine, and joint defense of local rights and freedoms.

Swiss asynchronism persisted during the nineteenth century, when sovereign, centrally governed nation-states were consolidating themselves all over Europe. Once again, the Swiss did the exact opposite: they created a federal state that is primarily a federation and hardly a state. The constitution of 1848, which is still in force today, leaves important sovereign rights with the cantons: taxation, education, jurisdiction, police powers, and others. The Confederation exercises only those functions explicitly assigned to it by the cantons under the constitution. Each canton has its own elected government and parliament. I know colleagues who decline to stand for the federal parliament. They prefer to remain cantonal councilors because, as they see it, genuine policy-making is carried on at canton level only.

The preamble to the Swiss federal constitution reads thus: "In the name of Almighty God, the Confederation, being desirous of reinforcing the alliance between the confederates and of preserving and promoting the unity, strength, and honor of the Swiss nation, has adopted the following constitution. . . ."

Thus the Swiss nation is an alliance between largely autonomous peoples, each of which possesses its own language and culture, religion and history. It is a confederation whose unity is dependent solely on outside pressure—an association formed for joint self-defense.

A European myth suggests that the Swiss Confederation subsists on its multiculturalism. This multiculturalism is a fiction, however. It does not exist. Although the great Romansh, French, Alemannic, and Italian cultures coexist within a very small area, light-years separate a winegrower on the shores of the Lake of Geneva from a shepherd in Uri, a Luganese corporation lawyer from a monk in Sankt Gallen, a hunter in the Bernina Alps from a Basel chemical worker or a Zurich bank clerk.

Switzerland is a defensive association, not a nation-state in the usual sense. We need foreigners, who alone prevent the Confederation from breaking up. But we demonize them in order to reinforce our alliance from within. In Bern, my native canton, the word "foreigner" is never used without an attributive adjective: di cheibe Usländer ("damned foreigners").

To the Swiss, xenophobia is not only historically logical; it is an inherent necessity.

3. Hubris

SWITZERLAND ESCAPED WORLD WAR II by virtue of shrewd, active, organized complicity with the Third Reich. From 1940 to 1945 the Swiss economy was largely integrated into the Greater German economic area. The gnomes of Zurich, Basel, and Bern were Hitler's fences and creditors. What exactly are gnomes? The dictionary definition: "A race of diminutive spirits reputed to inhabit the interior of the earth and to be the guardians of its treasures." The last five words are peculiarly apt.

In 1943, when the Allies began their terrible saturation bombing of German cities and industrial and mining centers, Switzerland remained Hitler's only unscathed industrial area: one in which, without prejudice to the Third Reich, munitions, precision equipment, optical instruments, and many other items of military importance continued to be manufactured. The Bührle-Oerlikon armaments firm delivered its last consignment of rapid-fire guns to the Wehrmacht in April 1945.

Why this complicity? The customary, semiofficial answer: because the Swiss had no alternative. They had been hemmed in by the Fascists since 1940. Hitler's pressure on Switzerland was irresistible.

Were the gnomes of Zurich victims of Nazi extortion? The records tell a different story. The overwhelming majority of senior bank officials, whether salaried under public law (at the National Bank) or privately remunerated (by the major banks), were willing accomplices and eager henchmen.

Hubris was at work—unbridled, soul-destroying greed and the (well-founded) hope of raking in exceptional profits in an exceptional situation. Many economic historians attribute the worldwide and impressive financial strength of the big Swiss banks to their wartime profiteering.

While Europe was subsiding into rubble and ashes, the Swiss National Bank's gold and foreign exchange reserves were mounting in a gratifying manner.

Throughout their history there have always been those who warned the Swiss against presumption. At the end of the fifteenth century, in a cave near Ranft on the Flüeli, high above the Lake of Lucerne, there lived a wise man, St. Nikolaus von der Flüh. He cautioned the Swiss, who had become embroiled in European (especially Lombardic) power politics, against rampant hubris and counseled humility and discernment. He urgently advised them "not to plant the fence too far away."

The Swiss ignored their prophet and plunged into a war of conquest. They allied themselves with the French king, the German emperor, and the pope, and dreamed of annexing Lombardy. Disaster overtook them in 1515, twenty-eight years after Nikolaus von der Flüh's death, when their dreams of great-power status were drowned in blood at the battle of Marignano.

In 1939 Switzerland's financial oligarchs were gripped by the same hubris that had set the Swiss authorities on the road to disaster at the end of the fifteenth century. Lured by the prospect of exorbitant profits, the banks could not resist the Nazis' offers.

"Nothing costs people more dearly," wrote Friedrich Dürren-matt, "than a cheap freedom."[7] Hitler presented the Swiss with a cheap freedom. Today, half a century later, they are paying a high price for it.

The hubris that gripped Swiss bankers in 1939 has never let go of them. The bank vaults of Zurich, Basel, Bern, and Lugano have become a kind of sewage system into which flow streams of filthy lucre from all over the world. The major Swiss banks are internationally powerful. They continue to rake in astronomical profits from looted gold, flights of capital, and "fencing" transactions. No longer called Hitler or Himmler, Göring or Rib-bentrop, their clients have names like Mobutu, Ceauşescu, Hassan II, Saddam Hussein, Abu Nidal, Duvalier, Noriega, Traore, Suharto, Eyadéma, Campaore, Marcos, and Karadžić. Thanks to the funds flowing in from these and other murky sources, Switzerland—though devoid of indigenous raw materials—is now the second richest country in the world. The World Bank measures wealth by per capita income. On its list of world rankings, Switzerland runs the United Arab Emirates a close second.

As early as the beginning of the 1950s, Friedrich Dürrenmatt indignantly complained that "Switzerland wanted to emerge guiltless from the war." He was angered by the discrepancy between the image of a small country under outside pressure and the (self-concocted) myth of "a history inflated to heroic dimensions."[8] Dürrenmatt likened Switzerland to a girl who works in a brothel but wants to remain a virgin. Having played whore to the Nazis in World War II, Switzerland is now trying to persuade us that it remained chaste—a tall order.

A parson's son from Konolfingen in Emmenthal, Dürrenmatt knew the location of the roots of Switzerland's living lie and the identity of its spiritual fathers: Jean Calvin and Ulrich Zwingli. Calvin, the Picard theologian who founded Europe's first theocratic republic at Geneva in 1536, published the *Institutes of the Christian Religion*. "All is grace," declared Calvin. Predestination governs the life of nations and individuals. Affluence is a mark of divine approval. Human beings cannot be guilty vis-à-vis other human beings, only before God, and then only when they oppose providence and reject predestination.

The Swiss are a friendly, peace-loving nation dominated by one particular desire: to slough off their guilt.

That British foreign secretary, Malcolm Rifkind—what was he really after? What does President Clinton want? What are they getting at, all these American journalists, these British members of parliament, these representatives of the World Jewish Congress? Why *should* we be guilty? Just because we escaped the war? Just because Hitler—divine predestination be praised!—was an Austrian who ran amok in Germany, not Switzerland?

In the stage adaptation of Dürrenmatt's *The Trial*, the play opens with the finale. Traps is dead, and the love-crazed prostitute Justine and Judge Wucht are seated on his coffin. Traps eventually emerges from the coffin, and the comedy begins at the beginning.

He is both acquitted and convicted by the same court. Everything is in a state of flux. Judge Wucht holds forth as follows: "In a world of *guilty innocents* and *innocent guilty,* fate has quit the stage and chance has taken its place." In other words, predestination.

No one has ever bettered Dürrenmatt's shrewd and accurate portrayal of the subconscious of Switzerland's great and good, their hubris and abysmal hypocrisy. Now, in 1997, disaster has finally struck: the foreigners have opened Pandora's box.

Well, it's out now: we're ensnared. Arrogant shrugs won't do any good, far less flat denials, because the Americans are in possession of intelligence reports filed by Allen Dulles, who lived and spied in Bern for a time during the war. The World Jewish Congress, too, with the backing of former British Foreign Secretary Rifkind and the Senate Banking Committee, has since the summer of 1996 been publishing almost weekly reports about the Jewish refugees who were shunted across the Swiss border, straight into the hands of SS murderers, and about the looted paintings and tons of jewelry that were sold off on behalf of Heydrich, Göring, and Himmler by Swiss art galleries in Lucerne, Basel, and Ascona.

Are our sins catching up with us? Not yet. After all, investigations are still at an early stage. The game isn't up.

The financial sharks are already closing ranks. Swiss bankers remain dangerous, even on the brink of the abyss. The spokesman of the Swiss Bankers Association, Heinrich Schneider, affected to be unconcerned. Writing in the *Handelsblatt* (September 13–14, 1996), he referred to the British Foreign Office's "so-called disclosures" and declared that the documents emanating from Washington and London appeared to be "diversionary maneuvers." As a rival financial center, he blustered darkly, Switzerland was being subjected to a vindictive campaign by the major U.S. banks....

Robert Studer is president of the Union Bank of Switzerland, our country's most powerful private bank. When confronted by foreign journalists with secret U.S. documents attesting the presence in Swiss bank vaults of "dormant" Jewish-owned assets worth millions, Studer contemptuously retorted that they amounted to "peanuts" and were unworthy of discussion.

The bank bosses have every right to feel confident. Major Swiss banks operate in a highly professional manner. The profits from Nazi gold are not simply lying around in their vaults; they have been invested and reinvested, laundered and relaundered by way of financial establishments in Liechtenstein, "mailbox firms" in the Caymans, and dummy corporations in Luxembourg. The vanished Holocaust funds have long ago been converted into real estate and portfolios under new names. They have been sold, reinvested, and resold as the state of the market prescribed.

Who, after half a century, would be capable of tracing the tortuous routes taken by these vast, vanished fortunes? Many of them have long been incorporated in the undisclosed reserves of public and private Swiss banks, insurance companies, trust companies, and financial institutions, or in the personal estates of corporation lawyers. At all events, Heinrich Schneider wishes the sleuths of the World Jewish Congress the best of luck.

Six separate investigations were in progress at the beginning of 1997:

1. Pursuant to a "Memorandum of Understanding" dated May 2, 1996 (see Appendix, p. 282), the Swiss Bankers Association and the World Jewish Congress have jointly established a "Committee of Eminent Persons" under the chairmanship of Paul J. Volcker, former chairman of the United States Federal Reserve Board. Performed with the aid of international auditors, its task is to unearth the so-called ownerless Jewish assets (securities, foreign exchange accounts, shares in real estate, precious metals, art treasures, jewelry, and so on) held by Swiss banks. The World Jewish Congress is acting in an official function: in 1992 the state of Israel entrusted it with the worldwide search for all the missing assets belonging to Jewish victims of the Nazis. The chairman of

the World Jewish Congress, Edgar Bronfman, estimates that "ownerless" assets worth around ten billion dollars are slumbering in Swiss bank vaults.

2. A Federal Act (see Appendix, p. 284) has provided for the appointment of a historians' committee charged with investigating the whereabouts of German-looted gold and moneys belonging to Holocaust victims held in Swiss bank vaults. Their work is funded by a budget of five million Swiss francs. Bank secrecy is annulled with respect to the period 1933–45 and of both categories of assets. The historians' committee is to remain in operation for five years.

The federal resolution is peculiarly Swiss in character: only government-selected historians are granted access to all the archives. These handpicked individuals can investigate, technically speaking, but the authorities are to decide what documents they publish.

This triggered a heated debate in historical circles, and rightly so. Professor Jörg Fisch *(Neue Zürcher Zeitung,* November 8, 1996) called for absolute freedom of research and publication and accused parliament and government of having "a dubious conception of the truth." It would, he said, be proper to open up the records completely and entrust supervision of the results to the public, not the state. The government stood firm, however: it alone would determine who should investigate and what names and documents should be disclosed to the public.

3. Speaking on behalf of the U.S. State Department, Nicholas Burns announced on October 4, 1996, that his superiors proposed to set up without delay a historians' committee of their own. On President Clinton's instructions, this would first comb the State Department's records for 1933–45 for information relating to the commercial relations between Swiss banks and the Third Reich, and then trace the whereabouts of missing assets deposited in Switzerland by Holocaust victims and others murdered by the Nazis.

4. October 18, 1996: documents unearthed in Washington

proved that Switzerland had concluded a secret agreement with Communist Poland in 1949. Under this agreement Switzerland assigned the Polish Communists Swiss bank accounts belonging to Polish Jews murdered by the Germans—and Poland returned the money to indemnify the Swiss banks and businesses in Warsaw, Kraków, and other cities, that had been expropriated by the new Communist regime.

Franz Egle, press officer of the Swiss foreign ministry in Bern, published a vehement protest the next day. The usual story: Washington's charges were unfounded. They constituted yet another intolerable attack on Switzerland concocted by the Senate Banking Committee and the World Jewish Congress. Twenty-four hours later the international news agencies received, from an American source, the text of the secret correspondence between the head of the Swiss delegation, Ambassador Max Troendle, and his Polish opposite number. Not for the first time, honest Franz Egle had been too quick to issue a denial.

October 23, 1996: Foreign Minister Flavio Cotti appointed a special board of inquiry. Its task: to examine all agreements between Switzerland and Communist, Eastern European countries concerning the use of murdered Jews' Swiss bank accounts to offset the expropriation of Swiss private property.

Denial is not, perhaps, the right word. The Bern authorities' technique is subtler and more complex. They want—honestly, truly, and in all good faith—to admit the truth, but they cannot do so under outside pressure. They would lose face in front of "all these foreigners," so they start by disputing the facts and defer their acknowledgment of the truth until later.

Bronfman of the World Jewish Congress puts it this way: "The Swiss are fighting us every centimeter of the way."[9]

5. Gizella Weisshaus is a sixty-six-year-old New Yorker of the Jewish faith. A Romanian-born survivor of Nazi genocide, she lost her parents and her six brothers and sisters in Auschwitz. On October 3, 1996, Mrs. Weisshaus filed a suit against Swiss banks in a New York court. Her attorney, Edward Fagan, is directing a

so-called class action suit against three major Swiss banks, the SBG (Schweizerische Bankgesellschaft, or Union Bank of Switzerland), SKA (Schweizerische Kreditanstalt, or Crédit Suisse), and SBV (Schweizerischer Bankverein, or Swiss Bank Corporation). Fagan is demanding twenty billion dollars' compensation for their complicity with the Third Reich. A class action suit is open to all concerned, and Fagan is presently mobilizing the creditors of the major Swiss banks. A second class action, in which several hundred creditors are participating, has also been launched against them by Michael Hausfeld, and Hausfeld isn't just any old attorney. A star lawyer in the class action field, he won millions in settlements from several multinational companies.

It is highly probable that a whole avalanche of similar demands for compensation will descend on the Swiss gnomes in the next few years, and that the competent courts—wherever they may be—will institute thorough inquiries. In October 1996, for example, President Carlos Menem of Argentina announced that all his country's archives and bank records will be accessible to such investigations. It is anybody's guess what offenses will come to light in the course of all these hearings.

6. In the fall of 1996 the chairman of the U.S. Senate Banking Committee threatened to reopen the bilateral negotiations between Switzerland and the Allies that led in May 1946 to the so-called Washington Accord. At that time the U.S., British, and French governments compelled Switzerland to hand over German assets as "war reparations" and pay compensation for looted gold.

Senator Alfonse D'Amato asserted that the Swiss had lied in 1946 and that the sum remitted bore no relation to the assets they actually held. Under international law, therefore, the Washington Accord was invalid.

The Swiss government indignantly rejected any form of renegotiation, but D'Amato isn't any Tom, Dick, or Harry of a politician. He happens to be chairman of the Senate Banking Committee and an influential member of the Finance

Committee—and committee chairmen wield considerable influence within the U.S. political system.

Swiss banks administer forty percent of all private funds deposited abroad, a considerable proportion of which derives from U.S. pension funds. Billions of dollars of their assets are annually invested—thanks to the competence of Swiss financial administrators—in Geneva, Zurich, Bern, and Basel. The Senate committee could legally prohibit these transactions at any time.

The course of 1998 will reveal whether Switzerland possesses the political, public relations, and economic muscle to resist the American demand (and any retaliatory measures arising from it). The official attitude is equivocal. On the one hand, there is a strong desire to get at the truth. Flavio Cotti and his six fellow ministers are hopeful that the historians' committee appointed by parliament will shed light on Swiss bank vaults in the next five years. Headed by Thomas Borer, a thirty-nine-year-old senior diplomat with experience of America, a task force is busy fending off attacks from abroad and combating unjustified international criticism. Ironically enough, the task force was initially based at 18 Bundesgasse in Bern, once the home of the consular protection service, whose principal function is to repatriate the corpses of Swiss who have died abroad.

On the other hand, Bern is spending taxpayers' money on vastly expensive American public relations firms and corporation lawyers. It is their task to try to win over the U.S. public, press, and Congress, and to prepare the members of the task force for congressional interrogation.

The Swiss government is also striving to combat foreign pressure, especially from the World Jewish Congress, by other, more discreet means: it is buying military equipment in Israel. In December 1966, for example, the defense ministry signed a contract worth 153 million Swiss francs with Elta Electronics, an affiliate of Israel Aircraft Industries, for some of the latest monitoring equipment developed by Israel to counter enemy radio communications.[10]

The accounts held in Zurich's Bahnhofstrasse are shrouded in secrecy. Only the gnomes themselves know what skeletons are buried in their vaults and what ghosts haunt the corridors of Crédit Suisse, the Swiss Bank Corporation, and the Union Bank of Switzerland.

At the time of this writing, we have no precise knowledge of the facts that will be unearthed by the international committees of inquiry, the national historians' committee, and the U.S. Senate's investigators. We cannot tell, either, what political battles waged during court hearings or behind the scenes will emerge into the glare of publicity. Light will be shed on every last corner, but no one yet knows exactly what it will reveal.

One glorious day in the late fall of 1996, I was invited to lunch by the Swiss ambassador to one of our larger neighbors. The trees in the embassy grounds resembled bursts of flame in the warm sunlight, and heavy-laden barges were gliding down the nearby river.

The ambassador, a shrewd and independent-minded but worried man, had spent the morning with his aides: fresh attacks on Switzerland had just appeared in the press of his host country. We discussed possible reactions.

"The thing is," the ambassador said suddenly, "we Swiss are innkeepers. . . ." Noticing my surprise, he went on, "It's true. The Swiss—and by that I always mean the German Swiss—make excellent innkeepers. They run their establishments admirably, welcome and wait on anyone who can pay. The service is excellent. And when the meal is over and the guests sit back and start philosophizing over coffee and brandy, the host discreetly retires to the back room, where he quietly and self-effacingly counts his francs."

Everything in this picture fits: the excellent service, the ecumenical hospitality (all are admitted, provided they can pay), the self-effacement, the discretion, and the lack of interest in any form of philosophical, ideological, or even theoretical debate. The counting of francs and love of bookkeeping, too, are right. Every aspect of the picture is right save one: many such innkeepers are very unpleasant customers—regular bandits, in fact.

To revert to the aforesaid Polish bank accounts and the bilateral compensation treaty between Bern and Warsaw in 1949: the Polish Communists had just nationalized or expropriated Swiss-owned businesses, bank accounts, property, agricultural enterprises, and other assets worth approximately fifty-three million Swiss francs. Being anxious to maintain good financial relations with Zurich (and obtain development and other loans), the Poles were prepared to indemnify Swiss companies and private individuals. But war-ravaged Poland had no foreign exchange.

For that reason, a secret protocol was added to the official, bilateral agreement. The Swiss government undertook to get the Swiss banks to liquidate the "dormant" accounts of Polish, mainly Jewish, citizens, and to transfer these assets—which consisted of convertible foreign exchange—to Poland.

The secret protocol prescribed that the Swiss francs and gold bars, securities, and other assets held in Polish accounts be remitted to Warsaw's central bank. It further prescribed that these assets be passed on to the descendants of the account-holders.

The Poles, for their part, undertook in the same protocol (strictly speaking, an exchange of secret letters between the two delegations) to indemnify the dispossessed Swiss in foreign exchange.

In concrete terms, the Poles paid these compensatory sums into an account, designated the "N" account, which the Swiss National Bank had opened at the headquarters of the Polish National Bank in Warsaw.

Switzerland liquidated its "dormant" Jewish accounts and remitted the funds to Warsaw—but omitted to enclose a list of the account-holders' names. This made it quite impossible to pay out these repatriated moneys to descendants of the victims of Nazi mass murder. It goes without saying that Switzerland *did* enclose a scrupulously accurate list of all the Swiss who had been dispossessed by the Warsaw regime and were thus in line for compensation. Everything went like clockwork. It was a strictly secret, highly efficient operation.

On the instructions of our federal government, Swiss banks quite illegally liquidated the Polish (Jewish) accounts—whereupon the Communist authorities in Warsaw promptly sent the money back (plus deliveries in kind) so as to indemnify the dispossessed Swiss.[11]

What can Ambassador Troendle, who headed the Swiss delegation in 1949, have thought when signing this secret protocol? Innkeeper Troendle probably told himself: "The Polish Jews are long dead, and so are their children. They aren't going to turn up in Zurich and ask to draw on their accounts. Besides, my protocol is secret."

But Innkeeper Troendle reckoned without the World Jewish Congress and the U.S. Secret Service.

PART ONE

Hitler's Swiss Fences

———

...What is here?

Gold! Yellow, glittering, precious gold!

[...]

Come, damn'd earth,

Thou common whore of mankind, that puts odds

Among the rout of nations, I will make thee

Do thy right nature.

WILLIAM SHAKESPEARE, *Timon of Athens*

1. The Bankrupt Führer

WORLD WAR II CLAIMED fifty-two million lives and maimed millions of men, women, and children, driving millions more from their homes. It laid waste to whole tracts of territory, and razed cities in Europe and Asia. It did not, however, devastate the entire world. However frightful the slaughter instigated by Hitler, it never encompassed the whole planet. Almost all of Africa south of the Sahara,[1] the whole of Southern Asia, extensive land masses in Central Asia, the Australian subcontinent, New Zealand and some Pacific archipelagoes, North and South America—all these were spared the bombs and shells that rained down elsewhere.

Throughout the six terrible years that elapsed between Poland's invasion by Fascist armies and the atomic mass murder of the populations of Hiroshima and Nagasaki, the inhabitants of our planet continued to trade, exchange commodities, transfer capital, make payments and purchases, and engage in insurance, transportation and service transactions spanning frontiers and continents.

It is impossible to understand the Swiss Confederation's central role in the slaughterhouse that Continental Europe had become unless we bear in mind the worldwide processes of commerce and freight traffic and the concomitant foreign exchange and barter transactions.

World War II was, first and foremost, a war of aggression and conquest waged by Hitler against Western and Eastern Europe, the Balkans, the Soviet Union, the Scandinavian countries, and the British Isles.

Hitler's Japanese accomplices waged similar wars of aggression in China and Thailand, Indochina and Burma, and throughout the Pacific as far as the western approaches to the North American continent. Fascist Italy invaded the countries bordering the east coast of the Adriatic. All these campaigns and raids by the Axis powers were resisted by the nations under attack.

But another war raged throughout the war years. Scarcely perceptible compared to military developments, deportations, industrial genocide, tank battles, and cities reduced to cinders, this was the trade war. Extremely complex and little documented, it was —unlike the military conflict—genuinely world-embracing. Indeed, some eminent historians believe that its influence on the outcome of World War II was greater than the battle of Stalingrad or the invasions of North Africa, Sicily, Southern France, and Normandy. More decisive, too, than the air war over Britain.[2]

Hitler was never, even at the height of his military successes, able to enforce German independence of the world market. Whatever areas rich in raw materials he conquered in Europe, the Near East, or the Balkans, his munitions industry was always reliant on purchases from outside the German sphere of influence. The economic historian Willi A. Boelcke cites some impressive examples, and the following particulars are taken from his book on the subject.[3]

In 1943 Hitler's munitions industry had to obtain the whole of its manganese requirements from abroad. Manganese is an exceptionally resistant metal, grayish white in color, that melts at a temperature of 1240° Centigrade. When combined with steel, it produces an alloy of extreme hardness and density used in the manufacture of gun barrels. Most of Germany's manganese was imported from Spain.

Likewise imported was 75.9 percent of its tungsten, also called wolfram. Tungsten—a word of Swedish derivation—is a grayish metal, somewhat softer than steel, that fuses at 3842° Centigrade. Steel-and-tungsten alloys are used in aircraft manufacture. The world's biggest producer of tungsten is China. But in 1943 that country was indirectly at war with Germany, having been at grips with the Japanese invaders since 1937, so Hitler had to procure his tungsten from Portugal. His munitions industry imported more than 4,000 tons of it in 1943 alone.

Stainless steel is an alloy steel containing chromium, a metallic element essential to the manufacture of ball bearings and used to reinforce shell cases. In 1943 the German munitions industry imported 99.8 percent of its requirements. Here again, however, the main producers were inaccessible. South Africa lay within the British sphere of influence and the Soviet Union was the Third Reich's enemy. That left only Turkey.

What applied to rare metals of strategic importance applied equally to common iron ore. The German munitions industry was structurally deficient even in this respect. German agents spent the entire war scouting around for iron ore, 40 percent of which came from Sweden. The Third Reich obtained diamonds for machine tools from South America, large quantities of oil from Romania, aluminum from Africa and Asia.

The German munitions industry's dependence on foreign supplies of vital strategic raw materials was a crushing burden.

Those who bought on the world market had to pay world market prices, not in homemade Reichsmarks, but in foreign currency and, above all, in gold.

To wage an effective war Hitler needed a banker—more precisely, a respectable, reliable, neutral banker. After running out of foreign exchange and almost out of gold by the time he attacked Poland, Hitler's invasion of the Low Countries, Norway, and other peaceful, prosperous states yielded a sizable quantity of assets. These had to be laundered by an unsuspicious accomplice, and the accomplice, in turn, had to introduce the stolen goods into the world market under a new identity.

The same went for the thousands of gold teeth extracted from their murdered victims by SS thugs, for the detainees' looted wedding rings and articles of jewelry, and for the personal fortunes purloined all over Europe by the Nazis' so-called foreign exchange protection teams.

Switzerland's financial sharps in Zurich, Basel, and Bern fenced and laundered the gold stolen from the central banks of Belgium, Poland, Czechoslovakia, Holland, Luxembourg, Lithuania, Albania, Norway, Italy, and elsewhere. It was they who financed Hitler's wars of conquest. Switzerland, the world's only neutral financial center of truly international standing, accepted Hitler's looted gold throughout the war years in payment for industrial goods or as bullion that was fenced and laundered and exchanged for foreign currency or traded off in other financial centers under new, "Swiss" identity. But for Switzerland's financial services and the willing fences of Bern, the zealous gnomes, Hitler would not have been able to wage his rapacious wars of conquest. Swiss bankers supplied him with the requisite foreign exchange. It was they who financed his wars of aggression.

When Hitler launched his invasion of Poland, the Third Reich was practically bankrupt, an almost financially ruined dictatorship that bluffed the democratic world with a monstrous show of military force. Economically speaking, Germany was down and out when Hitler made his bid for world supremacy.

On January 7, 1939, eight months before the invasion of Poland, Reichsbank President Hjalmar Schacht handed the Führer a remarkable memorandum.[4]

From:

President of the Board of the Reichsbank

Berlin SW 111, January 7, 1939

Confidential Reichsbank Matter

To:

The Führer and Reich Chancellor

Berlin

The Reichsbank has long drawn attention to the dangers to our currency arising from excessive public expenditure and short-term credit. At the end of 1938 the monetary and financial situation has reached a danger point that renders it our duty to request decisions[....] Accordingly, the overall German monetary situation appears to be as follows:

1. Externally: The Reichsbank possesses no more gold or foreign exchange reserves. The deficit of imports over exports is rapidly increasing. Exports are no longer attaining the value of the imports we require. The reserves formed by the annexation of Austria and the calling-in of external securities and domestic gold coins have been used up. The vast majority of the foreign exchange certificates for imports issued by the supervisory authorities are now no longer covered by guaranteed receipts of foreign currency, and thus present a danger that they will sometime be impossible to meet for want of foreign currency. This would also eliminate our last remaining foreign credit for the importation of goods.

2. Domestically: The Reichsbank's assets consist almost entirely of government securities alone (Mefo bills [Metallurgische Forschungsgesellschaft] in the main). The central bank is completely choked with them, and will not, if called upon again by industry, be in a position to grant the requisite loans. Some six billion Mefo bills are held outside the Reichsbank. These could at any time be presented to the Reichsbank for discounting in ready cash, and thus present a constant threat to our currency. On January 1, 1933, banknotes in circulation amounted to 3,560

million Reichsmarks. This figure had risen by March 1, 1938, to 5,278 million Reichsmarks. This increase of around RM 1.7 million in over five years need not arouse misgivings as regards monetary policy because German industrial output almost doubled within the same period and embodies an increase in consumer goods as well as in the production of capital goods. In the period between March 1 and December 31, 1938, however, banknotes in circulation rose to RM 8,223 million, that is to say, not counting those required for Austria and the Sudetenland, by a further RM 2 billion. The figure has, therefore, risen faster in the last ten months than in the whole of the preceding five years.

[. . .]

Backing issued paper money with state-owned land, government bonds, etc., cannot maintain its value, as the history of the assignat economy of the French Revolution very clearly demonstrated.

While an increase in public expenditure was inevitable during our two large-scale foreign policy operations in the Ostmark [Austria] and the Sudetenland, the fact that no restraints on public expenditure policy can be discerned since the end of those foreign policy operations, and that everything tends to suggest that a further increase in public expenditure is planned, renders it our bounden duty to draw attention to its monetary consequences.

It is not our place to prove the extent to which an unrestrained public expenditure policy accords with the revenues and savings of German industry or with the social requirements of the population. It is, however, our responsibility to point out that a further strain on the Reichsbank, whether direct or occasioned by the cornering of the money market elsewhere, cannot be justified.

The undersigned members of the Reichsbank board are cognizant that they have gladly collaborated to the utmost on behalf of our ambitious objectives, but that a halt must now be called. No increase in the production of goods can be achieved by increasing the amount of paper money.

In short, the Reichsbank was at the end of its rope. Hyper-inflation and an economy backed by paper money threatened:

> The Führer and Reich Chancellor himself has publicly condemned inflation, over and over again, as foolish and futile. We therefore request that the following steps be taken:
>
> 1. The Reich, together with all other public authorities, may not undertake any more expenditure, guarantees, and obligations that cannot be effected by raising loans without disrupting the long-term capital market.
>
> 2. For the effective implementation of these measures, the Reich minister of finance must reassume full financial control over all public expenditure.
>
> 3. Price and wage control must be effectively planned. The defects that have crept in must be eliminated.
>
> 4. Calls on the money and capital market must be subject to the decision of the Reichsbank alone.

Board of the Reichsbank

Dr. Hjalmar Schacht		Dreyse
Vocke	Ehrhardt	Puhl
Hülse	Kretschmann	Blessing

Schacht's ill tidings seem all the more surprising because, from the banker's point of view, an extremely fortunate event had occurred the previous year: the Nazis had annexed Austria, abolished its national independence, and incorporated it in the Reich as a country, nation, and economic zone. The Österreichische Nationalbank was taken over, free of charge, by the Reichsbank. Its reserves amounted to some billion gold marks, but not even this injection of gold had restored the Reichsbank to health.

Schacht's message could not have been clearer. There were no gold or foreign exchange reserves left. The Reich was "on the verge of collapse," with a balance-of-payments deficit amounting to several billion marks. Thanks to a policy of unbridled public expenditure, its financial position was "alarming" in the extreme.

Germany's rearmament during the 1930s had reduced unemployment, set the wheels of industry in motion, and transformed the Wehrmacht into Europe's premier military force. It had, however, played havoc with the Reich's finances.

Willi A. Boelcke estimates that between 1933 and August 1939 the German armed forces swallowed up 51.9 percent of all public expenditure.[5]

How did Adolf Hitler react to the Schacht memorandum? He stormed and raged, beside himself with fury. Criticism of his "economic policy" was intolerable to him. He couldn't grasp that the Reich was insolvent and his war machine threatened with ruin. Hitler's brain, befogged by Aryan racial mania and Germanic Herrenvolk mythology, was quite unable to perceive the financial facts advanced by Schacht.

The Führer promptly dismissed Schacht from his Reichsbank post. Five of the seven directors were also removed, the only ones to remain in office being Puhl and Kretschmann. Hitler's new appointee as president of the Reichsbank and minister of economics was the Nazi big-shot Walther Funk. Emil Puhl became his vice-president.

An alcoholic of unstable character, Funk was financially illiterate, and his forecasts were so inaccurate that they would have bankrupted Croesus himself. But Funk was now the economic supremo of a Third Reich destitute of foreign exchange and dependent on the world market. Disaster was inevitable, especially because Funk became transfixed with awe whenever he entered the Führer's presence.

Boelcke paints the following picture of Funk:

After the outbreak of war, Funk, who made an even more diffident impression, showed himself less and less equal to his post as Reich minister of economics, which was increasingly dependent on the Four-Year Plan and the Party Chancellery. [. . .]

Whenever he was in Berlin and his capacity for work not
overly impaired by his alcoholic excesses, he would spend the
morning as Reich minister of economics in his luxurious Unter
den Linden office.

Around noon he would leave the ministry and fulfill the, to
him, far more congenial function of Reichsbank president in
the nearby Reichsbank building. When Funk went to report
to Hitler—as State Secretary Landfried noticed on numerous
occasions—he would be so impressed by the ideas Hitler evolved
that he never got around to voicing his questions at all, even
during an audience lasting several hours. Later on, too, when
visiting the Führer's headquarters, Funk the Hitler devotee proved
to be more of an enthusiastic listener.

Hitler had expounded his "financial theory" to the minister
of economics in October 1941: "He is delighted, and says that in
ten years Germany will have eliminated the burdens of war without disrupting our internal purchasing power."

The minister happily left it to his representatives or the
relevant heads of department and advisers to discuss technical
questions at the ministry in accordance with the guidelines
of the Four-Year Plan. In his ministerial office Funk surrounded himself with loyal and devoted henchmen. His former
chauffeur and friend, Horst Walter, functioned from 1938 to
1943 as head of the ministerial office and drew a head of department's salary. From 1938 onward, Dr. August Schwedler
acted as his aide-de-camp and indispensable traveling com-
panion. Being suspicious by nature, Funk never signed auto-
graphs on principle; on business trips, his aide would fob off
autograph hunters by handing out five-mark bills, which—
because Funk was president of the Reichsbank—bore his signature.[6]

Ever wary and disinclined to pit himself against the crafty
gnomes of Bern or Zurich, Funk seldom showed his face in
Switzerland. The man who dined and conversed with the bank

bosses of Zurich and Bern, the Bahnhofstrasse launderers and Paradeplatz speculators in raw materials, was Emil Puhl.

From his office on the second floor of the Reichsbank, Nazi Puhl waged a secret war on Nazi Funk. Puhl never attended tea parties at Berchtesgaden, nor was he summoned to the Reich Chancellery at night. Hand-kisses for Fräulein Eva Braun? Puhl dreamed of them, but only Funk was invited to take tea with the Führer. Only he was privileged to pat Hitler's Alsatian bitch and, attired in lederhosen, to enjoy the view of the Obersalzberg under SS protection. Puhl did not belong to Hitler's inner circle. His only knowledge of the gangster supremo derived from the radio and mass rallies.

Puhl was an ambitious, industrious, levelheaded individual. Photographs of him also convey a faintly mocking impression. Whether or not he detested his boss, he certainly envied him. Anyone who took tea with the Führer and fantasized with him about the forthcoming thousand years of Germanic world domination belonged to a milieu that had always been inaccessible to the aspiring Emil Puhl.

But Puhl's word was law in the palatial old Reichsbank building in the heart of Berlin. He was its secret ruler. He maintained excellent relations with Himmler, Heydrich, and the Economic Administration Department of the SS. It was Puhl who proposed that the SS executioners open a deposit account at the Reichsbank for the "dead men's gold" from Auschwitz, Maidanek, and Buchenwald.

Emil Puhl was the sympathetic friend and wily business partner of the gold barons of Bern. He knew and appreciated their competence. He was alive to the gnomes' mentality, which had taken shape over the centuries—above all, to their abysmal hypocrisy. He knew that they would perform any service, however cynical, if only they were supplied with an adequate pretext, a "moral" argument in its favor.

He played like a virtuoso on the Swiss neutrality myth. He provided the bank tycoons of Zurich with the fictions they needed to justify their business dealings to themselves and allay their consciences.

Puhl made the gnomes' task easier. Alfred Hirs, a director general of the Swiss National Bank, always took great pleasure in making a note of Puhl's visits to Switzerland. Preserved in the National Bank's archives, several of his memorandums record Puhl's comments on the international situation, Germany's war aims, and the European New Order. They also convey covert admiration on Hirs's part.

The specific nature of bankers was a matter of concern to Voltaire. As one who spent the last twenty-three years of his turbulent life in Geneva and its immediate vicinity, he viewed Calvinist bankers like an entomologist observing rare butterflies. His verdict on them: "If you see a banker jump out of the window, jump after him.... There's sure to be money to be made."

Puhl helped the gnomes to endure their hard lot. The opportunistic, competent type of functionary described by Hannah Arendt,[7] he had joined the Reichsbank as a young man in 1913 and gradually ascended the professional ladder by dint of hard work, self-effacing humility, and strict obedience. Being canny as well, he had joined the Nazi Party just in time.

Walther Funk, listed as one of the major war criminals, sat in the dock at Nuremberg. For unaccountable reasons, Emil Puhl was not sitting beside him. An invited witness for the prosecution, he incriminated Funk to the best of his ability.

According to Puhl, the Reichsbank president (and minister of economics) bore sole responsibility for the SS deposits of dead men's gold at the Reichsbank, for shady deals in looted gold with the Swiss, for raw-materials rackets—for everything. Vice-president Puhl had either known nothing about these things, or, if he harbored suspicions about them, had acted in good faith....

Funk was gravely prejudiced by his former vice-president's testimony on May 15, 1946: the court sentenced him to life imprisonment.

But justice of a kind did prevail. Puhl was, after all, brought before a court at a later stage and sentenced to five years' imprisonment.

Reich Marshal Hermann Göring became de facto master of the German war economy in 1939. On August 30 of that year the Führer issued an edict under which the Reich Defense Council, hitherto subordinated to the High Command of the Wehrmacht, was transformed into a ministerial committee. It comprised six members—Martin Bormann, Wilhelm Keitel, H. H. Lammers, Wilhelm Frick, Funk, and Göring—and was chaired by the last.

After the Polish campaign the Wehrmacht vigorously advocated converting the economy into an all-out war economy. Funk hesitated, being reluctant to write the Führer a memorandum and suffer the same fate as Schacht. He had no wish to attract Hitler's ire, particularly because there were widespread fears within the Party that the general public's appetite for war, which was not too great in any case, might be still further diminished by an unduly massive economic changeover and its attendant sacrifices.

Göring tackled the problem with great diplomacy and powers of persuasion. He backed the Wehrmacht's demands with Hitler and simultaneously placated the Party. The "Führer directives" instructing industry to switch over to war production were issued on November 29. Göring thereupon laid down precise guidelines under which all economic resources (labor, capital, industrial installations, and so on) not productive of vital goods and services were to be made available to the munitions industry. "The decline in nonessential production associated with this measure," he decreed, "must be accepted."[8]

It has been proved that Göring required the help of the Swiss in order to mastermind his conversion of the economy into a war economy. The good business relationship he developed with the bankers of Zurich and Bern from 1939 onward was to stand him in good stead later on. At the end of 1944 and early in 1945 he transferred his substantial personal fortune to private and cantonal Swiss banks.

Emil Puhl and Walther Funk were Hitler's most prominent contacts with the fences in Switzerland. However, the strategy of cooperation was worked out at another, higher level: the compensating credits to the tune of billions granted by Switzerland to the Third Reich, the consignments of munitions, optical instruments, precision machinery, trucks and tractors, and the foreign exchange deals and purchases of looted gold were negotiated between Reich Marshal Hermann Göring and Hans Frölicher, the Swiss envoy in Berlin.

Minister Frölicher (the Swiss foreign service had no ambassadors in those days) headed the Swiss legation in Berlin throughout the war. He was a friend and admirer of the Nazis. The Bern authorities did not share his attitude, but they needed him. Like his closest associate, Franz Kappeler, Frölicher was on friendly and sometimes intimate terms with the leading Nazi bigwigs. His relationship with Göring proved especially valuable.

We shall reencounter Hermann Göring several times in the course of this story. The Reich's number two man, he was a morphine addict and Hitler's faithful assistant. His admiration for the Führer knew no bounds: "From the very first moment I saw him, I was utterly bewitched by him." And again: "I have no conscience; my conscience is called Adolf Hitler."[9]

The Swiss operatives had chosen the right business associate.

That Swiss bankers were substantially responsible for prolonging World War II and, thus, for the deaths of unknown numbers of servicemen and civilians is confirmed by a memorandum of German origin dated June 3, 1943, drafted by Ministerial Director Karl Clodius. Entitled "Note on the current status of economic negotiations with Switzerland," it was addressed to Ribbentrop's undersecretary "with a request to forward it by teleprinter to the Reich Foreign Minister."[10]

A brief historical digression: the year 1943 marked a turning point in the war. Hitler's triumphant advance in the east had been checked and the battle of Stalingrad lost. The Soviet offensive that had been making rapid progress since January 1943 was driving back the German invaders on all fronts. In North Africa, Hitler's war was already over.

The Allies were exerting pressure on the Swiss government. No more German gold must be accepted, and exports to the Reich of industrial and precision goods and military hardware must be drastically curtailed.

Great uncertainty reigned in Bern. Should the Swiss knuckle under to the Allies and incur the wrath of their German business associates, or should they put up with the Allies' threatened countermeasures and grant the Germans' request for even larger consignments?

Part Three of this book ("Economic Warfare") contains an account of the Swiss government's decision. Suffice it here to say that on May 25, 1943, the undersecretary at the foreign ministry in Berlin sent for Frölicher and sharply criticized his government's irresolution. Switzerland's attitude, he declared, was "unsatisfactory."

Meantime, a German delegation was negotiating in Bern. In the version of it I possess, Clodius's memorandum runs to six pages. Its purpose was to present the foreign minister with a general analysis of the state of negotiations and also the importance of Swiss gold transactions and industrial consignments.

In drafting his memorandum, Ministerial Director Clodius consulted the Berlin authorities particularly interested in dealings with Switzerland, namely, the Reichsbank, the Ministry of Munitions, the Wehrmacht, and the Ministry of Transportation.

The Reichsbank's statement could not have been clearer. To quote Clodius:

The representative of the Reichsbank board stated that, even regardless of the munitions ministry's position, he could not consent ... to the discontinuance of negotiations because Switzerland represents our only means of obtaining freely disposable foreign exchange.

To be on the safe side, Clodius personally consulted the minister of economics and president of the Reichsbank:

Reich Minister Funk, whom I also questioned in person about his position, fully confirmed the statement of the representative of the Reichsbank board, and added that he could not, even for two months, forgo the possibility of effecting foreign exchange transactions in Switzerland (above all, the conversion of gold into freely disposable foreign exchange).

Wehrmacht High Command and the munitions industry authorities also made it clear how much they needed the Swiss in order to carry on the war. Clodius again:

I began by once more discussing, at a meeting of the Commercial Policy Committee attended by representatives of the Wehrmacht High Command and the ministries involved, the attitude to be adopted in the light of these circumstances. The Ministry of Munitions stated that negotiations ... cannot be broken off ... because not even limited Swiss deliveries can be dispensed with, especially in the next few months. The Wehrmacht High Command and all the other ministries cited the munitions ministry's statement and expressed themselves in similar terms.

Clodius then presented a rather pessimistic account of the state of the German munitions industry, which had evidently been hard hit by Allied bombing. Arms production was being subjected to "ever increasing strains," and the Ministry of Munitions, in particular, could not dispense with Swiss arms deliveries.

In support of its view, the Ministry of Munitions went on to state in detail that [as regards the arms contracts awarded to Switzerland] what were involved were particularly important consignments of special, technical equipment whose shortfall, especially in the next few months, would seriously affect, inter alia, the German tank and remote-control programs.

The Clodius memorandum also referred to the economic position of Germany's Italian allies. Strong German forces were stationed in Italy in the summer of 1943.

Another important aspect is the threat to our [monthly] coal deliveries to Italy. The Reich Ministry of Transportation estimates that only around half of the *c.* 470,000 tons of coal currently being dispatched to Italy via Switzerland could be conveyed there by other routes. An Italian shortfall of over 200,000 tons of coal would not, however, be tolerable, especially at the present juncture. Moreover, the other routes would be so overburdened by rerouting half of the consignments hitherto traveling by way of Switzerland that the slightest disruption of those routes would result in more substantial shortfalls.

Finally, Clodius alluded to Hitler's personal position:

At an earlier stage in negotiations the Führer decreed that negotiations with Switzerland be conducted in such a way as to lead to as amicable a settlement as possible. In the light of the circumstances detailed above, I consider it unwarrantable to advise the Führer to depart from that position.

Clodius's memorandum leaves one in no doubt that in 1943, a crucial war year, Swiss gold-laundering services and Swiss deliveries of arms and industrial goods to the Third Reich were of vital importance to Hitler's prosecution of the war.

Our present state of knowledge confirms Switzerland's complicity in prolonging World War II. But for the effective gold-laundering services provided by the Swiss National Bank, and but for Swiss arms deliveries and loans to Berlin, the war would have ended earlier—probably in 1944. Swiss bankers, in particular, were responsible for millions of deaths. (The horrifying theory that Switzerland prolonged the war has just received additional support from Stuart E. Eizenstat, U.S. Department of Commerce undersecretary, and William Z. Slany, the State Department's chief historian, in a report commissioned by President Clinton and published in May 1997: "U.S. and Allied Efforts to Recover and Restore Gold and Other Assets Stolen or Hidden by Germany During World War II.")

A case in point occurred in April 1944, when the Allied offensive in Northern Italy ground to a halt along the Rimini-Bologna-Pisa line. Large German formations entrenched in strong defensive positions inflicted heavy casualties on Allied troops. Many American soldiers in particular were killed while repelling a German counterattack in the region of Bologna.

The German units had been reequipped and were in possession of almost unlimited quantities of arms, ammunition, spare parts, and gasoline transported via Switzerland. President Roosevelt and Prime Minister Churchill made representations to Bern, but in vain. The transportation capacity, especially of the St. Gotthard rail line, had been increased by 1944 to many times its prewar figure. It was not until October 1944 that the Swiss government declared itself ready to discontinue supplies of gasoline.

2. Resistance

HITLER'S SWISS FENCES WERE motivated not by any ideological agreement with the Nazi Party or personal affection for the Führer, but by unbridled greed. Only the Swiss were prepared to buy, launder, and trade in his looted gold. For the Third Reich, the equation was a simple one: no laundered gold, no foreign exchange; no internationally disposable foreign exchange, no purchases of strategic raw materials on the world market; no strategic raw materials, no Wehrmacht. Hitler was at the mercy of his fences. In their pockets from 1940 onward, he was a powerful client, yes, but dependent on them—in other words, every banker's dream. Astronomical profits beckoned.

The Swiss National Bank directors, government ministers, senior officers, arms manufacturers, private bankers, corporation lawyers, industrial tycoons, and traders who assisted the Third Reich were not, with a very few exceptions, Nazis. Local Nazi organizations never really gained a foothold in the Swiss ruling class or in the population at large.

"Fronts" did flourish in Switzerland immediately after Hitler's legal coup d'état in 1933, and "Frontists" was the name given to the Swiss Nazis who held their inaugural meeting at the Merchants' Guildhall in Zurich in April of that year. Uniformed storm troopers guarded the hall and ejected undesirables with cries of "Harus!" *("Out!")*. Colonel Emil Sonderegger, who had helped to break the general strike of 1918, delivered a disjointed speech entitled "Order in the State." The Zurich lawyer Robert Tobler, Gauleiter of the Front, condemned left-wingers, democrats, trade unionists, Jews, Freemasons, pacifists, and liberals, and proclaimed the advent of a "New Switzerland." Several hundred Swiss army officers were confederates of Tobler's, among them Colonel Wille, influential son of Switzerland's commander in chief during World War I. The Frontists, who maintained their headquarters at the German sanitarium in Davos, were closely associated with the German Nazi Party. They dreamed of making Switzerland a *Gau*, or province, of the Greater German Reich, paraded through the streets of Zurich, and greeted one another with the Hitler salute.

Geneva's Géo Oltramare, who came from a traditional upper middle-class family, inveighed against Bern, democracy, and the Swiss Confederation. (He became a Vichy radio correspondent and was later sentenced by a Swiss court.)

Despite sporadic local election successes, mainly in the early 1930s, the Frontists never achieved a breakthrough in Switzerland. Why were her homegrown Nazis so unsuccessful?

One answer may be found in the Swiss Confederation's cultural history. Anyone dependent on Berlin—any puppet who disseminates Greater German propaganda—comes up against the Swiss immune threshold. Switzerland's spiritual and psychological relations with its powerful neighbor in the north have been strained for centuries.

To describe those relations in a nutshell is impossible. German is my mother tongue and the language of my forebears. My father, a lawyer, studied at Dresden. My paternal grandfather, a country doctor, studied at Leipzig. As a child I would hike on Sundays from Thun to Aeschi, where the novelist Ricarda Huch was living in retirement. In short, I feel an affection for the spiritual Germany of Thomas Mann, Ricarda Huch, and Bertolt Brecht, as do many other German Swiss.

But the Germany of unbridled economic, political, and (erstwhile) military power has been, and continues to be, regarded with suspicion—indeed, hostility—by the Alemannic Swiss. What applies to the Alemannic Swiss applies in equal measure to their Ticinese, Rhaeto-Romanic, and Romand fellow citizens.

The arms of the Genevese republic comprise an episcopal key on a yellow ground and a black eagle. Geneva was a free imperial city ruled by a prince-bishop. It was in opposition to the bishop and the emperor that Jean Calvin proclaimed the independent theocratic republic in 1536.

As a child during the dark years 1939–45, I heard countless proverbs and legends that expressed this ambivalent, neurotically complex relationship with Germany. One saying current at the time was full of self-mockery: "We Swiss are neutral—it's all the same to us who defeats 'di Schwobe' [the Germans]."

An anecdote of the heroic variety, but one that is historically documented, concerns a visit to some Swiss army maneuvers by Kaiser Wilhelm II. Standing on a hill in eastern Switzerland with members of the Swiss government in attendance, Wilhelm delivered the following verdict: "Your army is impressive, but mine is twice as numerous." Whereupon one Swiss minister retorted: "That being so, Your Majesty, we'll order our soldiers to fire twice."

Seventeen traitors were executed by Swiss army firing squads between 1939 and 1945. The condemned men were either Nazis or poor devils like Ernst S., an unskilled laborer from eastern Switzerland. While serving in the army he had offered the German consul at Sankt Gallen a few shells—shells that had long since been demonstrated to German arms experts and sold to the Wehrmacht by arms supplier Emil Bührle.[11] Treason is a serious offense, but Swiss traitors were remarkably few in number.

The conservatives of Geneva referred to Géo Oltramare's Fascists as "Nazillons," or lousy little Nazis. The Ticinese detested Mussolini and his local propagandists. The overwhelming majority of German Swiss regarded the Frontists as noisy beergarden bruisers and low-down, unrepentant stooges of Party headquarters in Berlin. As for Dr. Robert Tobler, the Frontists' self-appointed Gauleiter, few Swiss felt anything for him other than disgust.

Switzerland's indigenous Nazis never succeeded in taking root in any part of the country or in any social stratum, high or low.

It would, of course, be naïve to claim that the Swiss ruling class consisted entirely of impeccable democrats. Like all the democracies of Western Europe, the Swiss Confederation had its right-wing extremists and reactionary, antidemocratic social groups. Much the most important extreme right-wing movement was the Ligue Vaudoise, under its longtime leader Marcel Régamey. The Ligue, which abominated the parliamentary system and the principle of popular sovereignty, revered Action Française, the monarchist, antirepublican movement in France, and its prophet, Charles Maurras.

Marcel Régamey, a gaunt intellectual, was a strange cross between a strict doctrinaire and an elegant, dandyish playboy. His publications *(La Nation, Les Cahiers de la Renaissance vaudoise, Écriture)* were worth reading for their stylistic brilliance.

Régamey and his "Liguards" became genuinely dangerous in 1940, when Hitler's troops paraded beneath the Arc de Triomphe and Marshal Pétain engineered France's submission. Régamey, for his part, planned a coup d'état with the aid of extreme right-wing officers in the Swiss army, then manning the frontiers.

His plan was to overthrow the government, suspend the constitution, and do away with parliament and popular sovereignty. All power would be assumed by a triumvirate: Philippe Etter, a reactionary federal minister, was to become Landammann (president); Colonel Andreas von Sprecher would take over the Foreign Ministry; and the Defense Ministry would go to Brigade Colonel Roger Masson, Switzerland's director of military intelligence.

The plan failed.[12]

Régamey was a dangerous Fascist and an anti-Semite of the most sophisticated variety. One of his leading articles in *La Nation* contained the following passage: "The naturalization of the Jews has never been more than a legal fiction, because the Jew remains forever symbolic of the unassimilable foreigner in our midst.... A middle-class Jew from Donafyre [a village in Canton Vaud] may speak with a Vaudois accent and serve in the dragoons or the artillery, but he remains beneath that mask a hundred percent Jew. The smallest incident, and you will see: his Vaudois amiability will at once give way to oriental nervosity and his pleasant Vaudois accent to a guttural, characteristic lingo."

Régamey, hero of one section of the contemporary intelligentsia of western Switzerland, was also responsible for this: "I prefer, any day, the Israelite horse trader to the Israelite philosopher. Our mistrust of the Israelite horse trader is instinctive. In the case of the wise rabbi, it smacks of prejudice.... But, whether one is dealing with Einstein the physicist, Benda the literary critic, or Bergson the philosopher, the Jew will always come out in favor of subversive ideas."

Régamey's hateful tirades helped in no small measure to legitimize the Swiss government's anti-Semitic refugee policy during the period 1938–45.

Militarism was rife in the higher echelons of Switzerland's officer corps. Many of its members admired the lightning victories of the Wehrmacht (and the SS), the courage of the ordinary German soldier, and the Führer's allegedly brilliant generalship. To many senior Swiss officers, their German counterparts personified military discipline and expertise, courage and efficiency. The Swiss army sent several medical missions to the Eastern Front in support of the gallant Wehrmacht—which was, after all, at grips with Bolshevism.

The enthusiastic commander of these missions was Divisional Colonel Eugen Bircher. Rudolph Bucher, a Zurich physician and founder of the army's blood donor service, accompanied the first such team. At Smolensk he witnessed the shooting of 260 hostages by the SS. He also saw some Jewish women compelled to dig their own graves and passed some deportation trains while in Warsaw. Swiss officers regularly joined the executioners for convivial evening get-togethers at which the black-uniformed killers happily drank beer with them when their day's work was done.

These atrocities were too much for Bucher. He not only talked about them on his return to Switzerland, but also delivered lectures intended to prick his brother officers' consciences. The military authorities and the minister of defense, Karl Kobelt, promptly threatened him with Article 16 of the military code, under which a soldier could be demoted or dismissed from the service.[13]

Hitler had attacked France by way of Belgium and Holland in the summer of 1940. On June 16 General Guderian's armored columns were in process of encircling the French army entrenched behind the Maginot Line, in Lorraine, Vosges, and Alsace. Tanks adorned with the swastika entered Besançon and Dôle. The same day, the German 29th Motorized Division received what was, militarily speaking, an utterly nonsensical order: "Imperative reach Swiss frontier June 16. Report back by radio."

Three light tanks under the command of a young lieutenant named Dietrich peeled off in the direction of Pontarlier, the small French frontier town in the Franche-Comté immediately opposite Vallorbe in Canton Vaud. Dietrich, with a big swastika flag flying from his lead tank, drove at maximum speed. There being no time to obtain local maps, he requisitioned them at a newsstand. The fuel tankers had not yet arrived, so he refueled at civilian gas stations.

The breakneck drive continued for 50 miles, straight through columns of French, Polish, and Moroccan combat troops. The three German tanks shot their way through villages with their heavy machine guns, firing on bewildered French units bivouacked beside the road. Fired on themselves, they survived and raced onward. Early on the morning of June 17 Dietrich came to a frontier fence in a valley in the Jura, and flying from a hut nearby was a red flag with a white cross. At 8:20 A.M. he radioed: "Have reached Swiss border."[14] At noon the same day his division established its headquarters in Pontarlier.

Why such a headlong dash through the middle of a combat zone? Adolf Hitler was anxious to hem Switzerland in, but he failed despite young Dietrich's suicide mission.

The French government had resigned on June 16. Pétain's questions concerning an armistice reached the Führer's headquarters at Brûly-de-Pêche in southern Belgium the next day, having been relayed from Bordeaux via Madrid.

Hitler flew to Frankfurt the same evening and traveled on to Munich by train. There, on June 18, he discussed the French armistice terms with Mussolini.

Mussolini was to blame for the failure to isolate Switzerland. French mountain troops had put up a stiff fight in the eastern and southern French Alps, and the Bersaglieri failed to reach the east bank of the Rhône. Hitler's plan had misfired. Although

Guderian's tanks held the entire Jura range from Basel to Pays de Gex and Pougny, the frontier village opposite Chancy, where the Rhône flows out of Switzerland, the whole of Haute-Savoie, Faucigny, and Dauphiné remained unoccupied. Not a single Italian soldier was to be seen there.

Although the encirclement plan concocted with Mussolini had failed, Hitler still strove to seal off Switzerland. General Wilhelm List's Twelfth Army was ordered to advance on Grenoble and Chambéry. If Switzerland's western lines of communication could not be lopped off in Haute-Savoie and Savoie, German forces would at least cut the transit routes further south, if possible in Dauphiné.

Too late: General List failed as well. French resistance held firm. One example: the fortress of Bellegarde, situated high above the Rhône between Geneva and Culoz, did not surrender until a week after the Franco-German armistice came into force. (The Franco-German armistice was signed in Rethondes at 6:50 P.M. on June 22, 1940, the Franco-Italian armistice in Rome shortly afterward.)

Hitler was furious. List's army had to withdraw to the armistice line, and the complete encirclement of Switzerland seemed impossible. It did not become a reality until late in 1942, when the Allies landed in North Africa and the Wehrmacht moved into southern France. Switzerland retained its road and rail communications with free Europe for almost two years. In particular, the Geneva/Eaux–Vives–Annemasse–La Roche-sur-Foron–Annecy railroad line operated without any form of German supervision. For a while, too, trains continued to run south and west along the Geneva/Cornavin–Bellegarde–Culoz route.

Swiss railroad cars and freight trains ran unchecked as far as Sète in southern France, the free port through which Switzerland obtained its imports. Passenger and freight traffic shuttled between Geneva and Port-Bou on the Spanish frontier, whence the cars traveled on to Barcelona. Even the immigration police profited from this open route: once a week they dispatched a sealed carload of German or Austrian Jewish emigrants to Lisbon. Switzerland had not been isolated after all.

The Führer's headquarters seethed with indignation at the "gap" in Haute-Savoie. Uncertainty surrounds Hitler's future plans for Switzerland. At dawn on June 23 he visited occupied Paris accompanied by Arno Breker, his favorite sculptor. On June 24 a special directive reached Army Group C: it was to hold itself in readiness for a Spezialmission Schweiz (special Swiss mission). Hitler had failed to seal the country off. Did he now propose to invade it?

A series of documents, entitled "Operation Tannenbaum," was found in German archives after the war, all of them relating to the possible conquest of Switzerland. Conquest, in fact, is not the right word.

The German staff officer responsible for working out these military contingency plans with respect to Switzerland was Captain Otto Wilhelm von Menges, who was killed outside Stalingrad on February 2, 1943. After the war his family made his papers available to the historian Klaus Urner.

Menges drafted three different operational plans, each of which contained the following passages: "I do not believe that Switzerland will defend itself by force of arms.... It is possible, given the the current political situation, that Switzerland will peacefully accept our ultimatum, and that, once we have crossed the border, we shall quickly be able to switch to a peaceful invasion."[15]

The "correct" analysis of these documents is disputed by various eminent historians. The military specialists Hans-Rudolf Kurz and Alfred Ernst, for example, hold that Operation Tannenbaum's numerous situation maps and details are merely war games and strategic studies such as all general staffs prepare against all eventualities. Jakob Tanner, Jürg Fink, Markus

Heiniger, and others are likewise doubtful that Hitler ever meant to invade. Switzerland functioned to his entire satisfaction as the Third Reich's bank vault.

Why should he have invaded, occupied, and—in the hypothetical event of resistance—devastated such a useful country? Switzerland was valuable to him as a sovereign, internationally recognized, "neutral" state. To invade it would have been a wholly counterproductive step, the more so since Federal President Marcel Pilet-Golaz had publicly, on June 25, proclaimed Switzerland's adjustment to the "New Europe."

Henry Picker's published record of Hitler's table talk at his headquarters includes a remark he made in the summer of 1940. According to Picker, Hitler stated that Switzerland was "far more valuable" as a foreign exchange turntable, a diplomatic protecting power, an international transshipment point for secret intelligence, and a supplier of precision equipment, munitions, and strategic raw materials of all kinds, "than as a satellite." It must not be attacked under any circumstances.

Historian Klaus Urner fiercely disputes this interpretation. He contends that, far from being war-game material, the Operation Tannenbaum documents are genuine plans of attack that Hitler refrained from converting into marching orders at the very last minute. Hitler definitely meant to invade, claims Urner.

While fully recognizing Switzerland's vital services to the Reich throughout the transcontinental economic war, Urner holds that Hitler was a pathological criminal whose mind and soul were badly deranged. Although quite capable of appreciating the, to him, vital functions of the Bernese gold-launderers, intact transit routes through the Alps, and Swiss precision equipment and arms deliveries, he was just as capable of decreeing the annexation of Switzerland from a variety of motives: hatred of a small democratic country, a sinister sense of his own omnipotence, and Greater German racial mania.

From 1940 on, the Bern regime bore many resemblances to that of Vichy France: close organic financial and economic cooperation with the Reich; discrimination against Jews inside the country and on its frontiers; authoritarian government camouflaged by democratic public debate.

The Bundesrat governed largely by executive decree during the war years. Radio and press were subject to efficient censorship, and civil liberties were restricted. The general public knew next to nothing about the Bernese gold bunker or the complicity of the great and good with Adolf Hitler.

When, on June 22, 1940, France signed the armistice agreement with Germany, General Henri Guisan sent the Swiss army home. Only 150,000 of its 450,000 officers and men remained mobilized. Broadcasting on June 25 from the three national radio stations, Beromünster, Sottens, and Monte Ceneri, Federal President Pilet-Golaz proclaimed Switzerland's intention of adapting to the new Europe and urged her citizens to trust their government like a "Führer." In short, he said, times had changed and collaboration with the Third Reich represented the road to the future.

To hundreds of thousands of inhabitants of the Swiss Confederation, Pilet-Golaz's speech implied a betrayal of the popular desire for national independence and sovereignty. Even at this distance in time, it still makes unendurable reading.

On September 7, 1940, the Aktion Nationaler Widerstand ("National Resistance Campaign") was founded at Zurich. Its inaugural proclamation was signed by three men of very different provenance: Hans Oprecht, trade union secretary and publisher, an elected national councilor from Zurich, and chairman of the Swiss Social Democratic Party; August Lindt, journalist and diplomat, who later became U.N. high commissioner for refugees; and Hans Hausammann, a Swiss officer.

The proclamation read:

The new alliance of Swiss [citizens] fights for the freedom, honor, and independence of the Swiss Confederation, for freedom of the individual and of conscience, for freedom of the community on a federative basis, for government by the people, for personal responsibility, for the guaranteeing of work and bread for every Swiss, against every defeatist, wherever he may be. Being resolved and ready, I vow, at the cost of any sacrifice, to commit myself to these aims.[16]

This book devotes far too little space to the "other Switzerland," the Switzerland of resistance, of the steadfast desire for liberty, of radical criticism. The organization of anti-Nazi resistance was widespread. Army officers made conspiratorial preparations to wage an underground war if the government capitulated to invading German troops. Courageous journalists defied the official, pro-Hitler censorship of the press. Albert Oeri, liberal editor of the *Basler Nachrichten*, and Peter Hirsch, alias Peter Surava, socialist editor of *Die Nation* (not to be confused with Régamey's smear-sheet), wrote truthfully throughout the war despite threats, sabotage, and official defamation. Under Surava's editorship *Die Nation* achieved the remarkable circulation of 120,000 sold copies. He was convicted on some absurd pretext, imprisoned, and hounded from his post, but his friends fought on.[17] As for the indomitable Oeri, the citizens of Basel regularly reelected him to the National Council (the Swiss federal parliament).

Social Democrats, Communists, trade unionists, Christians, Jews, men and women of all social classes, all cultural groups and languages, opposed the government's collaborationist policy wherever and however they could.

I may have contrasted the National Resistance Campaign with the government's policy of collaboration too schematically—even erroneously. The Swiss reality of the war years (and of the present time) is infinitely more complicated.

The inaugural proclamation of the National Resistance Campaign summoned people to fight for "the freedom, honor, and independence of the Swiss Confederation," for "government by the people," "personal responsibility," and "the guaranteeing of work and bread for every Swiss."

It would be unwarranted to claim that the ministers of the Swiss government, the corporation lawyers, bankers, industrialists, and National Bank bosses condemned these demands on principle. Even Emil Bührle, the pro-Hitler arms supplier, Alfred Hirs, the National Bank director, and the other esteemed dinner-table guests of Otto Köcher, the German envoy to Bern, spoke out in favor of preserving Switzerland's honor and independence.

So why the split? Why was Switzerland divided into two camps? Why the persecution of Peter Surava? Why the constant denigration to which men like Hans Oprecht and Albert Oeri were subjected? Why, by protesting against their employers' privileged business relations with the Third Reich, did ordinary bank employees and industrial workers risk instant dismissal and, on occasion, criminal proceedings for industrial espionage? Why did they have to establish contact with Allen Dulles at his Herrengasse headquarters in secret and by night?

The Swiss ruling class possesses a coherent system of self-interpretation. This is best defined by the word "fideism." Deriving from *Summa Theologiae* by Thomas Aquinas, this term was construed by him as approval of ideas that are acknowledged to be correct but held to be impracticable.

Swiss independence, absolute neutrality, a refusal to assist the Nazi Reich, criticism of its tyranny? Although right in themselves and morally justified, desirable, and good, these were either not practicable or only partly so. Their realization was inhibited by overriding constraints.

Swiss fideism gave rise to some peculiar individual behavior patterns during World War II. One example was Max Huber, a distinguished, influential, and highly qualified professor of jurisprudence. Subjectively an unmistakable democrat and anti-Fascist, humanitarian, and philanthropist, he functioned simultaneously as president of the International Committee of the Red Cross

(ICRC) and chairman of Alusuisse, the aluminum concern whose works at Singen employed several hundred Ukrainian slave laborers bought from the SS.[18]

The divide of 1940 was a deep one, and it imperiled Swiss unity. Why? First, we must reconstruct the economic, social, and psychological situation in which the inhabitants of the little country found themselves. The Swiss heard Hitler's ravings on the radio, saw newsreel shots of brown-shirted hordes parading through German cities on the occasion of Nazi rallies and remembrance days. These spectacular parades and insane speeches aroused the deep-rooted, instinctive fear in the few of the many. The Bern regime had little difficulty in fomenting that fear and converting it—by government decree—into obedience and submission.

The Swiss Confederation does not appoint a commander in chief of the army except in wartime. Once general mobilization, or so-called active service, has been decreed, the Combined Federal Assembly (the two houses of parliament) elects a general. On August 30, 1939, it elected Henri Guisan on the first ballot and by a large majority. Guisan, a kindly, upstanding sixty-five-year-old from Canton Vaud, was a gentleman-farmer by profession. He ran Bellevue, a farm at Chesalles-sur-Oron, and had simultaneously climbed the ladder of Switzerland's citizen army until, by 1932, he was a corps commander.[19]

Official propaganda promoted Guisan into an omniscient hero, a moral authority, and a figure symbolic of national unity.

A second factor: a large proportion of the population came of farming stock and had only recently been caught up in the process of industrialization. Social conflicts were numerous and violent. In 1932, soldiers of the Swiss army had shot thirteen workers and injured another sixty-five during a peaceful demonstration in Geneva. Labor disputes were fierce, and resistance to employers' exploitation was strong. World War II and its concomitant threat to the nation furnished the ruling class with an ideal opportunity to reassert its social and ideological control over workers and employees. The families of laborers, peasants, and white-collar workers were particularly hard hit by general mobilization, and it was, of course, the humblest social categories that suffered most from the imposition of food rationing.

The ruling class waged a class war from above. Any protest aimed at poor working conditions, low wages, and economic exploitation was branded an attack on national security. Many workers remained mobilized for the full duration of the war.

The officer corps was entirely middle-class. Active service provided its members with an opportunity to reinforce the old, unjust social hierarchies. Authoritarian government and press censorship served to stifle social debate, suppress any statements that conflicted with the official view, and control refractory political movements.

The Swiss tolerance level is in many respects very low. The ruling class tolerated no qualitative opposition in 1940, nor does it do so today. But it is equally true that Swiss democracy is founded on explicit respect for divergent opinions. A puzzling paradox: the acceptance of unlimited pluralism and the existence of a regime based on consensus and unity seem mutually exclusive. But this pluralism itself is standardized, not unlimited. Only those opinions and ideas, statements and actions that refrain from questioning the system's fundamental structures, in other words, the oligarchs' supremacy and their daily pursuit of fideism, are acknowledged to be "democratic" opinions and ideas, statements and actions. Any other utterance, however well-founded, is accounted "undemocratic." Naturally enough, the system encounters fierce opposition within its standardized domain, and this opposition is attacked and suppressed to the extent that it assails and imperils the system's unjust and oligarchic foundations.

The exalting of secrecy and opacity into a moral virtue, the equating of consensus with national unity, and the standardizing of freedom of opinion—such are the three ideological pillars that

underpin "Swiss democracy." In other words, the ruling bourgeoisie, whose hard core—the financial oligarchy—is endowed
with the weapons of symbolic authority, has erected a system of
unanimity and spurious equality.

The sociologist Pierre Bourdieu supplies a convincing definition of the term "symbolic authority": "All power is symbolic
authority; that is to say, all power that succeeds in enforcing
symbols on people and passing them off as legitimate by disguis-
ing the power relationships that form the basis of its power, adds
its own power to those power relationships."[20]

This term thus defines instruments that conduce to the
same end, on a symbolic plane, as others do on a material
plane—the end in question being domination. Like their material
counterparts, these symbolic weapons have their history, institutions, and custodians. Among those who guarded them most
vigilantly between 1940 and 1945 were the censors of the mass
media.[21]

A final word on the subject of fideism: it draws a sharp distinction between "positive" and "negative" criticism.

Positive criticism is permitted, even welcomed. It is inherent
in the system. In order to function as a democracy, the regime
requires opposition, criticism, dissent—but only within the standardized domain of reality. Anyone who questions the system
itself is "pathologized."

A subtle dialectic prevails in the aforesaid domain. "Standardized" and "aberrant" behavior are not straightforwardly
antithetical. The relationship between "positive" and "negative"
criticism is complex, contradictory, and forever reversible. The
opponent of the system is primarily a troublemaker who disrupts
the celebration of the cult, an unbeliever who abruptly tears the
curtain asunder to disclose a reality that was meant to remain
hidden. He resembles the sixteenth-century Anabaptist who proclaimed, at the top of his voice, that the dignitaries of Münster
were sinners and that the world was coming to an end.

The opponent is tolerated so long as he turns up in the place assigned him at certain times and on condition that he, too, employs the ritual language expected of him by his listeners. But as soon as he starts to inveigh against public institutions and endeavors to gain access to decision-making authorities by submitting unforeseen and socially unsupervised proposals, he becomes plain dangerous and is destroyed like the Anabaptist leader Thomas Müntzer.[22]

Relevant examples abound. Peter Surava was hounded from his editorial post, convicted, and imprisoned. Diplomat Carl Lutz, who had saved the lives of tens of thousands of Jewish men, women, and children at Budapest in 1944, was severely reprimanded by his Foreign Ministry superiors three years after the war's end. Police Superintendent Paul Grüninger suffered demotion, criminal prosecution, and social ostracism for having enabled Jewish refugees from Austria to cross the Rhine into Canton Sankt Gallen.

Paradoxically, however, the powerful know in their heart of hearts that they are sinners. However strong, well-tried, and effective may be the mechanisms that erase and suppress unpleasant facts—mechanisms developed in their consciousness in the course of an unacknowledged process—there are bankers and arms dealers and their political backers who know full well that their actions are at odds with the ethics proclaimed and believed in by themselves. The Anabaptist is perceived in a fideistic manner.

To the ruling class, qualitative opposition to the federal consensus represents a threat not only to their political objectives, but also to their very existence. Consequently, they bring all the negative fixations of official society to bear on that opposition. The critic is brutally and irrevocably expelled. But singular changes occur on the unconscious plane: the condemned protester becomes the bearer of a message, and that message sows doubts. What if—in theory, beyond the bounds of what is currently practicable and feasible—the protester was right after all? The fideistic perception of reality is rooted in that doubt.

3. The Gold-laundering Machine

THE BUNDESHAUS IN BERN is an imposing sandstone edifice embellished with wondrous stained-glass windows and a wide variety of escutcheons. The symbolic, mythical figures that adorn its façade include Mother Helvetia, armed with shield and spear, and some brooding legislators of heroic dimensions, each with a cast-iron toga richly draped over his bare right shoulder. Standing in the lobby are the three original Swiss who allegedly swore the first Swiss League into being on the Rütli meadow on August 1, 1291. Massive stone figures with blank expressions and outstretched arms, they are referred to by a young and irreverent female colleague of mine on the National Council as "The Three Rapists."

The Bundeshaus stands silhouetted against one of the finest scenic backcloths in the world: the Bernese and Valais Alps.

The main frontage, with its black iron gateway and rows of lofty windows behind which crystal chandeliers shimmer when darkness falls, faces north toward the Bundesplatz, or Federal Square.

The square is ringed with banks. On the east side, the Bern headquarters of the Swiss National Bank. On the north, the stone fortress of Crédit Suisse and the Bern Savings and Loan Bank. On the west, also adorned with mythical heroes, the façade of the Bern Cantonal Bank. Glittering a few hundred yards away are the windows and marble halls of the Union Bank of Switzerland, where Adolf Hitler kept his personal account.

At the market held in the Bundesplatz every Tuesday, farmers, horticulturalists, and market gardeners from the Bernese Mittelland offer their flowers, vegetables, fruit, meat, and dairy products for sale. Slumbering far below the asphalt on which their wares are displayed are the gold reserves of the National Bank.

The Swiss National Bank is a rather complicated structure. It was founded in 1905, and its principal stockholders—aside from private individuals—are the cantons. The Confederation itself holds no stock, but exercises a monopoly on the issuing of bank notes (which it delegates to the National Bank) and nominates twenty-four of its forty board members. The three senior executives, one of whom officiates as president and another as vice president, are appointed by the government on the board's recommendation.

The president of the National Bank is based in Bern, and part of its executive office is in Zurich. By law, 40 percent of the money in circulation must be backed by actual gold bars.

Although the National Bank is a modest concern compared with the major private banking empires—in 1997 its employees numbered a little more than 500—it occupied a dominant position where the gold trade is concerned. The private banks bitterly resisted its attempts to gain a monopoly of that trade during the war. In the end a gentlemen's agreement was concluded under which the private banks accepted a ceiling price for all their transactions in gold.

Hitler launched his Western blitzkrieg on May 10, 1940. From that day on, the National Bank's premises were guarded around the clock by units of the Swiss army.

None of the countries in which Hitler and his emissaries purchased strategically important raw materials was willing to accept payment in Reichsmarks. The Germans had to pay in gold or some internationally acceptable foreign currency, preferably Swiss francs. (The same applied to the Swiss. They too wanted their exports—munitions, optical instruments, and industrial goods of all kinds—to be paid for not in Reichsmarks, but in gold or foreign currency.)

When war broke out the Deutsche Reichsbank had a deposit account with the Swiss National Bank. Legally assigned to the Bank for International Settlements (BIS) in Basel, this account was empty.

The first gold deliveries were credited to this account on January 14, 1940. Hitler had meantime invaded Poland, and his depredations in the East were beginning to yield dividends. In May of the same year the Deutsche Reichsbank opened directly a deposit account in its name with the Swiss National Bank.

Bars of looted German gold traveled either by rail or, more often, by road to the vaults in Bern. Convoys of trucks crossed the Swiss frontier at Basel. At the entrance to the subterranean vaults in Bern, which was guarded by Swiss soldiers, the boxes were transferred from the trucks to low handcarts. Then, propelled by Swiss bank officials, the gold disappeared below ground. Werner Rings was the first to provide a detailed account of the manner in which the German gold in Bern was registered and stored.[23]

The bars were counted, classified, and registered below ground, then stacked on shelves. Their "marvelous sheen" was described to me—fifty years after the event—by a witness whose eyes still shone at the recollection.

"Looted gold," incidentally, is the correct term. The Reichsbank's gold reserves were almost exhausted by 1939. In the next chapter we shall see how Hitler repeatedly strove to pass off his loot as legal gold from Germany's prewar reserves. The Reichsbank board had the bars melted down at the Prussian mint and adorned with prewar German serial numbers, but these verification stamps were false.

Some of the looted gold became the property of the Swiss National Bank, which exchanged "German" gold for the Swiss francs used by Nazi purchasing agents for their transactions on the world market. Swiss francs were the only currency acceptable worldwide throughout the war. The National Bank bosses also accepted "German" gold in payment for Swiss exports to Germany. That there was never enough gold available is attested by the fact that Swiss exports of arms and industrial goods were bought largely on credit.

The Swiss granted Hitler so-called compensating loans worth

hundreds of millions of francs. By 1945 the Nazis were indebted to the Swiss to the tune of over a billion francs.

Where another proportion of the looted gold was concerned, the National Bank acted as a transshipment point—a gold-launderer, to be exact. The Third Reich's foreign suppliers were mostly unwilling to accept German gold. Take Portugal, for instance. Although Antonio Salazar, the Portuguese dictator, declined to accept Reichsbank gold because of British pressure, his country remained one of Nazi Germany's major suppliers. The wolfram for the German munitions industry came from Portugal and its overseas territories. The Reichsbank's truck convoys delivered German gold bars to the underground vaults in Bern. German purchasing agents, who received Swiss francs in return, used them to pay the Portuguese, and the Portuguese, having delivered the wolfram to Germany, used the Swiss francs to buy the gold deposited in Bern.[24]

In 1940 the Swiss gold-launderers imposed the following scale of charges on their Nazi clients: for taking receipt of the gold (in concrete terms, for unloading the bars from German trucks and loading them onto handcarts), 0.03 pro mille; for placing them on deposit, 0.015 pro mille; and for dispatching them, 0.9 pro mille.

The largest quantities of gold bars and sacks of coins were received in 1943, the year when the tide of war turned. It was a year of misfortune from Hitler's point of view. His Sixth Army was destroyed at Stalingrad, Rommel's Afrika Korps had sustained a crushing defeat at El Alamein, and the Allied navies were gaining the upper hand, especially in the north and south Atlantic. In short, Hitler was striving harder than ever to gird himself for the final and decisive phase of the war. Arms production was going full blast, with correspondingly heavy demands for strategic raw materials from abroad and, thus, for Swiss francs, freely negotiable gold, and foreign exchange.

More looted German gold disappeared into the Bern vaults in

1943 than at any other period: gold bars and coins to the value of nearly 529 million Swiss francs.

How much looted gold passed through the Bern gold-laundering machine? It is to be hoped that the inquiries instituted by the historians' committee—and doubtless by the Volcker committee as well—will elucidate this question in the next five years.

On December 13, 1996, the obscurity enshrouding the National Bank was pierced by a ray of hope. A new board had been appointed under a new president, Hans Meyer. He displayed courage—by Swiss standards. "Our predecessors," he conceded, "made mistakes."

Meyer confirmed at the same press conference that the bank had accepted gold from Nazi Germany to the value of 1.7 billion Swiss francs—a figure that had long been common knowledge.

The board of the National Bank was running no risk: prior to 1990, Swiss banks could not be prosecuted for laundering the proceeds of crime. Even if such an offense was committed fifty years ago, it would long have been subject to the statute of limitations.

Meyer's behavior was thoroughly in keeping with Swiss atavism: gnomes always confine themselves to admitting what cannot be denied—in other words, what the "damned" foreigners can prove beyond doubt.

To summarize: between 1939 and 1945, gold bars and coins then worth at least 1.7 billion Swiss francs were deposited in the vaults at Bern. This was equivalent to approximately one third of the world's entire gold production during the five years in question. To this must be added an unknown quantity of looted gold deposited with, or sold direct to, trustees and private banks, by members of the SS or agents operating on their own account.

These transactions paid off in a gratifying manner. While Europe was subsiding into rubble and ashes, undreamed-of treasures were accumulating in the vaults of the Swiss National Bank.

Its reserves of gold and foreign currency more than doubled between 1939 and 1945. Stuart Eizenstat and William S. Zlany's May 1997 report for President Clinton, to which we have already alluded, states that "Switzerland ended the war as one of the [world's] richest nations."

Swiss bankers possess one indisputabie attribute: loyalty to their clients. They took delivery of the last truckload of looted gold from Germany on the morning of April 6, 1945, a mere three weeks before Hitler committed suicide.

How much was gold worth during the war years? What was its average value? The following figures emerge from research conducted by the U.S. Federal Reserve: 1 ounce (28.35 grams) fetched, on average, $35. In 1946 the U.S. dollar was worth 4.20 Swiss francs.

Looted gold was usually laundered by means of so-called triangular transactions. The Germans delivered it to Switzerland and were reimbursed in Swiss francs. These francs were used by them to pay for their imports of strategic raw materials and numerous other goods from Turkey, Portugal, Sweden, Spain, and elsewhere. The central banks of the exporting countries thereupon used the Swiss francs they had earned to buy the very same gold with which the Reichsbank had originally purchased the very same Swiss francs. This relieved the exporting countries of a dangerous problem. They could claim to have purchased gold from Switzerland in the normal course of international trade—an effective means of countering Allied rebukes and pressure.

On January 11, 1997, the World Jewish Congress in New York published a secret report submitted by an OSS agent stationed in Bern. He described the convoys of trucks—each identified by a large Swiss flag—that transported laundered looted gold from the National Bank vaults beneath the Bundesplatz, across France and Spain, to Lisbon. From 1944 through March 1945 the agent counted 280 trucks, all owned by private Swiss firms.

Here is one example of a typical triangular transaction. Francisco Franco, Spain's dictator, liked to style himself a

personal friend of Hitler's. He assured the Nazis of his ideological solidarity. He even dispatched a division of Spanish combat troops to the Eastern Front. Notwithstanding all this, he
steadfastly refused to launder German gold.

The Reichsbank delivered looted gold to the Swiss National
Bank and received Swiss francs in return. These it used to purchase tungsten in Madrid. Spain's central bank thereupon exchanged the Swiss francs for gold in Bern. The gold now bore the
Swiss national emblem, or was at least accompanied by a Swiss
verification certificate. Franco was thus insured against Allied
countermeasures.

In January 1997 Ana Fernandez published an exposé of
Franco's gold transactions in the Madrid newspaper *El Pais*.
According to her, he acquired laundered German gold from
Switzerland worth, in 1945, 187 million Swiss francs.[25]

Were the bankers of Madrid (Lisbon, Stockholm, Ankara, and
elsewhere) any more "ethical" than their counterparts in Bern?

Of course not.

Were they afraid of Allied countermeasures and potential
claims for compensation from injured parties when the war
ended?

Naturally.

But the Swiss, too, were threatened by countermeasures and
claims for compensation, yet they blithely continued to launder
looted gold.

What accounted for this contradictory behavior?

A belief in predestination. The incredibly robust ideological
superstructure of Switzerland's collective consciousness. Last but
not least, arrogance.

Swiss bankers tend to be extremely cautious. How could they
have accepted Hitler's looted gold so indiscriminately and on such
a scale?

"Triangular transaction" is an analytical term. The National
Bank authorities denied, and continue to deny, its validity. Their

line of defense was, and continues to be, quite clear. First, the National Bank was committed to the gold standard, and gold standard regulations prescribe that a central bank must accept the gold it is offered. Second, the Reichsbank must surely have had undeclared reserves of gold. Third, Hitler's foreign policy had presented the Reichsbank with additional gold of an entirely legal nature; further legal transfers to Berlin took place after the Austrian gold reserves were transferred there in 1938. Another example: Czechoslovakia. The Wehrmacht marched into Prague on March 15, 1939. The Czech territories were proclaimed the Protectorate of Bohemia and Moravia, and Slovakia became an independent state. Twenty-four hours after the invasion, Prague's central bank gold reserves were transferred to the Reichsbank— quite legally, since the transaction had been decreed by the government of the Protectorate.

Strangely enough, Swiss banks never requested official confirmation from the Germans that the gold transferred to them was legal, not stolen. The government and the national Bank authorities contented themselves with Emil Puhl's assurances. The British economic historian Harold James, who teaches at Princeton, explains this omission as follows: "Should they ever be confronted after the war with a demand that the gold be returned, they would have to prove that they were acting in good faith. But if they submitted a written statement, that would naturally be regarded as evidence, not of good faith, but of great doubt."[26]

The Bern gold-laundering machine functioned in a highly professional manner. Although the launderers knew where the gold came from, they nearly always succeeded in maintaining their "neutral banker's" front.

They could also react swiftly in critical situations. For example, the minutes of a National Bank board meeting on June 18, 1942, record an intervention on the part of the vice president, Paul Rossy. Some potentially explosive freight had arrived in the shape of a Reichsbank consignment of gold bars bearing stamps that clearly indicated their places of origin, the United States and France. They were, in fact, bullion seized by the Germans in Holland. The Royal Netherlands Central Bank had quite legally purchased them in Washington and Paris before the war and added them to its reserves.

Rossy was perturbed: Funk's instructions were that the looted gold should be passed on to Portugal in a classic triangular transaction. Berlin would use the gold laundered in Bern to purchase fresh supplies of urgently needed wolfram from Lisbon.

The trouble was the gold stolen from Holland, some of which bore U.S. and French stamps. Lisbon was positively swarming with Allied agents, so there was a danger that the Allies would get wind of the Bern transaction and claim the looted gold as their property. Rossy blenched at the probable consequence: the Swiss National Bank would have paid its German friends millions of Swiss francs for looted gold that might very soon prove to be nonnegotiable and, thus, worthless.

As launderer in chief, Rossy was unprepared to expose his bank to such a risk. He recommended to his colleagues that the stolen bars from Holland bearing American and French stamps be melted down at once in Bern and adorned with Swiss stamps. The National Bank board agreed, but resolved to await Allied reactions before completing the deal.

It is very probable that the Nazis' theft of gold from Holland was known to the American and Free French secret services. The Dutch resistance movement was strong and, by 1942, well organized. It maintained agents not only in Holland's central bank, but also in various private banks and at the port of Rotterdam.

But there was no reaction from either of the relevant envoys in Bern, American or French. Relieved, the Swiss gold-launderers dispatched the laundered gold to Lisbon, and Hitler was free to purchase fresh supplies of raw materials for his armed forces.[27]

Nine A.M., Monday, January 20, 1997. The foreign affairs committee of the National Council has convened in Conference

Room No. 3, a paneled chamber on the ground floor of the Bundeshaus in Bern. Gray winter mist is drifting past the tall windows. The atmosphere in the room is tense. Hans Meyer, president of the National Bank, and Georg Krayer, millionaire private banker from Basel and president of the Swiss Bankers Association, are being questioned on the subject of looted gold.

Hans Meyer is wearing a gray suit. Beads of sweat glisten on his bald head as he gives his answers in a flat, militarily terse tone of voice. Seated beside him is the vivacious Krayer, whose dark, melancholy eyes roam the long table in quest of sympathy and understanding.

Meyer admits that the National Bank has always known the identity of every gold bar that passes or passed through its vaults. Every bar in Bern (as in every other central bank in the world) possesses its own identity card. The alloy of a bar enables its origin to be defined.

Meyer and Krayer are decent men. Looted Nazi gold in Swiss banks? No such thing has ever existed.

4. Three Sinister Swiss

WHO PRESIDED OVER BERN'S depository of looted gold? Three men: Ernst Weber, Alfred Hirs, and Paul Rossy. It was they, under Weber's chairmanship, who formed the executive of the Swiss National Bank during the war.[28]

Although the National Bank is a private joint-stock company, the government appoints its chief executives on the recommendation of the board and of the head of the Federal Department (i.e., Ministry) of Finance. Their appointment is governed by the numerical strength of their parliamentary party, their religious affiliation, and their geographical origin. The wartime board of the National Bank consisted, needless to say, of solidly middle-class men, whether liberal Protestants or Catholic conservatives.

It never occurred to any member of the Swiss parliament that a woman could conduct business at boardroom level, and women are excluded from the National Bank board to this day.

The board was, and still is, technically subordinate to a bank council whose composition also accords with the political, religious, and regional proportionality so dear to the Swiss Confederation. The bank council was chaired by a conservative, Professor Gottlieb Bachmann of Zurich University.

Bachmann evinced some uneasiness about doing business with the Nazis, but Weber stuck to his guns. He told Bachmann what he had told Yves Bréart de Boisanger, the governor of the Banque de France: "Switzerland is on the gold standard. The Swiss National Bank accepts gold from all countries and transmits it to all countries. It would be impossible to refuse to accept gold from one particular country. That would conflict with Switzerland's neutrality."

And again: "The National Bank cannot have regard to the provenance of the gold that is sold it by the Deutsche Reichsbank."

Switzerland was Hitler's safe-deposit box. The National Bank was supervised between 1939 and 1945 by two ministers of finance in turn. Although quite different in background, personality, and political affiliation, both men gave their blessing to Switzerland's laundering operations with an inertia worthy of the three wise monkeys. Bundesrat Ernst Wetter, elected to the government in 1938, was a typical Zurich economic free trader: to him, the profit-seeking interests of the big banks were always identical with the welfare of the Swiss people. Having begun his career as secretary-general of the Ministry of Economics, he went on to become director of the Department of Trade. Later still he became secretary of the Trade and Industry Association, the employers' umbrella organization. In government Wetter remained true to his former patrons: he never departed so much as a millimeter from the line laid down by the *Neue Zürcher Zeitung*.

Ernst Nobs, elected on December 15, 1943, was the first Social Democrat to enter the federal government. His socialism was a front, however. Formerly a schoolteacher and editor of the Zurich periodical *Volksrecht*, then mayor of Zurich, Nobs had long forgotten his ideological origins. He administered Hitler's safe-deposit box quite as efficiently as Wetter, the Bahnhofstrasse stooge.[29]

That the Banking Council and its committee failed to oppose the board's complicity with the Nazis goes almost without saying. Both are typical of those assemblages of languid dignitaries that abound in the Swiss Confederation. Their principal function is to rubber-stamp decisions already taken elsewhere.

But what really shocks and dismays one when reading the minutes is the passive, not to say mute way in which the government ratified the National Bank's underhanded dealings.

Messrs. Rossy, Hirs, and Weber did just as they pleased. Their cupidity was unbounded, their hubris infinite, their blindness absolute.

Who were these three sinister characters, and where did they come from?

Paul Rossy was undoubtedly the shrewdest, most adroit and cultivated of the trio. A lawyer with an honorary doctorate from Lausanne University, he hailed from Cossonay, a small town in Canton Vaud, where he was born into a prominent local family in 1894. At the National Bank he functioned as vice president and general manager in charge of Department No. 2, the chief cashier's department. Rossy was responsible for administering the looted gold. His patron at Bern was Marcel Pilet-Golaz, the Vaudois radical.

In 1940 Pilet-Golaz was federal president and foreign minister. It was he who greeted the German entry into Paris by delivering an ill-starred speech advocating submission to the "New Europe."

Pilet-Golaz was forced to resign in 1944. The nimble Rossy,

who survived unscathed, did not leave office until 1955. He was a talented cynic.

A settling of accounts took place when the war ended, even in Bern. The fences sprang at each other's throats, each determined to salvage his own career. Paul Rossy succeeded brilliantly. National Bank archives contain a letter from him in French dated June 19, 1946. "I can no longer work with Herr Hirs," wrote the bank's general manager, "because of his attitude in Washington, but above all because he bought stolen Belgian gold from the Reichsbank in 1943 and 1944 in full cognizance of the provenance and nature of that gold.... In my view, the Bundesrat cannot tolerate such conduct. It cannot permit Herr Hirs to remain a member of the board.... Should the Bundesrat leave Herr Hirs in his post beyond the year's end, I myself would feel compelled to quit the bank. I cannot under any circumstances run the risk of compromising myself because of the intrigues of the head of our most active department."[30]

National Bank President Ernst Weber, born in 1881, was an introverted, hidebound, pigheaded man with a rather unhappy personal life. His stern mouth was surmounted by a small gray mustache, glassy eyes expressive of insecurity, a broad, high forehead, and a domed cranium sparsely thatched with gray hair.

Weber had worked his way up inside the National Bank. He was an ambitious philistine of a functionary who couldn't even speak English. That he overcame those disadvantages sufficiently to become president of the bank was testimony to his patience, determination, and excellent political connections.

Weber's two obsessions were neutrality and monetary stability. If he defied the Allies, it was because of his sense of divine mission. He saw himself as the grand custodian of the national currency—indeed, he perceived inflation as the sole threat to Switzerland throughout the war.

Weber was also circumspect. He had sent two thirds of the National Bank's gold reserves westward before the war, dividing them equally between the United States and Great Britain. He had no liking for the Germans and did not trust his Reichsbank colleagues one inch, but he transacted some lucrative deals with them. Devoid of any sense of right and wrong, Weber was an apparatchik pure and simple.

Alfred Hirs, born at Zurich in 1889, was a suave, wily operator cut from altogether different cloth. In charge of foreign exchange transactions from 1942 on, he was neither a political protégé nor a central bank careerist. Having been a private banker, he liked to regard himself as a competent, objective, apolitical technician.

Hirs's milieu was the quick-dealing world of the foreign exchange and stock markets. Politics were alien to him. He never mastered the Bernese power machine; as far as he was concerned, the big guns of the Bundeshaus might have been on another planet. He seldom patronized the public houses or the Bellevue bar, where important political deals were transacted after midnight. Those were Rossy's stamping grounds, and that was why Rossy got the better of him.

The foreign exchange specialist wore hornrims over his small, fishlike eyes, had a strong nose, short brown hair, and a sensual mouth. He never thought in strategic terms, whether on his own or the National Bank's behalf. He favored swift, duplicitous action, which made him the ideal partner for Puhl. Cold and arrogant toward his subordinates, he aspired to be the perfect, dispassionate banker.

In order to characterize Alfred Hirs, I must anticipate an event to which we shall revert in detail in Part Five of this book: the Swiss-Allied reparations talks at Washington in 1946.

Rossy the cunning cynic, backed by Weber the melancholy bureaucrat, dispatched Hirs to Washington to conduct these difficult negotiations with the victorious Allies. Hirs did his utmost: he lied and cheated and sabotaged the reparations agreement to the best of his ability.

Marco Durrer gives the following account of Hirs's preliminary appearances at Washington in his standard work on Swiss-American financial relations during World War II:

> Hirs addressed the first session of the Gold Subcommittee on March 26, 1946. The general manager of the SNB [Swiss National Bank] began by stating that he had come to Washington merely as a "technical member" of the Swiss delegation.... It was not for him to defend the SNB's policy. He repeatedly stressed, in the course of his remarks on the development of Swiss-German gold transactions, that Switzerland had never had anything to do with looted gold; that was why he would not go into the question. Hirs did, however, mention that, according to the SNB's information, two thirds of the Belgian gold were in the United States and one third in France. He presumed that, like Switzerland, other countries had shipped the bulk of their gold reserves overseas prior to the German offensive in the west.
>
> At the second session on March 29, Hirs went more closely into the principles governing Switzerland's monetary policy. The SNB had been unable, from considerations of neutrality, to decline German gold.... Besides, various Reichsbank representatives had affirmed that the gold dispatched to Switzerland came from the Reichsbank's prewar holdings.[31]

Alfred Hirs was a professing Christian and a keen churchgoer. Was he anti-Semitic? There are many indications to that effect. From Washington he wrote long letters—surprisingly naïve and sometimes spiteful—to the colleagues who had remained at home. On March 18, 1946, he wrote to Zurich: "The American delegation makes a very congenial impression...although most of them have a touch of Jew."

On the 27th of the same month Hirs complained of the searching questions put to him by one particular member of the

American delegation. He knew why the American was being so unpleasantly inquisitorial: he was "an Austrian Jew from the Treasury." Hirs's September 1944 report on the money market, in which he strove to explain the monetary and foreign exchange policy pursued by the provisional French government, contained a passage expressive of incredible stupidity. The minister of finance in de Gaulle's provisional government was Pierre Mendès-France. Hirs attributed current French policy partly to the fact that Mendès-France was "a wealthy Jew."

Alfred Hirs's latent anti-Semitism was typical of a whole category of conservative Christians in Switzerland, both Catholic and Protestant. The serpents of racism slumber on in the catacombs of their subconscious. As children they rattled off the Good Friday liturgy's slanderous dicta about the Jews: the Cross a symbol of Jewish guilt; the Jew a scapegoat, the murderer of Christ.

Hitler, on the other hand, espoused an anti-Semitism that was purely Aryan, not Christian. His anti-Semitism was the expression of an Aryan master-race mania that combated any belief in God. His god was the Aryan race; that was why he fought the Christian churches as well.

For all that, the latent Christian anti-Semitism of many Swiss believers diminished their immunity to Aryan racial mania.

Hirs exemplifies this process very well. His Christian faith was sincere and deeply felt, I am sure, and I have no right to question it. It was the Church under whose influence he had grown up that imparted the racist poison. In contact with Emil Puhl, the German envoy Otto Köcher, and other Nazi dignitaries, he did not flinch when conversation turned to the persecution of the Jews. He was merely a technician, after all—and a professing Christian. Although well informed about Auschwitz, Maidanek, and Treblinka, he continued—with an unalterably clear conscience—to do business with the mass murderers' emissaries. Christian anti-Semitism had deprived him of his immunity to Nazi racial mania.[32]

———

On September 18, 1944, the vice president of the Reichsbank and his staff conferred with the board of the Swiss National Bank. Puhl stated for the record what the Swiss wanted to hear: he assured them that the Reichsbank had never dealt in stolen gold. If gold (and foreign exchange) from foreign central banks had turned up in Berlin, this was only because it had been legitimately and voluntarily transferred there by the relevant central bank. This gold from the occupied territories had been carefully weighed, paid for, and purchased by the Reichsbank in the ordinary course of business.

As for the gold garnered by the SS, the so-called *Totengold*, Puhl advised his Swiss friends to consult the relevant authorities at the SS Economic Administration Department. The Reichsbank was merely a depositary; it had never, at any stage, sent them gold of an illegal nature.

The eternal implication was that all the gold sent to Switzerland by the Reichsbank came either from Germany's prewar holdings or from gold reserves that had been voluntarily relinquished—and to believe that assertion bordered on the irrational.

Swiss archives contain another interesting document. Drafted by the National Bank's legal department and dated April 5, 1944, it presented an overall legal evaluation of the gold transactions conducted between Switzerland and Nazi Germany.[33]

The National Bank's lawyers urged that, where every future purchase of gold was concerned, the Reichsbank must be requested at once to confirm that it was legal German property. Henceforward, only gold bearing German stamps and accompanied by German documentation should be accepted. The National Bank should not, from now on, touch any gold bars that bore the national emblems of occupied countries. The board did not comply with this recommendation.

Embodied in the same legal opinion was a political analysis. The Swiss bank lawyers presented a thoroughly realistic account of Greater German occupation methods, notably the deportation of conquered peoples and, in particular, the persecution of the Jews.

The Swiss government and its three front men—Weber, Rossy, and Hirs—clung desperately to Emil Puhl's web of lies and entertained him royally whenever he visited Switzerland. Here, written in 1945, within weeks of Hitler's death and the Third Reich's downfall, are two letters from Party Member Puhl to his boss in Berlin, Walther Funk. On March 30:

> I think I can say that the Swiss are showing me every consideration. Yesterday, for example, they gave a banquet in my honor, which naturally came at once to the attention of our enemies. It's remarkable the way Swiss bankers and industrialists keep calling on me, although I'm under constant surveillance by the enemy's secret service.

Puhl's second letter looks to the future. The Swiss bankers evidently believed, even at the eleventh hour, that the Thousand-Year Reich would somehow survive. True to the admirable precept that enjoins the Swiss to remain loyal to their clients to the last, they were hoping for further good business in the years ahead.

Even Puhl could hardly believe his ears. Here he is, writing to Funk on April 6:

> Many people will think it scarcely possible that I have managed, in the present military and political situation, to conclude a written agreement with a Swiss institution [the Swiss National Bank].... Weber pointed out that an agreement concluded under present circumstances between the National Bank and the Reichsbank possesses a far-reaching importance that transcends the immediate present.... However the situation develops, such relations will always subsist between our countries....[34]

But Emil Puhl, alas, was not to be relied on. As soon as Hitler's Götterdämmerung was over, the arch-Nazi underwent a miraculous transformation: he placed himself entirely at the service of the victorious Allies.

The Nuremberg War Crimes Tribunal heard much about German thefts of gold reserves held by the central banks of occupied countries and of gold privately owned by their inhabitants, likewise about the Reichsbank deposit accounts opened by the SS with gold garnered from the concentration camps. This applied particularly to the hearings that concerned the machinations of Walther Funk, the former Reichsbank president and Reich minister of economics.

Invited to give evidence, Puhl told of the Reichsbank's gold transactions.[35] Yes indeed, he testified, the SS had deposited gold and other precious metals in the form of dental crowns, pieces of jewelry, wedding rings, spectacles, et cetera, at the Reichsbank's headquarters in Berlin. Yes indeed, thefts of gold reserves had occurred far and wide—in Norway, Belgium, Poland, Lithuania, and elsewhere. The Reichsbank had had the bars melted down and adorned with prewar stamps. Most of the looted gold had reached the world market by way of Swiss banks.

The witness was asked a direct question: Could the Swiss have known that the gold was stolen? Yes indeed, they were fully aware of the gold's provenance.

The court demanded to know who had informed Puhl of this.

"The president of the Swiss National Bank," stated Puhl, "Ernst Weber."

The three sinister but very dissimilar Swiss men who, in Switzerland's name and under the Swiss government's supervision, presided over vaults filled with looted gold and kept a worldwide gold-laundering system in operation for Hitler's benefit, had no particular liking for Nazi ideology.

Although they often enjoyed the lavish hospitality of the German envoy to Bern, Otto Köcher, and although they conscientiously supported German interests on the board of the

Bank for International Settlements, they did so only because the Reichsbank was a good customer of theirs.

Reich Minister of Economics and Reichsbank President Funk put it down in black and white: without the Bern gold-laundering machine, the Reich could "not survive for longer than two months."[36] The document in question is authentic and the facts are established, but Hitler's three Swiss henchmen were not Nazis. They were average citizens who had been washed up on the shores of power thanks to proportional representation, cronyism, and magisterial irresponsibility. Rossy was the gambler and cynic, Hirs the cold, unemotional technician, Weber the colorless, pen-pushing apparatchik.

Hannah Arendt asserts in *The Origins of Totalitarianism* that every nation, whatever its political culture and democratic tradition, harbors enough unstable people to provide a totalitarian system with the nucleus it needs.

This is undoubtedly true of Switzerland as well. The Frontists, or avowed Swiss Nazis, were never numerous. Their main characteristics were arrogance, stupidity, and rowdyism. In the entire course of the war, Swiss courts-martial passed thirty-three sentences of death for treason, seventeen of which were carried out. Most of the condemned men were confused, pigheaded individuals.

But the willing functionaries, the potential desk-delinquents and docile opportunists described by Hannah Arendt were thick on the ground in Switzerland.

Even the Bundesrat, the seven-strong government that functions as an executive and collective head of state, included some alarming figures: Philippe Etter, archconservative Catholic, minister of the interior, and enthusiastic advocate of a corporate state of the Austrian type; Ernst Wetter, who regarded Fascism as a bulwark against Bolshevism; Eduard von Steiger, minister of justice and police, a Bernese patrician of reactionary complexion who thought little of plebeian democracy and all the more of corporatist, authoritarian government; and Marcel Pilet-Golaz, friend of the Vichy regime. One serious blow to the government, and one from which it suffered throughout the war, was the resignation in 1940 of Defense Minister Rudolf Minger, the popular, shrewd, and patriotic agrarian politician.

In short, had Hitler invaded Switzerland and proclaimed the Gau Helvetia of which the Frontists dreamed, he would have found willing and well-qualified personnel to serve him.

One factor that seems unimportant in 1997, but clouded the horizon of many West Europeans in the 1930s and early 1940s, was the real or imaginary threat presented by Bolshevism.

Zurich's liberal party, the State Party of the Confederation, created the constitution of 1848 and has always been steadfastly democratic in its beliefs. In 1933 it joined with the Swiss Nazi Party (the Frontists) in putting up a combined list of candidates for the Zurich municipal elections, which took place immediately after Hitler seized power. The party's newspaper, the *Neue Zürcher Zeitung*, applauded this step on the grounds that Zurich had to be preserved from Bolshevism.

Hirs, Rossy, and Weber—the gold-launderers of Bern—regarded Hitler as the lesser evil. Supporting the Nazis meant saving Switzerland from the Bolsheviks, and the Bolsheviks, of course, included the Social Democrats.

It is worth taking a look at Switzerland's power structure from this point of view. As solid, immutable, and oppressive as the Gotthard massif, it has preserved the same stratification for nearly 200 years: the same oligarchic groups, the same financial networks, the same families, the same mentalities. In Switzerland reactionary and conservative are terms that can no longer be employed for purposes of differentiation.

All over the Continent—in France, Germany, England, Spain, Italy—the edifices of power have collapsed, been reconstructed in a different way, and collapsed once more. New class structures and social groups have come into being; new ruling elites have taken shape, seemingly out of nothing, seized the reins of power, and been overthrown by war, revolution, economic crises, hyperinflation, foreign occupation. Nothing of the kind has happened in Switzerland.

The last foreign soldier on Swiss soil had been one of Napoleon's men. He quit Geneva on December 31, 1814.

Since 1814 Switzerland has witnessed no violent demolition of its power pyramid, no modification of its social strata, not the smallest tremor in its class edifice. The same ruling class has wielded political, economic, ideological, and military power for almost two centuries. Its limited objective awareness is remarkable, and continues to operate unchanged to this day.

The Swiss newspaper that has made the fullest and most persistent efforts to refurbish Switzerland's conduct during the war is the *Neue Zürcher Zeitung*, the mouthpiece of the said ruling class, the permanently dominant bourgeoisie. One of the most intelligent, technically well produced, and best informed newspapers in Europe, it thoroughly merits its international reputation.

But it is incapable of understanding Switzerland's wartime history.

On October 22, 1996, for example, it published an extremely well-informed editorial of considerable stylistic elegance. Its title: "Shades of World War Two—Speechlessness and Helplessness." The editors' intention was to deal with the Swiss government's speechlessness and helplessness vis-à-vis attacks from abroad. All they did, in fact, was to reveal the newspaper's own helplessness and inability to understand the past:

> Constantly to react on the defensive is a reflex that may, perhaps, be beneficial to the relations between host and guest in a land of tourism like Switzerland. In foreign policy it earns little sympathy, either abroad or at home.... In respect to dormant assets and transactions between the Deutsche Reichsbank and the Swiss National Bank during World War Two, which have been—

somewhat precipitately, perhaps—lumped together under the catchphrase "looted gold," the Swiss Ministry of Foreign Affairs last Friday provided another example of communicative incompetence.[37]

I could scarcely believe my eyes: in October 1996, and despite its detailed knowledge of the facts, the *Neue Zürcher Zeitung* could still print the words "looted gold" in quotes.

5. Willful Ignorance

IT IS STILL UNKNOWN exactly how much looted Nazi gold the Swiss hoarded, fenced, and laundered. A dense pall of mist enshrouds nearly every aspect of the Bern gold-laundering machine and the gold transactions of the private banks, trustees, company lawyers, fund managers, and finance companies.

Consequently, every new publication that addresses the subject arouses the greatest agitation in the Bundeshaus, on Zurich's Paradeplatz, and in the higher reaches of the National Bank.

One example was the British Foreign Office indictment published on September 10, 1996, modestly entitled "Nazi Gold: Information from the British Archives"[38] and signed by Foreign Secretary Malcolm Rifkind.

From the strictly legal standpoint, this document—which became known worldwide as the Rifkind Report and resurrected ghosts that Bern had long thought laid to rest—was merely a straightforward ministerial reply to a question raised by a member of Parliament.

The shrewd and courageous parliamentarian concerned, Greville Janner, who also heads the Educational Holocaust Trust and is a vice chairman of the World Jewish Congress, had sent the minister a written request for information about the quantity and location of looted Nazi gold, most of which was stashed away in Switzerland.

Although a source of extreme danger to Swiss bankers, the Rifkind Report was really quite a commonplace document. No far-reaching research went into its preparation. It was a shot from the hip typical of British parliamentary practice. A Labour member with many international connections and, no doubt, some sound inside information, had accused John Major's Conservative government of conspiring to deprive the survivors of the Holocaust or their heirs of millions of pounds that were rightfully theirs.

Major's prospects in the parliamentary elections scheduled for early 1997 were poor. Most of the polls correctly predicted an overwhelming victory for Tony Blair's refurbished Labour Party. As a vice chairman of the World Jewish Congress and a well-respected figure on both sides of the House, Janner was not just any old backbencher. In Britain, in contrast to the United States, many Jews hold conservative views and vote accordingly. John Major could not afford to dispense with the Jewish vote.

Consequently, Janner had to be handled with kid gloves. Instead of answering him orally in the Commons or briefly by letter, Rifkind instructed his civil servants to examine the relevant documents. The resulting twenty-four-page report was not, for all that, a product of thorough historical research.

Rifkind's staff based their estimates on a hitherto little heeded remark made by Alfred Hirs, Swiss National Bank director and friend of Puhl's, who had sat across the table from the victorious Allies at Washington in 1946. The Americans had blacklisted more than a thousand Swiss concerns as "war profiteers" and blocked their overseas assets. The Swiss were now requested to hand over German assets to the Allies as war reparations.

Questioned as to the whereabouts of the gold the Nazis had stolen from Belgium's central bank, Hirs lied for all he was worth, until suddenly confronted with a deposition of Puhl's. "Are you trying to ruin my bank?" cried Hirs, on the verge of a nervous breakdown. "You expect me to hand over 500 million gold francs? Never!"

Rifkind rightly estimated that 500 million francs[39] in 1946 would now be worth approximately seven billion dollars.

Why did the rather unsensational Rifkind Report cause such a stir? Why the thunderclaps in the international press? Why the earthquake in Zurich's Paradeplatz, the panic in Bern? The Foreign Office people hadn't dug deep, after all, so why the tropical tornado?

British and American journalists are sleuthhounds by tradition. The Rifkind Report had scarcely been published when reporters from the *Evening Standard*, the London *Times*, the *Guardian*, the *Financial Times*, the *Independent*, *Newsweek*, *Time*, and the *New York Times* started delving into the records of the Washington reparations conference of 1946. And lo, the Swiss delegation had solemnly sworn that the quantity of looted Nazi gold they had traded in was so small as to be almost nonexistent. On the last day, under extreme pressure, the honest Swiss shelled out a mere 250 million francs. Looted Nazi gold? Not on your life! That sum—to cite the minutes—was "a voluntary contribution to the reconstruction of Europe."[40]

But Hirs, when questioned about the stolen Belgian gold alone, had admitted to having 500 million gold francs in his vaults. The sleuthhounds' conclusion: the Swiss at Washington had lied.

For the financial sharps of Zurich, Basel, and Bern, the Rifkind Report could not have appeared at a more inopportune juncture.

Some seven million Jews belong to that part of the Jewish people referred to by Elie Wiesel as "the Jews of silence."[41] They are the Jewish communities resident in the territories dominated by the former Soviet Union. Before the Soviet empire collapsed, to contact any Swiss bank was a potentially lethal undertaking for them. The sons or daughters of Jewish Holocaust victims who put through calls to Zurich or engaged attorneys there, let alone made trips to the West, rendered themselves suspect in the eyes of the East German Stasi, the Romanian Securitate, or the Soviet KGB.

Everything has changed since 1991. Freedom of movement prevails, and travel restrictions have been lifted. Every week since 1991, Zurich's Bahnhofstrasse has been visited by dozens of those whose parents or grandparents were murdered at Auschwitz, Buchenwald, Treblinka, Babi-Yar, and elsewhere. They come bearing information, sometimes vague, sometimes precise, about the assets their relatives deposited there for safekeeping.

They are met with legal quibbles and coolly turned away.

If the son or daughter, sister or cousin of a Holocaust victim who opened a deposit account with a Swiss bank (insurance, trust company, or other institution) turns up at the counter and asks to withdraw the money, the bank clerk's first question is: "Can you produce the death certificate of the alleged account holder?"

Swiss bank clerks seem unaware that no death certificates were issued for their victims by the commanders of SS death squads, the Gestapo thugs who operated in the torture chambers of Vienna, Berlin, and Amsterdam, the men and women who ran Auschwitz, Maidanek, Treblinka, and Mauthausen, the SS troops who liquidated the ghettos.

Now and again the descendant of a Holocaust victim succeeds in obtaining a legally valid declaration of presumptive death, but not even that will satisfy the bank clerk. "And now," he says, "kindly produce proof that you're the deceased's sole heir."

Since it was customary for entire families—men, women, children—to be massacred by SS squads or gassed, shot, or beaten to death in the extermination camps, the sole surviving heirs are in a hopeless position. They have to try to obtain death certificates, valid under Swiss law, for all the murdered members of their family. This being impossible, of course, the money remains in the Swiss bank, where—God be praised—it continues to earn good interest, year after year, as it has done for the past half century. The interest, of course, is pocketed by the bank.

In 1992 the World Jewish Congress, acting on behalf of the Israeli government, took up the cause of the rejected heirs. The murky past, the looted gold, the hypocrisy and lies—all these abruptly became a topic of worldwide interest.

Two ultraofficial, highly qualified committees of inquiry have now started work with the aid of international trust companies, auditors, and topnotch financial experts. No less a person than Paul J. Volcker, former chairman of the U.S. Federal Reserve Board, presides over one of these committees, which is composed of equal numbers of representatives of the Swiss Bankers Association and the World Jewish Congress. Volcker himself came to Zurich in October 1996 to negotiate with the international auditing firms that were to assist him. In other words, he has made it his personal business to track down the looted assets and so-called dormant accounts of Nazi victims that are salted away in Switzerland or have been sold off by the Swiss.

Experts and investigators of the Senate Banking Committee are at work in New York, Tel Aviv, and throughout the world.

Elan Steinberg, executive director of the World Jewish Congress in New York, has assembled a young and enthusiastic team of investigators in conjunction with Washington's Holocaust Museum. They have already unearthed thousands of documents in the war archives of Washington, Paris, Moscow, and London.

At the time of this writing I should be rash to talk figures. It is very probable that more alarming documents, more figures, more vanished fortunes in looted assets and fresh information about the sums handled by Hitler's Swiss fences will come to light every week for a period of several years. That is why I shall here dispense with quantitative arguments. The purpose of this book is to analyze sociological factors and human behavior, complicities and constraints, but also to draw attention to isolated acts of moral resistance in those dark days half a century ago.

The Swiss Confederation is a highly industrialized country. Politically it is a very old democracy, ideologically a society that bears the impress of Western, Christian morality.

It keeps records, reveres its own collective memory, and preserves the documentary evidence of its dealings. Miraculously enough, it has escaped every European war for the past two hundred years. Its archives, therefore, are intact.

The Swiss Confederation is not a Stalinist dictatorship—one that periodically, in accordance with the political climate, crops photographs, airbrushes out inconvenient figures, or renders documents illegible by obliterating undesirable passages. Most of those who work in the Federal Archive at Bern (and in the archives of the national and private banks, insurance companies, and so on) are competent, well-trained archivists.

Switzerland suspended free convertibility in the financial sector during World War II. The country was subject to foreign exchange control. The government established a so-called clearinghouse whose headquarters employed eighty or more highly qualified men and women. Every movement of capital in every direction was recorded. Although the authority itself no longer exists, the records of the Federal Clearinghouse are fully intact.

These Swiss archives—the wartime ones are not, admittedly, computerized—are all very difficult of access. They cannot be researched by just anyone. The government (or, in the case of private banks, the board) decides who can see and read which documents, let alone photocopy them. Thus the archives of the Federal Clearinghouse are still largely unexplored terrain. As strange and unfamiliar to historians as Tierra del Fuego, they may well yield gems enough to excite any seeker after knowledge.

Each category of documents is protected by a maze of regulations that prohibit publication before the expiry of a certain period. Anyone venturing into this jungle is well advised to secure the goodwill of the powers that be.

The Federal Archive stands on a hill on the south bank of the Aare. Immediately opposite, on the north bank, is the Bundeshaus. Both palatial edifices are constructed of the pale gray sandstone that has for centuries been excavated from the nearby quarries of Ostermundigen. Alike in period and style and possessed of a certain quiet charm, they are patriotic piles embellished with statues of heroes, warriors, and sturdy women. The similarity between the two buildings demonstrates that the young, nineteenth-century Swiss Confederation held its memory and history in high esteem. The Federal Archive had thus to be as majestic as the seat of government: a token of respect and symbol of national identity.[42]

There is, however, one minor difference: beneath the Bundeshaus is the government's atomic-bomb–proof shelter; beneath the Federal Archive are four reinforced concrete shafts, allegedly filled with papers.

The Federal Archive stands on Archivstrasse, surrounded by trees. The district is called Kirchenfeld, or "Church Field," a reminder that the dead were buried there in medieval times.

The archivists of the world's second richest country keep their documents in cardboard boxes—some twenty-two miles of them, and every passing year they devour another mile or so of shelf space. The boxes contain tons of paper, a mine of information humanly impossible to evaluate unless the millions of documents were to be computerized—and that, because of an inadequate budget, is not the general rule.

The reparations agreements with Poland and Hungary alone occupy more than 6,500 boxes. Forty additional personnel would be needed to get them into some sort of order, but the Federal Archive is underfunded: a staff of thirty-nine, an annual budget of 4.5 million francs.

Its director, Dr. Christoph Graf, is an extremely able, well-meaning historian. He knows what lies beneath the surface. "During the 1940s," he says, "Switzerland wasn't in the world's good graces. Our reputation was lousy. Then came the Cold War, and anti-Swiss resentment dissipated. But it was bound to return some day. That's what is happening today, and we suddenly feel powerless."[43]

The Swiss National Bank, too, has its records. Unlike those

of the Federal Archive, they are in a wretched state. When asked why the National Bank neglects to organize its records and fails to make them genuinely accessible to historians, the man in charge came out with a response that almost beggars belief: "It's true we spend very little on evaluating our archives.... That's because we have always preferred not to seem an extravagant institution."

The publication of documents is governed by terms laid down in an arbitrary manner. One of the most mysterious cadavers preserved in the vaults of the Federal Archives is the Dossier Interhandel, or "Interhandel File."

In 1948, at one of the subsidiary war crimes trials, twenty-three I. G. Farben executives were brought before an Allied war crimes tribunal at Nuremberg, charged with "enslavement and homicide." Their firm had manufactured Zyklon-B gas for the SS death camps and brutally exploited tens of thousands of deported slave laborers in its factories.

I. G. Farben was the largest chemical company in Germany and one of the largest in the world. In 1929 it founded the Gesellschaft für Chemische Unternehmen AG, known as I. G. Chemie, in Basel. To evade subsequent Allied countermeasures, I. G. Chemie changed its name and legal structure several times. By 1940 it was called Internationale Industrie- und Handelsbeteiligungen AG, or Interhandel for short.

At the Washington reparations conference in May 1946, the Swiss delegation stated that Interhandel was a purely Swiss concern, quite unconnected with the Nazi gas manufacturer. The Allies reluctantly and dubiously accepted this story. In 1966 Interhandel merged with the Union Bank of Switzerland, and the latter became, overnight, the country's most powerful bank.

Historians suspect that the Swiss statement in Washington was a brazen lie and that Interhandel was enemy-owned to the last. This is confirmed by a 500-page audit report prepared in 1945–46 by the firm of Albert Rees.

Under the terms of a special federal act, access to the Dossier Interhandel in the Federal Archive at Bern is prohibited for an indefinite period.[44]

Does the Swiss government impose censorship on its archives? Does it disregard freedom of scholarly research? Does the Bundeshaus operate like the Vatican?

Not at all. The government's methods are subtler. It maintains a few court historians and a handful of court lawyers. They are well funded and continually extolled in government speeches. Like Amalekite high priests, they not only know a great deal; they know what the ordinary folk around them, their inferiors and associates, are entitled to know—or, rather, are capable of taking in. One can't tell everyone everything, they argue—one never knows if people are capable of correctly understanding what they hear. That's why interpretation, discreet precensorship, and mental reservation are essential. Those in the know are responsible for the wider picture, after all. They have to be careful.

Edgar Bonjour was one such court historian. Professor of modern history at Basel University for decades, he is a national monument and the author of a monumental *Geschichte der schweizerischen Neutralität*. Commissioned by the government and comprising no less than six volumes, it is the conclusive, definitive history of Swiss neutrality, the preeminent scholarly reference book that soars above all ideological lowlands.

Bonjour spent decades of his life delving into Switzerland's archives, yet he found no trace of any looted Nazi gold, nor of the "dormant" accounts belonging to East European Jews that were arbitrarily liquidated four years after the war. He detected no evidence of the valuable and effective alliance maintained between Switzerland and Nazi Germany throughout the Allied economic blockade. Capital transfers by the SS, Hermann Göring's looted art treasures, Joachim von Ribbentrop's and Franz von Papen's ill-gotten fortunes, which were hoarded, or disposed of, in Switzerland from 1944 on—all these escaped his notice.

The man who functioned as court lawyer to the Bern authorities until his death in 1948 was Dietrich Schindler, a Zurich university professor and a widely respected expert on international law. Steadfastly friendly to the government and gratifyingly cooperative, Schindler would swiftly supply legal arguments of all kinds and for all seasons, whenever called upon to do so by the republican monarch in Bern. The fact that his scholarly argumentation invariably legitimized, clarified, and approved government decisions, past and present, was nothing more, of course, than a fortunate coincidence.

The term "court lawyer" is not, by the way, a polemical invention of my own. Quasi-official in character, it is employed by Robert Urs Vogler, archivist of the Swiss National Bank.[45]

One of Schindler's legal opinions, dated July 22, 1944, proved especially disastrous. When the Allies protested to Bern about transfers of looted gold, notably of bullion stolen from Holland, even the Bundesrat, whose seven members were always hard of hearing, became faintly uneasy. They consulted the board of the National Bank. Were these lucrative gold transactions with Berlin genuinely legal? "Of course," the answer came back—on the strength of Schindler's expert opinion. Weber's and Hirs's reply could not have been more explicit or categorical: "The requisitioning of gold is a right to which an occupying power is entitled under the provisions of international law."

Schindler based his opinion on the Hague Land Warfare Convention of 1907, which related to the public property of occupied countries. However, except for the Deutsche Reichsbank, from 1939, all the European central banks were and are civil institutions, mostly joint-stock companies. The Hague Land Warfare Convention's right to requisition did not apply to them. What could Dietrich Schindler have been thinking of when he submitted his opinion?

PART TWO

The Murderers

———

Who would respond at this time

to the terrible persistence

of crime, if not

the persistence of testimony?

ALBERT CAMUS

1. The Dakar Raid

IT IS AN ESTABLISHED fact that as soon as Hitler's armed forces, the SS, and the Gestapo invaded a country, they proceeded to loot it thoroughly and systematically. Their first step in every case was to raid the gold and foreign exchange reserves held by the central bank of the country in question.

This chapter presents a detailed analysis of one such operation: the theft of the bullion and foreign exchange holdings of Belgium's central bank in Brussels.

First, though, a preliminary remark. Much useful work on this subject has been performed by Werner Rings, now an eighty-six-year-old living in retirement in Ticino. In *Raubgold aus Deutschland* ("Looted Gold from Germany"), first published twelve years ago, he presented an important and estimable account of the problem based partly on existing secondary sources and partly on sources researched by himself.[1]

Rings, born at Offenbach in 1910, is an interesting man. A staunch anti-Fascist, he fled Germany and joined the French Foreign Legion before becoming a Swiss citizen. As a journalist, he has done much to help his adoptive country to acknowledge and rise above its conduct in the war.

Rings's interpretation of the standard investigations by Pierre Arnoult and P. Kauch into the subject of the looted Belgian gold differs from mine. He accepts that the bankers of Bern and Zurich and the then Swiss government acted in good faith.

I do not. Where the gold stolen from Belgium and Holland is concerned, Michel Fior's work (see Part One, note 27) has since dispelled all doubt.

Unlike the theft of gold and foreign currency reserves from many other central banks, which is still shrouded in obscurity, that of the Belgian gold has now been documented in considerable detail. In this respect, particular importance attaches to the study by the historian P. Kauch, to which I was kindly given access by my colleagues at Liège University.

The "phony war" on the Western Front came to an abrupt end in 1940, when Hitler, instead of breaking through the Maginot Line, sent his tanks through the Ardennes Forest and overran Belgium. Sedan soon fell, followed by the whole of northern France.

The Belgian army, with French support, held out bravely for eighteen days. The military situation was confused. The Belgian General Staff, being obsessively determined to render Belgium's neutrality credible, had stationed some of its forces in the southeast, along the frontier with northern France, as well as on the German and Dutch borders.

This division of forces contributed to the relatively swift disintegration of the Belgian army. Although most of its units laid down their arms after less than three weeks, others put up a stubborn fight in various strongpoints, most of them—like the fortifications around Namur and Liège—dating from earlier centuries. They continued to resist after their country had capitulated.

At the time of the surrender, Belgium's gold—more than 221 tons of it, worth approximately one billion Swiss francs—was in the safekeeping of the Banque de France, where the country had opened a deposit account.

The political situation in Belgium after the surrender was

equivocal and complex. The government had fled to London, but King Leopold III and his court were prisoners of the Wehrmacht at Laekan Castle. Theirs was no ordinary captivity, however. Hitler treated Leopold with the respect due to a head of state. He personally dispatched an "honor guard" to protect (and keep tabs on) him.

The occupying power had indigenous allies inside Belgium itself, where Christ Roi (from Christus Rex), an extreme right-wing movement, had been founded before the war. Its leader, Léon Degrelle, quickly became a true-blue Fascist, and he and his "Rexists" lent major support to the Wehrmacht and the SS. The SS Division SS-Wallonie, recruited from Rexists and other Belgian collaborators, served under German command on the Eastern Front. Gauleiter Degrelle not only survived the war, but died a happy exile in Franco's Spain.

Belgium was and still is a multiethnic, multicultural state. Hitler treated the Flemish and Walloon areas of the country differently. German racial theorists regarded the Flemings as Germanic cousins, whereas the Walloons were classified as hated Latins.

But civil resistance was widespread nonetheless, and many of those involved in it risked death throughout the long years of Nazi occupation. At the beginning of the winter semester of 1996–97, I delivered a guest lecture in the great auditorium of Liège's ancient university. The walls of the entrance hall are covered with big marble plaques bearing the names of hundreds of students, teachers, and administrators of both sexes and varied origins, all of whom were murdered in German concentration camps and Gestapo cellars or killed while conducting underground operations against the Wehrmacht and the SS.

This is not the place to criticize Leopold's political sympathies, his bad relations with the government-in-exile, or his weakness toward Hitler. The Belgians themselves decided that issue when they compelled him to abdicate in 1951.

The fact is that Leopold was worried about his country's gold.

Through the German liaison officer at his court he requested a personal interview with Hitler, his aim being to persuade the Führer to have the Belgian gold in France brought back to Brussels. Leopold believed that the boxes were in Bordeaux, whither the Third Republic's last government, the Reynaud cabinet, had fled after the Germans broke through on the northern front.

In France, of which only half was initially occupied, the area south of the Loire was governed, courtesy of Hitler, by Marshal Philippe Pétain, hero of World War I and ex-ambassador to Franco's Spain.

The French Third Republic was dead. In mainland France and the French colonies there had come into being an "état national" founded on a corporative, racist ideology. After June 18, 1940, however, another France existed in exile in London—one that rejected Pétain's claims to legitimacy: the Free France of Charles de Gaulle.

The Franco-German armistice agreement, which was signed on June 22, 1940, recognized Philippe Pétain as head of state and confirmed the legitimacy of his government at Vichy, a health resort south of the Loire.

Technically speaking, normal interstate relations existed between the Third Reich and Vichy France.

The Germans adopted a legalistic approach. They did not, for example, dispatch the Gestapo to the Banque de France. Instead, they sent the Vichy government a questionnaire through diplomatic channels. What gold was held by the Banque de France? Where, in particular, was the Belgian gold?

Vichy readily supplied the requisite information. The executive board of the Banque de France gave a detailed breakdown of its existing deposit accounts: they comprised the aforesaid Belgian gold, fifty-seven tons from the National Bank of Poland, and more from the central banks of Norway, Lithuania, Czechoslovakia, Luxembourg, and Latvia.

The Banque de France further stated that the depositors' motive in opening all these accounts had been the desire for security.

The gold had consequently, for safety's sake, been sent off to sub-Saharan Africa.

What had happened?

When France's defeat became a foregone conclusion, the board of the Banque de France, most of whose members were men of patriotic disposition, got in touch with the British and arranged for the French and foreign gold to be evacuated to the United States. But something went wrong. The Royal Navy, preoccupied with covering the evacuation of British troops from Dunkirk and organizing the naval and coastal defense of the British Isles, did not send the stipulated ships—or not, at all events, until too late.

The boxes of gold bars, which were already in Brittany, were loaded into French warships, the Belgian gold being put aboard the cruiser *Victor Schölcher*. On June 18 the ships left their berths in Lorient and Brest and sailed for Dakar.

France's colonial empire in Black Africa comprised two large administrative blocs, the federations of French West Africa and French Equatorial Africa. Madagascar, Djibouti, and the Indian Ocean islands were separately administered. Dakar was the seat of the governor general of the West African Federation, Brazzaville that of his opposite number in Equatorial Africa, but only Dakar possessed an efficient harbor, railroads, and an infrastructure sufficiently sound for gold storage purposes. Also based at Dakar—or, rather, in the barracks at Ouakam—was by far the strongest colonial garrison in Vichy's army.

The *Victor Schölcher* put into Dakar on June 28, 1940.

Hitler was neither Attila nor Genghis Khan. More precisely, even though his personality may have resembled that of the aforesaid "Scourges of God," he was operating in the new, extremely complex Europe of the twentieth century, not in the bleak and inhospitable steppes of Mongolia or the Syrian desert.

If he wanted to secure his rear in the west, he would have to treat Pétain with consideration. Germany's diplomats duly set to work.

What were their arguments? That Leopold III wanted the gold returned to Brussels carried little weight. The king was discredited, even at Vichy, and the Belgian government-in-exile in London naturally opposed such a step.

The Germans' legal position was unfavorable. The central bank authorities in Brussels and Paris, who knew their international law, refused to return the gold voluntarily. The Hague Land Warfare Convention of 1907 clearly distinguishes between public and private property. An occupying power can confiscate the former as war reparations, but not the latter.

To repeat: nearly all Europe's central banks—Belgian, French, Polish, Czech, Latvian, Lithuanian, and others—were and are joint-stock companies. They do have certain prerogatives, such as issuing national currency and setting the discount rate, but structurally they are legal entities under civil law. To this day, for instance, the Swiss National Bank belongs to the cantons and the various private individuals and firms that constitute its stockholders. Even the Deutsche Reichsbank remained a legal entity under civil law until 1937, when Hitler transformed it into a state institution subject to government authority. A still more drastic reform ensued in 1939: thereafter the Reichsbank was directly subordinate to the Führer and the Reich Chancellery.

The German occupying power was prohibited, under the Hague Convention, from mounting a raid on the gold depositories at Dakar. Bréart de Boisanger, presiding governor of the Banque de France, and Belgian National Bank governor Janssen were shrewd lawyers. They resisted with great ingenuity.

But the wily German diplomats soon came up with another argument. Was it for safety's sake that the Banque de France had shipped part of its own gold and all of the gold entrusted to it to Africa? The French West African Federation was threatened with chaos, they pointed out, and security prevailed only in Europe under the "New Order." Ergo, the boxes of gold must all be shipped back to Europe.

The Germans had a point: by the fall of 1940, General de

Gaulle was already preparing to launch a commando operation against Dakar.

Cape Verde, the inhospitable peninsula on which Dakar stands, juts into the south Atlantic at the westernmost tip of Africa. Everywhere along its countless bays and beaches—at N'Gora and Ouakam and on the Corniche—Lebu fishermen put to sea before sunrise in their traditional dugout canoes and paddle back at noon. The currents around the peninsula are dangerous. Weather conditions are forever changing, usually in an unpredictable way.

At dawn on September 23, 1940, three British warships neared the coast. It was the end of the rainy season, and the red cliffs and hills were veiled in mist.

De Gaulle, who wanted to avoid bloodshed, appealed to the garrison to surrender peacefully. A battalion of the Foreign Legion commanded by Gaullist officers attempted to land, but in vain: the flotilla was bombarded by coastal batteries under the command of officers loyal to Vichy. That ended any hope of capturing Dakar, and the ships withdrew three days later.[2] More than 600 people were killed.

An important interjection: General de Gaulle was not, of course, a would-be looter of gold. He mounted his Dakar expedition for quite another reason: a wish to rally the French West African authorities and their troops to the cause of Free France.[3]

In fact, de Gaulle's expedition to Dakar proved counterproductive. Johannes Hemmen, who headed the economic section of the armistice commission based at Wiesbaden, cited it to the Vichy regime as evidence of the allegedly "chaotic conditions" prevailing the France's Black African colonies.

The political and military situation in France's sub-Saharan colonial empire in the middle of 1940 was certainly confused. On August 26, 1940, Félix Eboué had risen in revolt at Fort Lamy, the dusty capital of Chad, the colony situated on the eastern edge of French West Africa. Eboué was governor of Chad, but he was also a black man from French Guiana. His decision in favor of de Gaulle and Free France was of the utmost political and symbolic importance. Vichy's colonial troops were ninety percent black or Arab. Hundreds of thousands of Africans found it inspiring that the only black man to attain so senior a post in the French administration should declare against Pétain and for de Gaulle.

From London, de Gaulle promised internal autonomy and a reorganized French commonwealth founded on equality. The French garrison in Chad rebelled. At Bamako, Libreville, Ouagadougou, Abidjan, Cotonou, and Lomé, black colonial troops refused to obey their Vichy officers. De Gaulle appointed Eboué governor general of the Federation of French Equatorial Africa. The revolt was soon joined by Congo-Brazzaville and Cameroun, colonies far richer than Chad. British troops stationed in Sudan and Kenya attacked and defeated the Italian armies of occupation in Eritrea and Abyssinia. Vichy's colonial empire in Africa had begun to totter. Marshal Pétain was having some sleepless nights.

German diplomats took advantage of the old man's panic. The Franco-German armistice commission and, more especially, Johannes Hemmen stepped up their pressure on him. After some initial hesitation, Pétain had become converted to a policy of total collaboration and was now convinced of Hitler's final victory. Gullible in the extreme and eager to wangle his defeated country a place of honor in the Thousand-Year Reich, he gave orders that the gold be returned to Europe.

How hungry they must have been, the robbers in Berlin! I am impressed, having personally delved into the archives of London's former Ministry of Economic Warfare and traced the organization and route of the gold shipments. The Nazis were thieves and murderers, but they were certainly talented organizers.

The German plan for the transcontinental transportation of the gold to Berlin reads like the script of a Hollywood B feature.

German agents were formed into armed, elite squads run on military lines but under instructions to wear "inconspicuous" civilian clothing. How white secret agents with German accents from Berlin were expected to remain inconspicuous and unrecognized among teeming masses of black Africans the organizers did not reveal.

German air force planes, also in civilian guise, were to fly the gold to Marseilles via Vichy airfields in North Africa. The French had to provide the fuel and ensure that the precious freight was guarded during intermediate stops.

Transportation by warship, the obvious and seemingly far more practical method, was ruled out because the Germans feared the British submarines patrolling the south Atlantic.

From Marseilles the gold was to be conveyed to Berlin by train. The plan envisaged that each airplane would carry a load of two to three tons and that the whole operation would not take longer than two months.

The reality was quite different. Only forty-nine tons of gold had been flown out by Christmas of 1940. It had safely crossed the Sahara and was now lying in storage sheds on the provincial airfield of Oran in western Algeria, guarded by French marines from the nearby naval base at Mers el Kebir. The gold bars remained temporarily grounded at Oran because of the air battles that were raging over the western Mediterranean. Before long Allied fighters rendered it impossible for lumbering German transport planes to cross the Sahara.

The Germans decided on a change of plan. The boxes of gold were put aboard the Dakar-Koulikoro railroad. First stop: Bamako, at that time a small colonial garrison town situated beside a ford across the river Niger, in the heart of the kingdom of the Bambara.

The gold traveled on downstream, still by train, to Koulikoro, then the railroad terminus and capital of French Sudan (not to be confused with Anglo-Egyptian Sudan), now known as Mali.

Koulikoro is some 900 miles from Timbuktu, the Tuaregs'

historic caravan city, where Saharan tribes mingle with the Songhai, Bambara, and Fulani. The only relatively safe means of transportation is the Niger, but the river, which flows first from west to east and then from north to south, is navigable between Koulikoro, Ségou, Mopti, Jenine, and Timbuktu for only five months a year. At Timbuktu the freight was loaded into smaller craft.

On it went, downstream to Tossay and Gao in the kingdom of the Songhai. Then began the arduous journey northward by truck through the mountains and sand dunes of the Sahara. The track from Gao to Colomb-Béchar is nearly 1,200 miles long, and the convoys were soon halted by frequent sandstorms. When the trucks got stuck, donkey and camel caravans were brought into play, urged along by German agents disguised as Bedouin. Knowing the area as I do, I can attest to its being one of the most godforsaken, inhospitable stretches of terrain in the world.

Colomb-Béchar was the capital of the Vichy-controlled Algerian Confins sahariens and the southern terminus of the West Algerian railroad. From there, 1,000 miles from the Mediterranean coast, the boxes were transported to Algiers by rail.

Less than one third of the entire hoard had crossed the Sahara by the end of December 1941. The last consignment reached Berlin, via Algiers and Marseilles, on May 26, 1942.

The German operation had taken a good eighteen months instead of the two originally envisaged. It was nonetheless a remarkable feat, when one considers how much willpower and talent for improvisation and organization were required to bring it to a successful outcome. There remained the knotty problem of how the Germans were to take possession of the Belgian gold reserves in a legally proper manner.

In July 1942 the Soviet General Staff transferred two reserve armies to Stalingrad. In September the front traversed the city's western suburbs. On September 27 fighting began in the industrial districts, notably inside the "Red October" and "Barricade" complexes.[4]

Time was short. With the decisive battle imminent, the German munitions industry was going full blast. Hitler was compelled—through the good offices of his Swiss business associates—to purchase increasing quantities of strategic raw materials on the world market. The gold-laundering machine in Bern demanded more and more looted gold.

In mid-September 1942 the Belgian gold was sequestered by order of Reich Marshal Hermann Göring, plenipotentiary for the Nazi Four-Year Plan. Belgian archives record that, on October 2, 1942, the Reichsbank gave Belgium's national bank a receipt for 198 tons of gold. The Reichsbank's quid pro quo: Germany would pay the Belgians 2,784 Reichsmarks per kilogram and credit their national bank at once with the sum of 500 million. Walther Funk, still president of the Reichsbank and minister of economics, imposed one condition: the Reichsmarks were to be used only for the purchase of German goods in Germany. The Belgians stubbornly refused. Once again, National Bank governor Janssen invoked international law.

The Reichsbank made two more offers, one to the Belgians in July 1943 and one in September of the same year to the Banque de France, which was still, after all, the depositary for the Belgian gold. Both offers were rejected. Yves Bréart de Boisanger, governor of the Banque de France, advanced the same argument as Janssen.

Early in October 1943 the Germans lost patience: they deposited Reich treasury bonds with Berlin's central court that roughly corresponded in monetary value to the sequestered Belgian gold. The gold itself was melted down by the Prussian mint, adorned with new stamps, and predated.

The Reichsbank had two objectives: first, to camouflage its theft in legal colors, and, second, to suggest to foreign clients that the remelted bars came from its legal prewar reserves and were not wartime loot.

The remelted gold was promptly sent to Switzerland in the usual way. And, in just the same way, Hitler's war machine acquired more of the universally disposable foreign exchange it so badly needed.[5]

The minutes of the Washington Conference of 1946 are particularly informative about the wide variety of depredations inflicted on all or part of the central bank gold reserves of other occupied territories, for example, Norway, Czechoslovakia, Albania, Lithuania, Latvia, Luxembourg, Italy, Greece, and Poland. It would, however, be inappropriate here to present a detailed account of all the "bank raids," extortionate diplomatic maneuvers, and spurious transfers to which the Nazis resorted in order to gain possession of those gold and foreign exchange reserves.

Where central bank gold is concerned, I shall cite only one more example. Like many other European central banks, that of the Netherlands managed to convey a substantial proportion of its gold to safety before the Germans invaded. London was already holding some of the Dutch bullion in 1939.

The neutral Kingdom of the Netherlands was invaded by the Wehrmacht on May 10, 1940. During the night of May 11 the royal family quit the country aboard a British warship. Also onboard were several hundred boxes containing more of the central bank's gold reserves.

However, approximately 100 tons of gold worth almost 500 million Swiss francs remained behind at the Rotterdam branch of the central bank. Although the Wehrmacht's swift and unexpected onslaught precluded its wholesale transportation to safety in England, part of the gold was put aboard a small craft berthed at Rotterdam with the intention of transferring it to a larger vessel at sea. The attempted evacuation failed when the boat struck a mine and sank. A few of the boxes were salvaged two months later under German naval supervision.

Holland had no Leopold III. The entire country resisted the

occupying power, and Hitler decreed that the Dutch should be brutally subjugated. Rost van Tonningen, a convinced Fascist and henchman of the Nazis, was appointed by them to head the central bank.

But even in Holland the Nazis observed certain legal formalities. The looted gold's access to the world market had to be preserved. More concretely, Swiss bankers had to be furnished with a semiplausible pretext for the Reichsbank's "legal" takeover of Holland's gold reserves.

In March 1941, pursuant to a judgment pronounced by a maritime court at Hamburg, the gold that had gone down with the Dutch ship was transformed into a lawful "prize." Anyone who seizes booty aboard an enemy vessel in wartime is entitled under international law to keep it.

That left the gold that had been stolen on land from the Rotterdam branch of the central bank. Again in March, and with the consent of the central bank's new boss, Rost van Tonningen, these bars were confiscated by the Wehrmacht as a "voluntary" contribution to occupation costs.

The looted Dutch gold, stamped with the royal insignia, was shipped off to Switzerland. The Swiss National Bank evidently gave credence to the "prize" and "voluntary" contribution myths.

The vast majority of the Nazis' looted gold, whether recast in Berlin or sold off abroad, mostly in Switzerland, consisted of gold bars purloined from the reserves of the central banks of occupied countries. However, consideration should also be given to another category of loot: the assets—foreign currency, precious metals, and so on—garnered by various occupation authorities from private individuals and private banks, commercial concerns, insurance companies, and the gold from the concentration camps.

By 1940 the Third Reich had special teams at work in the occupied territories charged with helping to combat its permanent balance-of-payments deficit. The job of these preposterously named Devisenschutzkommandos, or "foreign-exchange-protection-task-forces," was to plunder private assets—primarily gold, jewelry, and foreign currency—in every corner of occupied Europe. They broke into savings banks, looted private banks, emptied jewelers' shops and private residences. They always gave their victims receipts and often went so far as to reimburse them in Reichsmarks or local currency. Legal formalities were almost invariably observed.

The Devisenschutzkommandos' forays were largely profitable. In Holland's case, for example, the licensed looters went to work on the country's towns and villages immediately after the Wehrmacht invaded in May 1940. Of the thirty-nine tons of gold they stole, a large proportion belonged to Jewish families and firms. They, too, were issued receipts. The Jews who lived and worked in Holland numbered 140,000, and many of their families had resided there for centuries. It was not long before the Nazis deported over 100,000 of them to extermination camps, where they were murdered.[6]

Most of the privately owned gold from Holland, too, found its way into Swiss bank vaults and was converted—thanks to Swiss business efficiency—into precious foreign exchange for Hitler's war machine.

2. Gold from the Death Camps

RUDOLF FRANZ FERDINAND HÖSS, one of the most abominable murderers the world has ever seen, in his capacity as camp commandant at Auschwitz was guilty of the deaths of more than 2.5 million people, mostly of Jewish descent. He appeared before the Nuremberg War Crimes Tribunal merely as a witness and was not sentenced to death by a Polish court until 1947.

Höss described in wholly unemotional language how gold was taken from his victims:

It took between three and fifteen minutes, depending on weather conditions, to kill the people in the death chambers. We knew when the people were dead because their cries ceased. We usually waited half an hour before opening the doors and removing the corpses. Once the bodies had been hauled out, our special squads removed their rings and extracted the gold from the teeth of these cadavers. An improvement on Treblinka was that we constructed gas chambers capable of accommodating 2,000 people at once, whereas the ten gas chambers at Treblinka held only 200 people apiece.[7]

Höss also supplied detailed information about the victims' jewelry:

Special trucks were employed to transport it, and we packed the rings, watches, and bracelets separately. Exceptionally valuable pieces were later sold in Switzerland.

The *Berner Tagwacht,* the official organ of Switzerland's Social Democratic Party, sent a reporter of its own to Warsaw to cover Höss's trial. He wrote on March 18, 1947:

Gold teeth were wrenched from the corpses and their valuables and jewelry removed. The gold was melted down into bars and sent to the Reichsbank in Berlin. Articles of daily use were carted off to the Reich by the carload and distributed among the population there. The valuables were dispatched to Switzerland to be exchanged for foreign currency via a special department of the Reichsbank.

How did the Swiss government react to the testimony of this mass murderer, who was executed at Auschwitz on April 16, 1947?

Werner Meister, a Conservative representative from Sumiswald, Canton Bern, put the question on the parliamentary agenda: "The government is asked for information on whether it had knowledge of the events described by Höss, if they accord with the facts, and what steps it took to penalize such transactions detrimental to Switzerland's honor."

The government came up with its official reply in May 1947: "Having no knowledge of the events that form the subject of National Councilor Meister's question, the Federal Council instituted detailed inquiries. These elicited not the smallest evidence to support the accuracy of the information referred to."

All the territories conquered by the Wehrmacht were encompassed by the SS reign of terror. In addition to six million murdered Jews, the dead included many millions of "inferior" Russian, South Slav, and Polish men, women, and children, hundreds of thousands of Gypsies, prisoners of war, slave laborers, and hostages of all kinds, and tens of thousands of resistance fighters, Germans among them. The SS state murdered fourteen million people in concentration camps, slave labor factories, and ghettos, many in the course of mass executions by shooting.

The authority responsible for the gold, silver, and other precious metals gleaned from the concentration camps was the Economic Administration Department of the SS. The SS bureaucrats sent monthly consignments of gold to the Reichsbank, which recorded their value. The gold was transferred to its reserves. Thereafter it very probably made its customary way into Swiss bank vaults (and from there onto the world market).

SS units not only robbed Jewish religious communities and prisoners in their charge in concentration, labor, and slave labor camps of all privately owned jewelry, gold, silver, watches, and any other salable items, but also systematically stole silver candelabra, lecterns, and other religious objects, not to mention art treasures such as sculptures, manuscripts, and paintings.

British researchers have investigated the official procedure whereby loot was converted into cash. The Wehrmacht's spoils went straight into the public exchequer, whereas those of the SS followed a different route. The Economic Administration Department kept a collective account at the Reichsbank for all its loot, code-named "Melmer." The proceeds (from bars composed of melted-down dental crowns, wedding rings, and so forth) went into an account, likewise kept at the Reichsbank, code-named "Max Heiliger."[8]

The SS was a well-organized band of thieves. Its agents sold semiprecious stones, eyeglass frames, and articles of jewelry containing little gold on the black market of the occupied country in question. It has also been established that such agents made business trips to Switzerland.

Israeli prosecutor Gideon Hausner describes the frightful procedures adopted by the SS who extracted prisoners' gold teeth at Maidanek, Auschwitz, Buchenwald, Treblinka, and almost all the camps. Inmates in penitentiaries, prisons, and other places of detention under SS supervision were also systematically robbed.

Here is Hausner's account of what went on at Maidanek:[9]

> Sometimes one of the SS men would go up to a batch that had just arrived, point to several healthy-looking arrivals, and order them to fall out. Now and then the Germans would sift a batch for carpenters, shoemakers, tailors, mechanics, and other craftsmen. They were then employed in the camp and had to keep it clean, sort out victims' belongings, transport corpses to the crematorium, or, where no ovens existed, bury them. Some of them were "hairdressers" who had to cut off women's hair; others were "dentists" who had to extract gold teeth from cadavers' mouths. They were the camps' "service squads"—poor wretches whose existence was sheer, unending hell. Sometimes, when they had to work outside like the men in the "forest squad," they had their legs chained. After the horrors they had seen on their arrival, most of them tried to commit suicide the very first night.

Camp inmate Abraham Lindwasser was employed as a "dentist." Hausner cites him verbatim:

> "I couldn't stand it anymore and tried to commit suicide. I was already dangling from my belt when a bearded Jew—I don't know his name—cut me down and proceeded to lecture me. It

was an ignominious job, he said, and one oughtn't to do it in the normal course of events, but one had to pull oneself together and make an effort to ensure that at least someone remained alive to describe what had happened here. And, since I had an easy job here, I could survive here and help others by so doing."

A few—a very few—other "dentists" also survived. Hausner:

It sometimes happened that a prisoner had to work on the corpse of a person he recognized: "I was a 'dentist' at Treblinka until, one day, I recognized the corpse of my sister. . . . I simply couldn't touch her, I simply couldn't go on. I asked the Kapo, a Jew, to transfer me to cleaning teeth instead, which he did. . . . We used to send two chests containing eight to ten kilograms of gold out of Treblinka every week."

Michael Podchlevnik, another of Gideon Hausner's interviewees, had a similar encounter at Chelm:

"I was in the party that had to handle burials. After some days I recognized my wife and two children among the corpses. I lay down beside them and asked to be shot. An SS man hit me twice, dug me in the ribs, and said: "You're still strong, you can still work. . . ." That night I tried to hang myself, but my friends took me down. . . . Three days later I jumped off the truck that was driving back from work and escaped."

The "service squads" were singled out for special torment in concentration camps. The SS made use of them, but bullied them in particularly hateful ways. Gideon Hausner again:

These people, of whom there were several hundred in every camp, were made the butt of all kinds of "amusements" by SS personnel off duty. They were ordered to put mice in their trousers, which were tied up below, and stand at attention without moving while the mice crawled around on them. The slightest movement triggered a whiplash. The SS men balanced bottles on prisoners' heads and fired at them. They ordered them to walk along a plank below the roof of the hut, more than twenty feet from the ground, and anyone who fell off was "an enemy paratrooper" and received twenty-five lashes or had a vicious dog let loose on him.

[. . .]

The SS kept dogs that were specially trained to attack people. One favorite name for these wild animals in the camps was "Barry." On the command "Jew!" or "Barry, come on, dog, attack!" the huge, calf-sized beast would rush at its victim and literally tear him to pieces. "When the dog attacked someone, he was helpless and couldn't do a thing. The dog knocked you down," said a survivor, "and you had to abandon yourself to it."

Service squads had to cart away the corpses of those who had been gassed and deliver them to the crematoria, cutting off their hair and examining their mouths for gold teeth en route. The prisoners assigned to perform such tasks were to be pitied most of all. They extracted the gold teeth of their companions in misfortune, thereby rendering themselves the SS Economic Administration Department's initial suppliers. Few of them survived. Most were gassed or hanged by the SS after three or four months' work.

After the war, a macabre communication reached the Anglo-Franco-American committee responsible for distributing the 337 tons of gold found in Thuringia by the Americans. The Greek government wrote: "In addition to our previous requests, we must revert to the subject of the dental gold of the 62,500 Greek Jews who were gassed. The assumption that this gold, which was extracted from the teeth of the Greek Jews, is worth approximately 100,000 Turkish pounds, does not seem exaggerated. This dental gold was cast into bars of rectangular shape. The work was performed by two deported French goldsmiths in a shed situated right beside the crematorium."

In 1947 the Polish government, too, got in touch: "On the assumption that the 3.2 million Jews killed represented 800,000 families each comprising four persons, and that each family possessed 100 grams of fine gold in some form or other, we conclude that the Germans stole at least eighty tons of Polish gold and regularly deposited it at the Reichsbank." The Poles enclosed some supporting evidence, to wit, an SS Economic Administration Department document dating from 1942: "Fifty kilograms of gold derived from dental crowns and plates found in deceased Polish prisoners are being deposited at the Reichsbank."[10]

The wedding rings, gold dental crowns, bracelets, gold watches, earrings, and other jewelry stolen from their victims by the SS and handed over to its Economic Administration Department were, as we have said, deposited at the Reichsbank, which melted them down into bars stamped with the German national emblem.

Large numbers of these bars, too, were dispatched to Switzerland, receipted by the Swiss National Bank, stored in private Swiss banks, and sold for foreign currency on the world market. Whether the National Bank purchased the bars or simply held them in trust, the foreign exchange was always remitted to Berlin for the benefit of the German war industry, the German intelligence services (whose operations abroad required large amounts of foreign currency), and the German army, navy, and air force.

In exoneration of National Bank directors Rossy, Weber, and Hirs, and of the numerous Nazi accomplices in law offices, major banks, trust companies, and finance houses, it must be said that no one could have identified the bars as gold looted from concentration camps. From 1941 on, however, Zurich and Bern were well aware of how the SS extorted gold, what physical methods it employed, and how its lethal bureaucracy functioned.

Gold came not only from the concentration camps, but from ghettos and places of execution in the open countryside. When

Hitler's Wehrmacht advanced into Russia in the summer of 1941, SS units and police battalions ran amok behind the lines, as they had in Poland. The Jewish inhabitants of occupied towns and villages were systematically rounded up. Hundreds of thousands of men, women, and children were shot to death en masse, and many thousands more were herded together in ghettos. Whether dead or alive, they were stripped of all they possessed.

More than 1.3 million Jewish men, women, and children were shot, beaten to death, drowned, or buried alive in Poland and Russia by SS units, police battalions, and Ukrainian, Latvian, and Lithuanian auxiliaries. Following hard on the heels of the advancing Wehrmacht, the so-called Einsatzkommandos, or special task forces, systematically exterminated the Jewish inhabitants of towns, villages, and hamlets. In the first six months of the Russian campaign, which was launched in June 1941, they murdered more than half a million Jews.

British radio interception experts succeeded in cracking the SS codes and deciphering the signals sent by Einsatzkommando chiefs to their headquarters in Germany. The messages they monitored were gruesome. In a speech broadcast on August 24, 1941, Prime Minister Churchill presented the British public with some examples:

". . . from the Arctic Ocean to the Black Sea, six or seven millions of soldiers are locked in mortal struggle. The tremendous battle rages along nearly 2,000 miles of front. . . . [Hitler] retaliates by the most frightful cruelties. As his armies advance, whole districts are being exterminated. Scores of thousands—literally scores of thousands—of executions in cold blood are being perpetrated by the German police troops. . . . We are in the presence of a crime without a name."

The Einsatzkommando signals picked up at Bletchley Park (home of Britain's codebreakers) in 1941 remained secret for fifty years. The following examples are taken from a preliminary volume of these documents published in 1996.[11]

The commander of Police Battalion 309 reported from

Bialystok on June 27, 1941, that he had liquidated 2,000 Jews in a single day, 700 of them in a synagogue reduced to ashes with gasoline and hand grenades.

On July 18, 1941, SS Lieutenant General Erich von dem Bach-Zelewski radioed Heinrich Himmler: "In the course of yesterday's mopping-up operation at Slonim, 1,153 Jewish looters were shot by Police Regiment Center." In August: "By noon today another 3,600 had been executed. That brings the number in my area to more than 30,000."

These radio messages usually ended: "Own losses: none."

The monitored operational orders from Berlin betrayed concern for the murderers' mental equilibrium. They offered the following friendly advice: "The day's impressions are to be effaced by holding comradely evening get-togethers."

The police battalions murdered hundreds of thousands of defenseless men, women, and children, but not before stealing their possessions. Anything convertible into cash was channeled into the SS distribution networks. If the looted assets included gold or other precious metals, pieces of jewelry, works of art, or foreign currency, SS agents often sold them via Zurich, Bern, and Basel.

Reich Marshal Göring set up a special authority, the Main Trusteeship Office East, for the confiscation and disposal of Jewish and other assets in Eastern Europe and Russia. Its task was to exploit such confiscated assets—especially articles of jewelry, coins, foreign currency, and gold—for the benefit of Germany's war economy.

One example: Lodz, known while under German occupation as Litzmannstadt, was Poland's second largest city. It was situated in that part of Poland which the Nazis incorporated in the Reich and renamed the Warthegau. Its Jewish inhabitants originally numbered 233,000. Of those, 226,000 were murdered and only 7,000 survived.

Early in February 1940 the Jews of Lodz were herded into a

ghetto and walled up. The official reason, here as elsewhere, was "racial hygiene," but the Germans' real aim, as in Lithuania, Russia, Latvia, and other countries, was to create the best possible conditions for the amassing of loot. A branch of Main Trusteeship Office East was installed inside the ghetto for this purpose. Bendet Hershkovits, an eyewitness of events at Lodz, recalled: "A section of the German Kripo [Criminal Investigation Department] was stationed on Kocielna Street. Its German personnel compelled Jews to hand over their jewels and other valuables. They beat and tortured them, sometimes with fatal results."[12]

Göring issued strict guidelines governing the collection, receipting, and registration of confiscated property. Trusteeship Office East maintained branches in nearly all ghettos. Like other looted gold, what they collected was conveyed to Berlin, deposited at the Reichsbank, and melted down. Although precise figures are unavailable, most of it was shipped off to Switzerland.

It is also certain that a great deal of the gold (jewelry, coins) stolen from individuals by the SS and police personnel who carried out mass shootings, and by the Gestapo and SS who ruled the ghettos, was never surrendered to Trusteeship Office East.

The SS maintained some distribution networks whose agents sold looted valuables abroad for foreign currency and paid it straight into private accounts. Looted valuables were also consigned to safe-deposit boxes rented from foreign, mostly Swiss, private banks.

In 1992 the American historian Christopher R. Browning published a report on the murderous operations carried out against the Jewish population of Poland by the German 101st Reserve Battalion.[13]

At dawn on July 13, 1942, members of the police reserve—older men unfit for combat duty, most of them husbands and fathers—surrounded the Polish village of Josefow and took 1,800 Jewish men, women, and children prisoner. Three hundred young men were selected as Arbeitsjuden ("labor Jews"); the remaining 1,500 people were taken to a nearby wood and shot in the back of the neck, one by one.

The battalion numbered 500 (Browning questioned 210 veterans). This relatively small unit wreaked terrible havoc among the Jews of Poland. While on the move for sixteen months, they detained 45,000 Jewish men, women, and children, thrust them into cattle cars, and sent them off to the SS extermination camp at Treblinka, where they all met their end in the gas chamber. The same German police officers, most of whom came from the Hamburg area, killed a further 38,000 Jews in the course of the war.

Browning also gives a detailed list of the homicidal operations conducted by German police battalions in south and central Russia.

Jewish men, women, and children were conveyed by truck to mass graves, where they were made to undress and deposit all their belongings on the edge of the trench. Other Jews, whose lives were temporarily spared, had to sort through the personal effects for articles of value. These valuables were confiscated by the commander of the Einsatzgruppe. If "honest" he handed them over to the nearest branch of Trusteeship Office East. If the personal profit motive prevailed he entrusted them to a fence, sold them to other SS officers or policemen, or tried to unload them on Aryan members of the local population.

From 1941 to 1944 SS Captain Eduard Roschmann commanded the concentration camp (originally the ghetto) at Riga, which functioned as a transit camp for most of the Jewish families deported from Germany and Austria. Roschmann, whose henchmen were Latvian SS troopers, practiced a merciless form of selection whenever another batch of prisoners arrived. All those not assigned to slave labor in the neighboring forests, fields, or factories were summarily shot or gassed in waiting buses. Other doomed Jews were lined up on the edge of a mass grave and machine-gunned by Roschmann's Latvians. Rank after rank of dead or only wounded people toppled into the trench, one on top of the other, having first been compelled to surrender all their possessions. Gold dental crowns were extracted from the mouths of the dead and dying by trustees. More than 80,000 people, mostly of German or Austrian extraction, were murdered at Riga.

Roschmann sold all their valuables for his personal benefit. The substantial fortune he amassed enabled him to evade the Allies after 1945. He sneaked across Europe and escaped to South America.

There is no documentary evidence as to the precise behavior of individual Einsatzgruppen commanders, concentration camp commandants, or Gestapo officers operating in ghettos. Except for Hoess, we cannot ascertain which of them handed over his victims' valuables to the relevant branch of Main Trusteeship Office East or sold them for personal profit. What has been established is the existence of SS distribution networks. The assets of the dead were marketed in Switzerland by SS agents or middlemen who sold them and credited the proceeds to their clients' personal accounts with trust companies, private banks, and corporation lawyers in Zurich, Basel, and Bern.

A U.S. Secret Service document dated May 28, 1945, and published by the World Jewish Congress in November 1996 proves that Swiss private banks began to be infiltrated by Gestapo agents soon after Hitler seized power. The Gestapo used the inside information they obtained to blackmail Jewish or other holders of Swiss accounts.

The secret American document details the case of an Austrian Jew named Henry Lowinger, the owner of a large laundry in Vienna and holder of a private bank account in Switzerland. When questioned by the Gestapo, Lowinger managed to save his own life and that of his family by signing over his Swiss assets to them.

In view of the Gestapo's notoriously brutal interrogation methods, it is highly probable that many reports from informants inside Swiss banks led to the torture or even death of account-holders arrested in territories under German control.

In October 1996 the 29,000 staff employed by foreign branches of the Union Bank of Switzerland received a memorandum from Gertrud Erismann, the bank's director of communications. Its purpose was to provide "the requisite background for discussions with clients, other employees, friends, and relations." The *Financial Times* of London obtained a copy of this document, whose existence Frau Erismann confirmed in the *Sonntagszeitung* (Zurich) on November 17, 1996. The memorandum's central assertion: Union Bank of Switzerland has nothing to do with looted gold—if at all, and at most, with "dormant" Jewish accounts. "German gold went to the Swiss National Bank alone."

The Erismann memorandum propagated an untruth: millions of francs' worth of ghetto gold and gold from places of execution found its way into the vaults and deposit accounts of Swiss private banks. To cite but one example: Deutsche Wirtschaftsbetriebe GmbH (abbreviated to DWG), an enterprise controlled by Reichsführer-SS Heinrich Himmler, functioned as a foreign sales organization for valuables belonging to murdered concentration camp inmates and slave laborers. DWB also supervised the manufacture—using hair taken from these murdered victims—of felt slippers for German submarine crews. Crédit Suisse of Zurich, which maintained active business contacts with DWB, granted it generous loans and held numbered accounts for the SS. SS Captain Leo Volk was a welcome client in Zurich's Paradeplatz. Early in 1945, when the Allies intensified their demands for the freezing of German assets in Switzerland, the SS officer wrote as follows to his friends in Zurich: "Please be careful to ensure that the designation Reichsführer-SS does not appear." Needless to say, the board of Crédit Suisse granted his request.

No one today can fail to wince when reading *Die Schweiz und die Juden, 1933–1945* by the Swiss historian Jacques Picard, who devotes nearly a hundred pages to "Messengers of the Holocaust".[14]

One of those "messengers" is Gerhart M. Riegner, now eighty-five years old and resident in Geneva. Riegner fled from Germany in 1933, first to France, then to Switzerland. Initially legal adviser to the World Jewish Congress, he later headed its Geneva office and served as the organization's secretary-general from 1959 until his retirement in 1983. Thanks to his close contacts with numerous delegates to the League of Nations, Riegner was well informed by the end of the 1930s about conditions prevailing in SS-run concentration camps. Early in the 1940s he began to receive precise, detailed and almost daily accounts of the mass murders perpetrated in the extermination camps.

Riegner was, and is, a stickler for accuracy. He regularly passed on his information to Allied diplomats in Geneva and Bern—and, what is more, to the Swiss government. One of the most warmhearted and courageous men I know, Riegner remains to this day, even in his ripe old age, an enthusiastic jurist and ultratypical German lawyer of the old school. He still reveres the memory of his friend Hans Kelsen, who taught him at the Geneva Institute for International Studies. To my surprise, Riegner assures me that he avoided all contact with Allen Dulles when the latter was resident in Bern. He preferred to steer clear of spies, even when they numbered President Roosevelt among their personal friends. Riegner's role was that of a messenger, a sentinel, a wise, courageous person who sounds the alarm, documents injustice, defends its victims, and indicts the monsters who prey on them.

PART THREE

Economic Warfare

The Swiss, neutral during the great revolutions in the countries surrounding them, have enriched themselves on the destitution of others and founded a bank on the misfortune of nations.

—FRANÇOIS RENÉ DE CHATEAUBRIAND

1. Switzerland Supplies the Tyrant

ON AUGUST 9, 1940, barely six weeks after the defeat of France, the Swiss Confederation concluded its most important trade treaty with Adolf Hitler. This, to cite the historian Hans Ulrich Jost, brought about Switzerland's "de facto integration" into the German economic area.[1]

The commercial and creditor-debtor relations between Switzerland and the Third Reich are a matter of record. In 1950 the Swiss Ministry of Economics published a volume—over a thousand pages long—entitled *Die Schweizerische Kriegswirtschaft 1939 bis 1948* ("The Swiss War Economy, 1939–48"). This volume shows that, prior to August 1940, Switzerland exported considerably more industrial products (including arms, detonators, optical instruments) to the Allies, and to Britain in particular, than to Germany. Jakob Tanner's comprehensive study presents an account of the logic inherent in Swiss economic policy.[2]

One of the great myths disseminated for over half a century by official government rhetoric—though Tanner refutes it—is that Switzerland radically redirected its exports in the summer of 1940 under irresistible duress. The premise that France was defeated and Switzerland encircled, so exports to the Allies were a practical impossibility, is simply untrue. German pressure existed, to be sure, but the Swiss hucksters acted on their own initiative.

What really happened? Pétain signed an armistice agreement with Hitler on June 22, and with Mussolini shortly afterward. Three days later, Federal President Marcel Pilet-Golaz delivered his notorious speech. From now on the watchword was an accommodation with Germany.

Official historians still try to represent the presidential address as an unfortunate, isolated initiative on the part of a pro-Vichy individual. Jean-Claude Favez rightly calls it "the speech of which it cannot be clearly enough stated that it was a speech [delivered on behalf] of the entire government."[3]

What change of heart had occurred in the Bundeshaus at Bern and in the executive suites of Switzerland's banks and industrial concerns? Hitler's victorious offensive in the West had convinced the Swiss ruling class of the Nazis' military, political, and ideological omnipotence. Hitler's final victory was assured. Europe was ruled by a new, integrated regime, and that regime would endure. The hucksters chose to ally themselves with the victor.

Switzerland was, in fact, far from encircled. As we have already seen, it had access to a railroad line that traversed the unoccupied part of France. Heinrich Rothmund's frontier police sent off a sealed carload of emigrants to Port Bou on the French-Spanish border every week. Trains exempt from German checks ran from Geneva's Eaux-Vives station to Lisbon via Annemasse, Annecy, Marseilles, and Sète.

The Geneva–Cornavin–Bellegarde–Culoz line was subject to intermittent German checks. In an attempt to counter the Allied economic blockade, the Germans insisted on strict supervision of Swiss exports to the West. The Allies were to be sold no more goods of military value (precision instruments, detonators among them). Berlin further insisted on the introduction of a certification system: all exports had to be rubber-stamped and travel via Basel. The Swiss government agreed to this. What was more, it cooperated with its Nazi business associates to an extent that raised eyebrows even in Berlin. It was going to take time to organize the certification system. "That's not a problem," said Bern, and complied with German customs regulations even before the certificates had been printed and the relevant authorities installed.

Here is another example of Switzerland's ultrafriendly cooperation in business matters. German agents discovered that David Kelly, the British envoy in Bern, was buying sophisticated firing mechanisms in Switzerland, dismantling them, and mailing the components to London in parcels or even letters. Swiss experts periodically traveled to England, and also the United States, to assist in reassembling these devices.

When German intelligence alerted Hermann Göring, he first considered assassinating Kelly, but then hit upon a more effective solution: he made representations to his business associates in Bern. The Bundesrat promptly banned all exports by mail and instituted strict checks in post offices. Swiss experts were forbidden to leave the country.

The Swiss government was more docile than that of Vichy France, as the historian Klaus Urner has demonstrated. On September 9 and 10, 1941, German agents intercepted eleven letters that had been mailed there from Switzerland. They were found to contain miniature, dismantled components sandwiched between sheets of cardboard: 1,044 specially ground industrial diamonds and 1,008 tiny screws with an average diameter of 0.5 millimeters. Berlin complained to Vichy and demanded that the mails be forthwith subjected to stringent checks along Swiss lines. Vichy rejected the request.[4]

Swiss arms manufacturers proved especially valuable to Hitler. Switzerland leads the world in precision engineering. The aiming devices of Swiss guns and the accuracy of Swiss mortars, machine guns, and quick-firing antiaircraft guns were, and still are, the finest available anywhere. Hitler ordered tens of thousands of them, and Wehrmacht and SS gunners were trained under Swiss supervision.

The Swiss munitions industry possessed another advantage: being on neutral territory, its factories escaped Allied bombing.

The largest private arms manufacturing company in the country—and one of the largest in the world—was owned by Emil Bührle, the son of German immigrants from Württemberg, most of whose workshops were situated in Zurich-Oerlikon. His business transactions with the Third Reich proved gratifyingly profitable. Between 1939 and 1945 his declared annual income rose from 6.8 to 56 million Swiss francs, and his personal assets, after tax, from 8.5 to 170 million.[5]

Emil Bührle was on friendly terms with Albert Speer, Hitler's minister of munitions and war production, and with Councilor Freiherr von Bibra, possibly the most important intermediary between the Nazi bosses and Swiss industrialists. He was also a welcome guest at the house of Otto Carl Köcher, the German envoy in Bern.

From the summer of 1940 until the spring of 1945, Bührle's armaments firm worked almost exclusively for Hitler. By 1941 it employed a staff of 3,761, or three times as many as it had at the outbreak of war. Bührle-Oerlikon was originally a machine tool manufacturer, but it converted itself into an arms manufacturer after Hitler's invasion of Poland. By 1940, 95 percent of its production consisted of arms and ammunition. Its bestseller was the 20 millimeter Oerlikon antiaircraft gun that earned high praise from Hitler for the large numbers of Allied aircraft it shot down.

Bührle was a belligerent employer. He detested trade unions in general and, in particular, Hans Oprecht, a Zurich trade union leader and courageous Social Democrat member of the National Council. Journalist André Marty has traced the development of the wage structure in the Bührle-Oerlikon machine tool and arms manufacturing concern. In 1940 an unskilled laborer earned a basic wage of 1.30 Swiss francs plus 7 centimes shift allowance for the first and second shifts and 25 centimes for the night shift. The danger money—accidents, some fatal, were of frequent occurrence in such a firm—amounted to 10 centimes an hour.[6]

Because of Germany's inconveniently rapid collapse, not all of Bührle's inventory could be delivered. Many guns that had been ordered by the Nazis remained stranded at Oerlikon. Even after his favorite customer's suicide, however, Bührle knew how to come up smiling: he exported his guns to the Third World. In 1969 the Ibo people rose in revolt against their oppressors from northern Nigeria, the Hausa, in alliance with the Yoruba. War broke out, and General Ojukwu proclaimed the independent state of Biafra west of the river Benue.

The United Nations imposed an arms and economic embargo on Biafra. The war killed two million people, mostly women and children, and the rebellion collapsed. Although Switzerland, too, had subscribed to the ban on arms exports, UN inspectors found dozens of Bührle guns in Biafra's military installations. Some of them still bore swastikas and German serial numbers. They were Oerlikon stock, ready for transportation to the Third Reich but never collected. The Nazis had already paid for them, but Bührle sold the same guns a second time to Ojukwu—an excellent business deal.

The Federal Supreme Court fined Dieter Bührle, Emil's son and heir, 20,000 Swiss francs for having broken the embargo.

The Swiss legation in Berlin was headed from 1938 until 1945 by Minister Hans Frölicher, who energetically promoted Swiss industry's integration into the German economic area. He was a welcome guest at the Reich Chancellery and on friendly terms with Göring and Himmler. The Bern authorities were well aware of Frölicher's pro-Nazi sympathies, as we have already said. They did not share them, but they left him alone.

In 1991 Thomas Hürlimann wrote *Der Gesandte* ("The Minister"), a documentary play about Frölicher, his activities in Berlin, and his reports to the Swiss government. I first saw it at Geneva's Théâtre de Poche in 1994. A deathly hush reigned in the auditorium when the curtain fell. There were tears in people's eyes—tears of anger and shame.

Frölicher's closest associate in Berlin was Councilor Franz

Kappeler. Urs Schwarz, Berlin correspondent of the *Neue Zürcher Zeitung* from October 1940 to December 1941, called on Kappeler at the legation immediately after the arrest of Maurice Bavaud, a young Swiss theology student from Neuchâtel who had narrowly failed to assassinate Hitler. Bavaud was tried by the so-called People's Court, which was presided over by the notorious Roland Freisler. Attorney General Lautz led for the prosecution, but Bavaud had no decent defense counsel. When he tried to explain his motives, Freisler shouted him down. Convicted and sentenced to death, he awaited execution in Berlin's Plötzensee prison.

Urs Schwarz had no knowledge of Bavaud's exact predicament when he entered Franz Kappeler's office. He recalls:

> I involuntarily overheard a telephone conversation in Councilor Kappeler's office at the Swiss legation. The phone rang while I was talking with Kappeler. He picked up the receiver. I rose, intending to withdraw discreetly, but Kappeler motioned me to remain seated.
>
> I gathered that someone was asking Kappeler what could be done for a Swiss in dire trouble. Kappeler's reply indicated that the Swiss in question was in prison and under sentence. Kappeler said (into the phone): "No, no, we won't do a thing. It's his own fault. He shouldn't have done it."
>
> The conversation concluded with the usual polite phrases.
>
> Unable to restrain myself, I asked Kappeler: "What was that about? Is it a serious matter? Is the sentence a severe one?"
>
> "Yes, of course," Dr. Kappeler replied.
>
> Then he laughed.
>
> He drew his hand across his throat in imitation of the guillotine. "He'll be beheaded," he said.[7]

Maurice Bavaud was guillotined in Berlin on May 18, 1941. He belongs in the ranks of anti-Nazi martyrs like Pastor Dietrich Bonhoeffer, Hans and Sophie Scholl, and Claus von Stauffenberg.

As for the laughing Franz Kappeler, he enjoyed a brilliant postwar career as Swiss ambassador to numerous countries, notably South Africa in the days of apartheid (of which he approved). He never displayed any remorse. Göring's friend Hans Frölicher was never called to account either. In 1961, after many years of well-earned retirement, he died peacefully on his estate at Ursellen, near Bern.

What never fails to fascinate me about Swiss business tycoons, industrial magnates and bankers is their combination of great professional ability and infinite political naïveté. Typical of this antithesis was Hans Sulzer, one of the four or five most powerful men in Switzerland during World War II. Joint owner of Gebrüder Sulzer AG of Winterthur, an engineering firm with worldwide business interests, he was president of his employers' association, the Verband Schweizerischer Maschinenindustrieller. A patriotic Swiss, he put his boundless energy at the service of the Swiss war economy as unpaid director of the Iron and Engineering Section and president of the Supervisory Committee for Imports and Exports.

In 1942, when the government appointed him to head a delegation to London, Sulzer was sixty-six years old and at the height of his professional experience and political power. By then Switzerland was providing Hitler with the foreign exchange essential to his war effort, laundering his looted gold, granting him loans worth many millions, and supplying Germany's armed forces and war economy with weapons, precision instruments, ammunition, trucks, and spare parts of all kinds.

Sulzer spent his nine months in London trying to convince the Allies of Switzerland's "good faith," but the Ministry of Economic Warfare had been keeping a close watch on Swiss industrial exports to the Third Reich. Sulzer retained his composure. He declared that the British statistics relating to those industrial exports were an "optical illusion." Of course current deliveries were at a high level, but only because the Swiss were working off German orders from way back....

The ladies and gentlemen from the Ministry of Economic

Warfare were unimpressed. They not only declined to relax the blockade against Switzerland in any way, but blacklisted Gebrüder Sulzer AG's engineering works into the bargain. The Winterthur firm was added to the British blacklist on October 26, 1943, and to the American on November 19 of the same year.

Sebastian Speich, the author of a subtle pen portrait of Sulzer, writes: "Hans Sulzer's world collapsed.... 'He bowed his head, and his eyes roamed around like those of some hopelessly cornered beast'—such is the dramatic description given of the humiliated giant's condition by the diplomat Ernst Schneeberger."[8]

Sulzer's response to Allied condemnation cannot be accounted for by rapacity, hypocrisy, and cupidity alone. The key words are political naïveté. To Sulzer, Herr Hitler was just a business associate like any other. There was a war on? So what? Gebrüder Sulzer AG was happy to supply all the belligerents—as long as they paid on time. Sulzer couldn't, or wouldn't, get it into his head that in 1942–43 the free world was battling for survival against a mass murderer.

Henry Guisan was a lieutenant colonel in the Swiss army and a director of Extroc AG, a firm based in Lausanne. The beloved son of General Henri Guisan, the universally respected commander in chief of the Swiss army, Henry (with a "y") had some excellent international connections.

In 1941, SS Captain Hans Wilhelm Eggen turned up in Lausanne with instructions to purchase 2,000 wooden huts. For these and other services Extroc AG charged the horrendous sum of 22 million Swiss francs. The Waffen-SS paid up without a murmur, and the bank transaction earned Henry Guisan a cool 13,000 Swiss francs. The huts, according to Eggen, were to be used "to accommodate troops on the Eastern Front."

Willi Gautschi, the biographer of Henry's father, comments: "The negotiators and suppliers concerned could hardly have been unaware of the purpose of the wooden huts supplied to the

Waffen-SS, because the existence of the concentration camps was also known in Switzerland by that time."[9]

What did Henry Guisan care about another concentration camp more or less? The SS were prompt payers and the deal smelled good.

The Swiss garage owners' association concluded a lucrative deal with Nazi Germany for the repair of thousands of trucks, Switzerland being a prime source of spare parts.

Another contract concerned gas engines, which the Swiss were particularly good at building. Though the Third Reich was short of gasoline after 1942, gas engines were much in demand, especially for Wehrmacht trucks. Feeling slightly uneasy, the garage owners inserted a clause in their contracts stipulating that the repaired and converted trucks must not be used at the front, only in "the German interior."[10]

Tractors, too, were supplied to Germany by Switzerland. Hermann, Freiherr von Wolff Metternich of Cologne, described just how useful they were in a letter to the *Frankfurter Allgemeine Zeitung* dated October 11, 1996:

I spent my childhood and adolescence at Wewelsburg, not far from Paderborn, a village whose dubious privilege it was to have been selected by Heinrich Himmler as the SS administrative center. It all began around 1935, when Wewelsburg Castle, once a seat of the prince-bishops of Paderborn, was developed into the SS Reich Leadership School and encircled by new SS administrative buildings. Gigantic plans in the Speer style were envisaged, and the villagers were to be compulsorily resettled. To obtain the requisite slave laborers, the SS had, from 1936 or thereabouts, established a concentration camp of its own on the outskirts of the village. Designated Konzentrationslager Niederhagen, this took its name from an expanse of communal woodland on the outskirts of the village.

The prisoners' main job was to excavate unworked travertine-like limestone from the neighboring quarries and transport it to the construction sites, a task that claimed many lives. To speed up the work, the SS had originally installed a small field railroad complete with dump cars that were usually propelled by prisoners, sometimes with the aid of a small steam locomotive. The dump-car track was amateurishly constructed and inefficient, however, and caused many accidents.

The situation changed abruptly in 1940–41. The railroad was abandoned and replaced with some brand-new tractors. These attracted attention if only because they were the last word in technological design, with chromium-plated headlights and fully enclosed cabs, a feature still uncommon at the time. Boldly displayed on the hoods was the name "Hürlimann," which surprised us, because modest Lanz and Deutz tractors were the only ones familiar to us in our rural neighborhood. It was not long before the word got around: they were vehicles of the finest Swiss manufacture and would help the SS to speed up their construction projects. The concentration camp prisoners may even have regarded this Swiss contribution to the development of the SS state as a form of humanitarian relief, because the dump cars no longer had to be propelled by hand.

Switzerland has been an exporting country for a hundred years —in fact, even today one third of its national income is attributable to the export trade. Germany was, and still is, its principal European trading partner.

Ernst Mühlemann, a national councilor from Thurgau, bank director, and brigadier general in the Swiss army, proudly declared in 1996: "We have a stronger balance of trade with Baden-Württemberg alone than with all the Third World countries put together."

He is right.

Wasn't it only natural, therefore, that the Swiss should continue to maintain commercial and financial relations with their

German neighbors during the dark war years—especially as they also went on doing business with the Allies, at least until 1940?

No, it was neither natural nor justified. What the stubborn defenders of mass exports to Nazi Germany from 1940 to 1945 refuse to concede to this day is that it makes a difference whether Swiss locomotives manufactured by Gebrüder Sulzer AG of Winterthur pulled regional trains from Stuttgart to Konstanz, or whether the same locomotives pulled trainloads of sealed cattle cars filled with doomed and despairing people from Budapest to Birkenau. Passenger traffic and SS death trains are not the same thing.

Volkswagen, the Nazi-run automobile manufacturer, was one of the largest industrial concerns in the Third Reich. Many large and medium-sized Swiss firms supplied it. In addition to automobiles, Volkswagen manufactured mines, V-1 rocket components, weapons of all kinds, and military vehicles.

The firm's workforce included slave laborers purchased from SS-run concentration camps, notably 800 Jewish men and women from Budapest whose murderous exploitation at the Volkswagen works subjected them to unremitting overwork and undernourishment. A comprehensive account of Volkswagen's employment of slave labor has been published by the historians Hans Mommsen and Manfred Grieger.[11]

One relatively unexplored chapter in the history of Swiss efficiency is the inexpensive acquisition by Swiss firms of "Aryanized" property formerly in Jewish ownership.

The Germans systematically expropriated Jewish assets—industrial enterprises, commercial concerns, real estate, and banks —from 1938 on. The Nazis sold off this loot to their Aryan German and foreign friends, usually at bargain-basement prices. Willi A. Boelcke reproduces the relevant statistics kept by the Reich Economics Ministry: no fewer than 39,532 Jewish-owned businesses were "Aryanized" within a single year (April 1, 1938– April 1, 1939).

Villiger, the Lucerne cigar manufacturer, is now a large, internationally active concern with an excellent reputation. Its international breakthrough came in 1935, when the brothers Max and Johann Villiger, who then headed the family, bought two of the best-known German cigar factories at Bad Cannstatt and Saarbrücken. These factories belonged to a Jewish family named Strauss whose members were being compelled to flee the country. They managed to emigrate, almost destitute, to the United States. The little the Villiger brothers had paid them for their business was taken by the Nazis as Reichsfluchtsteuer (literally, "Reich flight tax"), the official term for the confiscation of Jewish emigrants' property.

The Villigers had made an excellent impression on the Nazis. When submitting his application, dated February 20, 1941, for a permanent visa to the Reich at the German consulate in Basel, Max Villiger proudly made the following entry under the heading "Descent": "Aryan-Catholic for four hundred years."

The impoverished Strauss family tried to obtain compensation in the courts after the war, but the Villigers successfully contested the suit. One promising sign, however, is that Kaspar Villiger, Max's son, now a member of the government and Switzerland's minister of finance, is willing to discuss the issue in public.

The following words appeared in the booklet that marked the hundredth anniversary jubilee in celebration of the founding of Bally, the Swiss shoe manufacturer (which now belongs to Bührle): "It seems scarcely conceivable today that our beloved country was spared these two catastrophes [the two world wars]. Is our own generation grateful enough to such a kindly destiny?" Then, after a long digression into the firm's century-old history: "As time went by, one or two more retail footwear stores were acquired, both in Austria and in Germany."

What delicate phraseology! In fact, the Swiss firm snapped up ten prosperous Aryanized retail footwear stores after 1938. The Nazis had taken them from their Jewish owners and sold them off to the Swiss. The Bally shoe store near the Theatinerkirche in Munich belonged to a half-Jewish woman who had to get out of Germany but was short of cash. At the last minute she sold a 50 percent interest in the store to the Swiss. Her 50 percent was, of course, confiscated by the Nazis.

The Bally shoe kings, father and son, maintained friendly relations with numerous Nazi bigwigs, thereby facilitating their inexpensive acquisitions of Aryanized Jewish property. Both were men of influence in Switzerland. Father Eduard played an important role in the Liberal Party, and son Iwan represented Solothurn in the federal parliament from 1937 to 1943.

Friendly relations with the Third Reich were also maintained by many other Swiss industrial tycoons, including such prominent figures as textile manufacturer Max Stoffel and Ovomaltine manufacturer Georg Wander.

Hitler himself had visited Switzerland as early as August 1923 at the invitation of some Zurich industrialists and bankers. He stayed at the Hotel Gotthard on Bahnhofstrasse and dined in select company at the Villa Schönberg, where his hosts were the Wille-Rieter family (Crédit Suisse and textiles), who showed considerable foresight: Hitler was only an obscure political agitator when they bestowed on him their first modest gifts.

2. Allied Countermeasures

HITLER'S BANDITS PILLAGED EUROPE and looted eleven European central banks. His "foreign exchange protection teams" filched and extorted millions of private assets in the countries subjugated by the Wehrmacht; SS troops ran amok in the concentration camps and stole whatever they could—and the Swiss converted their spoils into foreign currency and remitted it to Berlin. Swiss industrialists supplied the Third Reich with machine tools, guns, and optical instruments.

Did the Allies simply look on?

It wasn't quite as simple as that. The strained relations

between the Western democracies and the Swiss money men passed through several different phases.

In the Allied camp the blockade was coordinated by Britain's Ministry of Economic Warfare (MEW) until 1941, when the direction and coordination of the Allied efforts was taken over by the U.S. Board of Economic Warfare.

Ever since the mid-1930s, when Hitler's rearmament policy became manifest, the British Foreign Office, the Treasury, and the Bank of England had been keeping as close a watch as possible on Germany's gold transactions. The British were aware of the Third Reich's perilous reliance on strategic raw materials from abroad and, thus, of the extreme importance to its war industries of Swiss francs and gold.

When war broke out the British were ready to impose an immediate naval blockade designed to cut off the Germans from their markets overseas. Throughout the world, attempts were made by British secret agents, bankers, and businessmen to sabotage German purchases of raw materials. Pressure was brought to bear on neutral countries, the object being to reduce their goods and services traffic with the Reich.

Problems arose first and foremost with the Swiss. Like all the industrial powers, Britain needed Switzerland in its capacity as a financial center. In particular, London needed Swiss francs. The British government also knew that the Swiss themselves were dependent on imports for foodstuffs and industrial raw materials. British representatives in Bern complained that their trade with Germany was unduly brisk and their loans to Germany were too extensive. But British pressure was gentle nonetheless. London credited the Swiss with good faith and even expressed sympathy for their predicament.

The Allies built up a highly effective worldwide surveillance network. Most German radio signals were monitored, recorded, and translated. A watch was also kept on communications between Berlin and Bern, Zurich and Berlin, and Zurich and the world. There were radio monitoring experts aboard Allied warships on the high seas, in all consulates and embassies, and all secret service stations.

Secret codes were ineffective. The Allies managed to crack the vast majority of them. At Bletchley Park, situated between Oxford and Cambridge some fifty miles northwest of London, the British authorities had assembled the most eminent mathematicians and cryptanalysts they could find. Their radio monitoring headquarters, code-named "Communication Section," had a worldwide network of 30,000 eavesdroppers.[12]

Hitler was satisfied that no one could defeat "Enigma," the German enciphering machine, but he was wrong. Even when German cipher experts developed a still more intricate and seemingly enemy-proof code, the British cracked that too. In short, British intelligence was privy to almost every telegraphic and telephonic communication emanating from Switzerland's bankers and industrialists.

On January 11, 1997, the U.S. Senate's Banking Committee published an OSS report from Bern citing a highly placed Swiss source and confirming an MEW decryption. Both documents referred to the same triangular transaction between Germany, Switzerland, and Portugal.

Thanks to successful monitoring and decrypting, MEW agents had identified three bank accounts held at the Swiss National Bank by the central bank of Portugal. One of them contained gold paid into it by the National Bank. For this gold the Portuguese supplied escudos. The second account displayed a series of complicated transactions: the Germans sold gold bars to the Swiss, who sold them off to the Portuguese, who in turn credited an existing Reichsbank account in Lisbon with escudos. The third account unearthed by British agents contained gold that the Swiss National Bank held for Portugal on behalf of the Reichsbank. All these transactions were effected in 1942 and 1943, and all were directly related to German purchases of wolfram in Lisbon.

In 1942 the Wehrmacht was advancing at breakneck speed—something it could never have done without the help of Hitler's Swiss fences, their purchases of raw materials and industrial exports. The Allies were gradually losing trust in Switzerland's good faith.

Winston Churchill went on the attack. In January 1943, at his request, sixteen governments signed the "Interallied declaration against acts of dispossession committed in territories under enemy occupation or control." The purpose of this interallied declaration was "to combat and defeat the plundering by the enemy Powers of the territories which have been overrun or brought under enemy control." The Allies reserved the right "to declare invalid all transfers of, or dealings with, property, rights, and interests of any description whatsoever which are, or have been, situated in the territories which have come under the occupation or control, direct or indirect, of the Governments with which they are at war."

Churchill's anger was directed in particular at Switzerland's gold-laundering transactions. The Allies were also worried by the vast loans being extended to the Third Reich. From Berlin's point of view, these were badly needed financial injections—in modern parlance, development aid.

Switzerland's massive arms deliveries and exports of mechanical devices, optical instruments, and so forth were partly offset by German deliveries of coal and other commodities, but they were often supplied on credit. The loans in question were long-term loans that granted the Germans many a valuable respite.

The Rifkind Report quotes an exchange of letters in April 1943 between Sir David Waley of the Treasury and a Mr. Gibbs of the Ministry of Economic Warfare. It shows how frustrated the Allies were. Gibbs wrote that the Swiss should be compelled to discontinue their purchases of gold. Waley replied that he shared Gibbs's belief that the warning to Switzerland could not be a hundred percent effective because, in his opinion, it would be a hundred percent *in*effective.[13]

Intelligence reports, notably from Allen Dulles in Bern, indicated that major Swiss banks were converting gold and other looted assets into cash on numerous international financial markets, and that they were doing so on a vast scale for the benefit of their clients in Berlin. Shanghai and Lisbon were the financial centers to which reference was often made.

The Allies regularly complained to the Bern authorities, but the Swiss government always had a twofold answer ready. In the first place, Switzerland represented Germany's diplomatic interests in several countries.[14] Second, strict bank secrecy prevailed in Switzerland, so Bern was unable to supervise the business dealings of major banks, private financial administrators, et cetera. Both answers were legally incontestable.

Half a century later, in 1996, the presidents of Crédit Suisse and Union Bank of Switzerland were confronted by American journalists with a U.S. Secret Service report of 1944 containing information about their financial dealings with the Third Reich. The bankers issued no disclaimer. A spokesman for Crédit Suisse stated tersely: "We had a businesslike relationship with Germany."[15]

The Allies' first priority was to impose as watertight a worldwide economic blockade as possible. The Germans had to be cut off from their sources of raw materials in order to starve their munitions industry. The Wehrmacht needed manganese for shell cases, iron ore for guns, wolfram for the optical gunsights on its tanks, chromium alloys for armor plate and gun barrels. Vast quantities of all these strategic metals had to be purchased from Portugal, Turkey, Sweden, and other countries beyond Hitler's grasp.

In Latin America, Switzerland, Spain, Portugal, and elsewhere in the world, Nazi agents had set up an unknown number of dummy corporations. They had also taken over legal, long-established foreign businesses and remodeled them. Many German firms had founded subsidiaries in Switzerland during the 1920s, mostly for tax reasons. All these and any concerns in other countries that worked with or for the Nazis—banks, insurance companies, industrial and commercial enterprises—were subject to a rigorous Allied boycott.

Blacklisting was restricted to firms whose volume of business with Germany had increased during the war years—and blacklisting here means entering on the blacklist compiled and daily updated by the U.S. Department of the Treasury. Where Swiss firms were concerned, the boycott was not lifted until June 30, 1946. The Allies kept other lists as well. London's Ministry of Economic Warfare, for example, maintained a "blacklist," a "suspect list," and a "statutory list." At one time or another, more than 1,600 Swiss firms or individuals appeared on the "statutory list" alone.[16]

The Allies were able to keep tabs on the volume of business transacted by thousands of firms, particularly Swiss, by an efficient espionage network built up by Secretary of the Treasury Henry Morgenthau and his agents.

In April 1943 Washington demanded that the Swiss reduce their loans to Germany. To enforce their demands, the U.S. authorities deployed a powerful weapon: Unless Switzerland complied, the Allies would cancel all contracts relating to shipments of foodstuffs.

The Allied weapon was the "Navicert," or navigation certificate. Landing rights at Genoa and Sète were useless unless freight bound for Switzerland (grain from Argentina, for instance) had been legitimized by the said certificate. Without a Navicert it would be confiscated. Switzerland was, and still is, dependent on sources abroad for up to two thirds of its food. The Swiss must stop trading or starve.

The British and Americans ruled the waves in 1943. The Swiss could not survive without food imports from overseas, but the government, and Walther Stampfli in particular, resisted stubbornly. He negotiated and played for time—with some success.

Walther Stampfli was chairman of the Federal Department of Economics, that is, minister of economic affairs, from 1940 to 1947. He came to the post from heavy industry, having previously been managing director of the Von-Roll-Werke. He was a Solothurn radical, a liberal of great intelligence, authoritarian manner, iron determination, and unbounded energy. One of the few great statesmen Switzerland has produced in the present century, he served his country well.

Stampfli managed to keep open the international trade routes that made it possible for Switzerland to import foodstuffs throughout the war. Yet he, too, was something of a vacillator. Although not neutral in his personal sentiments and aware that World War II was a fight to the death between civilization and Fascism, he was nevertheless averse to acting accordingly. On the contrary, he publicly voiced the following angry remark: "Just imagine, the Allies are demanding that we join in the war against Germany! Germany has never treated Switzerland as badly as the Allies are doing now."

Switzerland eventually signed an agreement with the Allies on December 19, 1943, pledging itself to reduce deliveries of arms and ammunition to Germany by 45 percent over the previous year. Exports of optical instruments, rocket components, and precision material were to be cut by 60 percent, and loans would also be trimmed.

The Allied resolutions of February 22 and August 18, 1944, left nothing to be desired in the way of clarity: they warned against accepting German gold, whatever its provenance. Gold transactions with the Third Reich were declared illegal. The Allies would not acknowledge the validity of such transactions, even in the far distant future, and even in the case of neutral countries.

In the knowledge that Swiss arms deliveries and financial aid to Germany were prolonging the war, the Allies made an appeal to conscience. In January 1945 President Roosevelt wrote to Federal President von Steiger:

> It would indeed be a matter of conscience to every peace-loving Swiss to have to live with the knowledge that he had in some way obstructed the efforts of other peace-loving peoples to liberate the world from a ruthless tyrant.... I express myself thus firmly because every day's prolongation of the war costs the lives of a number of my fellow countrymen.[17]

In London, Foreign Secretary Anthony Eden summoned the Swiss envoy, Walter Thurnheer, and told him that "every franc's worth of war material dispatched by Switzerland to Germany prolonged the war."[18]

At the beginning of 1945 Hitler still controlled—on paper—more than 10 million soldiers. He had 290 divisions, or roughly twice as many as on May 10, 1940, but the Third Reich was already in its death throes.[19]

Five million Red Army soldiers were advancing on the Baltic front. The German armies facing them numbered 1.8 million, but they were hungry and exhausted, demoralized, and short of supplies. Stalin brought up 7,000 tanks including a large number of those bearing his own name, each with a range of 150 miles and weighing in at 46 tons. Hitler had only 3,500 tanks on the Eastern Front, many of them lacking fuel, ammunition, and spare parts.

It dawned on the Swiss government that something was amiss with its current policy. On February 16, 1945, it resolved to freeze all German assets in Switzerland. An official investigation was launched of the gold and other assets consigned to Swiss bank vaults by the Nazis.

On March 2, 1945, Switzerland banned all dealings in foreign banknotes. On March 8 the Swiss government concluded an agreement, known as the Currie Agreement after Laughlin Currie, the chief Allied negotiator, with the Allies. The other subscribers to this document were the United States, Great Britain, and France. Bern promised to take steps to identify and freeze German assets. It would then ascertain which of them constituted "looted property" and inform the Allies accordingly. The Swiss government was thus creating a legal basis for the return of those frozen assets that had been seized from their rightful owners. Finally, as specified in the Currie Agreement, Switzerland promised not to purchase any more gold from Germany, effective immediately.

The Currie Agreement was dated March 8, 1945. The last consignment of looted gold from Berlin, escorted by armed German agents, reached Bern on the morning of April 6.

The Swiss had by no means capitulated. The Bern government voluntarily declared itself ready to freeze all German assets in Swiss bank vaults, but it wouldn't hand them over on any account. That would have been the worst of all sins: a violation of Switzerland's sacred neutrality.

Then came the meeting at Potsdam, July 17 to August 2, 1945. Hitler was dead and the Thousand-Year Reich lay in ruins. Roosevelt was also dead, so the conference table was occupied by Churchill, Stalin, and Harry Truman. Churchill having been incomprehensibly defeated in the British parliamentary elections, he was replaced on July 28 by Clement Attlee.

It was resolved that the German assets in neutral bank vaults in Western Europe should be handed over to the Western Allies, as well as to fifteen other allied countries, excluding the Soviet Union and the countries of Eastern Europe. The Allied Control Commission's Law No. 5, of October 30, 1945, stipulated that German creditors could not draw on their assets abroad. Power of disposal was assigned to the Control Commission.

The great reparations conference was held in Paris during November and December of the same year. This set up an international authority, the Interallied Reparations Agency (IARA), based in Brussels. The participants also reached agreement on the percentage distribution of the total sum to be paid in reparations.

The United States, Great Britain, and France were empowered on the same occasion to open negotiations with neutral countries, and with Switzerland in particular, concerning the handover of German assets.

3. Henry Morgenthau, Jr., and the Safehaven Program

A SPECIAL ROLE IN the whole complex strategy of Allied commercial and financial retaliation against Hitler's Swiss accomplices was played by Operation Safehaven, under the direction of Secretary of the Treasury Morgenthau.

Henry Morgenthau, Jr., was a strong-willed, extremely dynamic and talented man. The son of German immigrants, born in New York in 1891, he at first devoted himself to agriculture. A personal friend of Franklin D. Roosevelt, he shared the latter's aversion to the speculative capitalism that ran riot during the late 1920s. Morgenthau believed in the state as a moral institution and in modern democracy's duty to mold society. The Wall Street crash of 1929 strengthened him (and Roosevelt) in that belief. On November 8, 1932, Roosevelt won the presidential election, and Morgenthau became one of his closest advisers. Together they devised the program that has gone down in history as the New Deal, a series of projects designed to revitalize the economy, combat mass unemployment, and assist the weakest social classes. In 1934 Morgenthau was appointed secretary of the treasury. He held the post until his resignation in July 1945, having shaped the financial and economic policy of the United States for eleven long years.

Morgenthau's name is indissolubly linked with the worldwide economic war against Nazism. In 1943 he drafted the so-called Safehaven Program, whose implementation he supervised and directed. Its aim was to prevent neutral countries, especially Switzerland, from becoming "safehavens" for the Nazis' spoils.

Assisted by their British and Free French colleagues, U.S. military and civilian intelligence agents infiltrated German front companies, neutralized German or German-employed raw-materials buyers, and sabotaged the Third Reich's international trade routes. They blew up countless factories, oceangoing ships, and railroad trains in third countries. Even the Oerlikon arms factory, situated near Zurich on neutral Swiss territory, was bombed "in error." Seymour J. Rubin, whom we shall meet later on, even managed to place agents in the New York branches of major Swiss banks. German businessmen or their foreign collaborators were murdered in Ankara, Lisbon, Rio de Janeiro, Djakarta, Shanghai, and Havana.

Once the tide of war in Europe had turned in favor of the Allies, the Safehaven Program was followed by the Reparations Program: the effective confiscation of all German assets, wherever they might be, as a means of offsetting Allied war debts. Underlying both the Safehaven and, later on, the Reparations Program was another motive hard to comprehend today.

Germany is now the largest and probably the most vital European democracy, but in 1943, 1944, and 1945 the Allies suffered from a traumatic fear that German militarism was ineradicable. The Third Reich's unconditional military surrender was within arm's reach, but Roosevelt, Churchill and de Gaulle (not to mention Stalin) doubted that this would set the seal on the problem of German militarism.

The Allies were haunted by the events of the 1920s and 1930s. The draconian clauses of the Versailles Treaty and the occupation of the Ruhr, Germany's industrial heartland, had served no purpose. Within the space of a single generation, the German military machine had arisen once again, more powerful, murderous, and aggressive than ever.

Morgenthau, himself of German-Jewish descent and profoundly mistrustful of all things German, submitted a plan for the complete and—so he hoped—final destruction of German industry. Europe's foremost industrial power was to be transformed by Allied decree into farmland. This would sever the roots of

German militarism and deprive it of nourishment in perpetuity.

The Morgenthau plan was rejected by the new president, Harry Truman, and its author resigned, embittered, in July 1945.

The minutes of the Yalta Conference, February 4–11, 1945, make interesting reading. It was an occasion fraught with tension and mistrust. Seated at the conference table were Churchill and Roosevelt, the two leading statesmen of the largest Western democracies, and Stalin, a man responsible for the deaths of millions of his compatriots. Though united in a military alliance against Hitler's wars of aggression, they were humanly and culturally light-years apart. But Stalin and his allies were agreed on two points: Germany must be occupied in toto after its defeat and, if possible, dismembered.

Stalin wanted to settle the partition issue right away. An American plan provided for the Reich's division into five or six parts. Churchill submitted a scheme that would have isolated Prussia and internationalized the Rhineland. He also proposed to create a Danubian Federation. Stalin was in favor of dismemberment but against the Danubian Federation.

Discussions eventually ground to a halt, and a committee was appointed to study the American program under the chairmanship of Anthony Eden, the British foreign secretary.[20]

The Allies' fear that German militarism might rear its head once more—with or without a new Hitler—persisted. It was not as utterly absurd as all that.

On the morning of August 10, 1944, a select gathering assembled at the Hotel Rotes Haus in Strasbourg. Seated at the table were senior executives of Krupp, Röchling, Volkswagen, Rheinmetall, Messerschmitt, and other industrial concerns. Also present were some gentlemen from IG-Farben, which supplied the SS with Zyklon-B gas for use in extermination camps. Most of these industrialists were personally indebted to the men who wore black uniforms with death's-heads on the lapels. They knew each other well and had worked together for years. Many of their companies employed slave laborers taken from concentration camps and sold to them by the SS. Also represented were the Reichsbank and the Ministry of Munitions. An SS general was the chair. The aim of the Strasbourg conference was to transfer German assets abroad, so that (to quote an OSS report) "a strong German Reich can rise again after the defeat."

The conference had a complicated prehistory of which only a brief outline can be given here. Italy had surrendered in 1943, and the Allies had landed in Normandy in June 1944. The belief was gaining ground, both in boardrooms and in Himmler's entourage, that Germany could not—despite secret weapons and total mobilization—win the war. Himmler's agents fanned out all over Europe, trying to establish direct or indirect contact with Allied representatives in Stockholm, Madrid, Bern, Lisbon, and Ankara. Himmler was obsessed with the crazy notion of persuading the Western Allies to conclude a separate peace. In return, he offered to continue the war against the Soviet "subhumans." In an attempt to save his own neck, he sent his confidential agent to Stockholm to see Bruce Hopper, the OSS chief in Sweden.

Seven hundred thousand Jews, the last surviving Jewish community in the Nazis' sphere of influence, were resident in Hungary in 1944. In Budapest the Swiss consul Carl Lutz and the Swedish diplomat Raoul Wallenberg were issuing thousands of passports to Jewish families at the risk of their own lives. The Reichsführer SS used these Hungarian Jews as a bargaining counter. He proposed to exchange them for money and a separate peace—indeed, he temporarily halted the death trains bound for Auschwitz.

On August 21, 1944, Himmler's emissary, SS Lieutenant Colonel Kurt Becher, negotiated with Sally Mayer, accredited representative of the Joint Distribution Committee, an American Jewish welfare organization, at Sankt Margarethen on the German-Swiss frontier, but to no avail. The death trains set off for Auschwitz once more. The SS bosses were also in active communication with Colonel Roger Masson, the Swiss military intelligence chief. SS General Walter Schellenberg had even dined with General Guisan, the commander in chief of the Swiss army, at the Bären, a country inn at Biglen.

Information about the Strasbourg conference is scanty. It derives mostly from fragmentary OSS reports published in Washington in 1996 and from Nazi-hunter Simon Wiesenthal's investigations. Leading historians of this period whom I myself have consulted—notably Jean-Claude Favez, Philippe Burrin, and Daniel Bourgeois—have no knowledge of any conference minutes. Burrin surmises, doubtless correctly, that the SS officers and industrialists at Strasbourg were at pains to keep their deliberations secret and confined themselves to passing an oral, unrecorded resolution. The modern history archive at Zurich's Federal University of Technology contains the report of an investigation, drafted in 1966, which also concerns Wiesenthal's research.[21]

It seems clear that no one has yet essayed a scholarly reconstruction of the conference discussions and decisions. I certainly know of no publications on the subject.

The main purpose of the Strasbourg conference was to organize capital transfers abroad, especially to South America, to create the preconditions for a resurrected Reich. Another aim was to organize and finance escape routes for senior members of the SS and Gestapo. Even in 1944, the Allies were making no secret of their intention to bring the perpetrators of war crimes to trial once Germany had unconditionally surrendered.

The SS was a state within a state, responsible for the Reich's security and charged with the destruction of all "worthless" lives, the subjugation of "inferior" Slavic peoples, and the final extermination of European Jews and Gypsies. The SS was responsible for the deaths of some fourteen million men, women and children, including six million Jews, five million Russians, two million Poles, more than half a million Gypsies, and hundreds of thousands of chronic invalids, resistance fighters, Social

Democrats, Communists, Christians, trade unionists, and anti-Nazis of every complexion, in Austria and Germany as elsewhere.

Department VI of the Central State Security Bureau under the command of SS General Schellenberg, was entrusted with the exportation of capital. Schellenberg worked closely throughout the war with the heads of firms and high finance houses. In addition to espionage and counterespionage, his responsibilities included the organization of the economic war, or "counterblockade," as it was known. SS Major Bernhard Krüger, one of Schellenberg's section heads, had millions of forged pound notes printed and distributed in an attempt to undermine Britain's currency. Krüger did an efficient job. As late as 1950, Scotland Yard confiscated some forged Nazi pound notes that had come from Argentina and were circulating in London.[22]

The senior executives of large German firms and banks, as well as of the Reichsbank and the Ministry of Munitions, who conferred at Strasbourg organized a massive flight of capital.

Also involved were personal friendships with, and loyalty to, the SS. One of Nazi Germany's unofficial but extremely influential associations was the Freundeskreis des Reichsführer-SS Himmler ("Reichsführer-SS Himmler's Circle of Friends"), which had been meeting regularly since the mid-1930s. This association, to which most of the industrialists and bankers in conference at Strasbourg belonged, doubtless passed resolutions on how to distribute the concentration camp slaves among its members' various manufacturing plants.

Legalistic to the bitter end, the Nazi bureaucrats prevailed on Hitler to issue an edict revoking the ban on private German capital exports that had been in force since 1933. The transfers of capital were to be effected through a third country—Switzerland, of course. The two Swiss banks selected to carry out this operation were the Basler Handelsbank and Crédit Suisse. Now that the Führer's ban had been lifted, the floodgates opened.

Goebbels continued to bellow into every available microphone, blustering about ultimate victory and summoning his compatriots to fight to the last. In the suburbs of Berlin a limping, bent-backed, ashen-faced Hitler inspected the companies of undernourished youngsters and feeble old men who were sent into action, and thus to certain death, in the final battle against well-equipped Red Army units.

Himmler's role was important. His betrayal of the Führer brought many Nazi bosses to their senses. It was a question of every man for himself—plus as much loot as possible.

To begin with they established personal caches in the areas under their control. On April 4, 1945, for example, U.S. infantrymen advancing through Thuringia came across a regular Ali Baba's cave. Near Merkers, in the subterranean galleries of a salt mine, they discovered a glittering hoard comprising thousands of gold coins and bars and silver ingots. The SS generals of the Central State Security Bureau had buried their loot some 2,800 feet up on the Blaa-Alm, near Altaussee in the heart of Austria. Information to this effect appears in a U.S. Counter-Intelligence Corps (CIC) report dated 1947. The cave filled with SS plunder was only a few miles from the Altaussee salt mine where the Nazi bosses had hoarded hundreds of stolen works of art (paintings, sculptures, drawings, manuscripts) in hopes of better days to come.

In the summer of 1996 some remarkable facsimile documents came to light in Washington's secret archives. One was an agent's report from the Davos branch of Graubünden's cantonal bank. Another insider's report, drafted by an OSS informant, tells of what went on in the Banque Cantonale Vaudoise at Lausanne. Hermann Göring's loot was involved in both instances. Evidently knowing how crafty the big Swiss banks could be, the Reich Marshal was wary of them and preferred to keep his treasures in smaller, cantonal banks whose confidentiality and loyalty he could fully trust.

We now have documentary evidence of many other operations of a similar nature. Vast fortunes were transferred by representatives of industry, commerce, and banking, as well as by members of the Nazi Party and SS.

Franz von Papen, the German ambassador in Ankara, was acquitted at Nuremberg. (He was later convicted by a German court but released in 1949.) The owner of a substantial fortune, Papen wondered how best to preserve it from Allied confiscation. He had a friend, a senior Swiss diplomat, who helped him to transfer it to Switzerland.

Published on December 4, 1996, was a secret American document from the OSS archives, dated April 1945. Relating to the Berlin office of the Dresdner Bank, it attested the transfer, via a Swiss trustee, of $20 million to a Buenos Aires account in the name of Joseph Goebbels.

Corporate lawyers (trustees, financial administrators, and so forth) in Zurich, Basel, Lugano, Bern, and Lucerne were kept extremely busy in late 1944 and early 1945. At that time, and until 1990, there existed in Switzerland a "Form B." This entitled an attorney to open an anonymous account for his client. More precisely, the attorney opened the bank account in a fiduciary capacity but withheld his principal's name and invoked his own duty of confidentiality. The gratifying advantage of this system was that it reinforced the already hermetic protection of bank secrecy with that of legal confidentiality. The client was thus enabled to conceal his loot behind a double wall of silence.

It is very probable that in the years to come the historians' committee appointed by the Swiss government and parliament will find an answer to the question of the extent to which this flight of German capital derived from the Strasbourg meeting. Another committee chaired by Paul J. Volcker, on which the World Jewish Congress and the Swiss Bankers Association are equally represented, will also be tackling this problem in the very near future. Most of the loot amassed by Göring and the other Nazi dignitaries was, after all, Jewish-owned.

South America, and Argentina in particular, was second only

to Switzerland as a favored port of call. Jorge Camarasa documents the nocturnal landings made by German submarines in the estuary of the Río de la Plata. Laden with boxes of gold, silver, and diamonds, the U-boats were accompanied by armed German agents.[23]

Argentina's Juan Perón first succumbed to the charms of Fascism as a youthful military attaché in Rome in 1933. Despite his belated, Allied-enforced declaration of war on Hitler in 1944, his country remained a favorite place of refuge for defeated Nazis. The Canadian historian Ronald C. Newton, who has devoted a book to the subject, analyzes the escape routes to Argentina taken not only by Nazi loot but by war criminals on the run from the Allies.[24]

We already have some knowledge of the effective way in which capital transfers to South America—especially to Argentina, Paraguay, and southern Brazil—were arranged by private Swiss banks, trustees, corporation lawyers, and financial administrators. They enabled numerous Nazis to rebuild their private lives after 1945. Adolf Eichmann, who headed the Jewish Section of Department IV of the Central State Security Bureau, was captured by agents of Israel's Mossad in Buenos Aires, but hundreds of other Nazi war criminals lived peacefully and unscathed—often in luxury—in Missiones, in the Brazilian region of Iguaçú bordering Paraguay and Argentina, or on handsome estates along the banks of the Paraná. Joseph Mengele, the concentration camp doctor, was never caught.

Among those who retired to South America were Eduard Roschmann, nicknamed the Butcher of Riga, Gestapo chief Heinrich Müller, and many other Nazi functionaries.

On February 2, 1996, the U.S. government published a secret document which, for the first time, puts a figure on the Nazi loot transferred to South America, in particular Argentina and Paraguay. In April 1945 alone, Argentinian insurance companies, banks, trust companies, financial administrators, and commercial firms took receipt of Nazi plunder worth approximately one billion dollars—a sum so alarming that it rightly gave the Allies nightmares. In 1945 German agents bought huge estates in Missiones, the aforesaid northern province of Argentina, where maté is grown. Today in Encarnación, the Paraguayan town just across the Paraná from Missiones, German—with a Berlin or Munich accent—is still the language most often heard.

No Fourth Reich has arisen, but loyalty to the past persists. As Wilfried von Owen, formerly Goebbels's press chief and now living in retirement in Buenos Aires, told the Madrid daily *El Sol* in 1992: "Not only do I not regret my past in any way, but I remain a great admirer of my erstwhile boss, Dr. Joseph Goebbels. He was a brilliant man. I'm not in hiding. I was a soldier, and subject to the orders of a legitimate government. I committed none of the so-called war crimes. No one can hold anything against me."[25]

The capital exports to South America and the massive transfers to Switzerland were nearly always arranged by Germans in positions of authority and only rarely by private German trustees. Göring, Ribbentrop, and many other Nazi higher-ups conveyed their treasures to safety with the active assistance of members of their own government departments or senior Party officials.[26] The accounts were opened by Göring's agents, who traveled on German diplomatic passports. Direct transfers were then carried out by German private banks, notably the Süddeutsche Diskonto-Gesellschaft of Baden.

Göring filched most of his treasures from Jews, but he also stole anything from anywhere he could: art collections from Polish, Hungarian, Russian, and Dutch museums, millions in foreign currency from the private banks of occupied countries, and many other things of value.[27] Convoys of trucks belonging to the Reichspost, the state postal service, were escorted by German police officers. Setting off from Nuremberg and Munich, they crossed the Swiss frontier at Buchs. Then, laden with Göring's stolen pictures, sculptures, jewelry, precious stones, gold bars, silver candelabra, diamonds, and foreign currency, they carted off their loads to Swiss bank vaults. Switzerland was not alone in harboring Göring's loot. Four tons of his gold went to Madrid.

Accounts were opened at Davos in the name of the German Sanitarium, which was wholly controlled by the Nazi Party machine. Other assets—the present running total amounts to sixteen million Swiss francs—were hoarded in a Swiss account under the cover name Dr. Ingmann.

The supposition that Göring's private flights of capital were connected with the strategy developed at Strasbourg in August 1944 is reinforced by other pointers. Many other Nazi bosses followed Göring's procedure. Ribbentrop, for example, favored the Basel-based Swiss Bank Corporation. Those who conferred with its directors were usually diplomats from the Foreign Ministry in Wilhelmstrasse, among them a man named Kurt Eichel. This was yet another instance where a Nazi bigwig conveyed his millions to safety through semiofficial channels. It seems inconceivable that Ribbentrop could have done so without Hitler's knowledge and the consent of the SS and the Gestapo.

Ribbentrop's dealings were highly professional. He operated not only through the big banks, but through private trust companies such as Wehrli & Co. of Zurich. Wehrli, which no longer exists, had good connections in Buenos Aires. Ribbentrop's millions wound up at the Banco Alemán Transatlántico, in a dummy account under the cover name Pedro Rodriguez Panchino.

Ribbentrop's hoard of gold had colorful origins. Italy changed sides and broke with Hitler on September 8, 1943, but the Wehrmacht and the SS did not pull out of Rome empty-handed: their trucks carried off a part of the gold reserves of Italy's national bank. In its vaults they found the gold and foreign currency holdings of the Albanian national bank, which Mussolini had previously seized. The SS squads purloined that gold as well, bringing their haul to a documented total of 475.8 million Swiss francs, a value equivalent to roughly 1.5 billion dollars today.

The Italian and Albanian gold was deposited in the vaults of the Reichsbank in Berlin. The Italian consisted largely of coins from a wide range of countries. Some of these were remitted to various intelligence services, government authorities, and Wehrmacht and SS departments for special use. Ribbentrop treated himself to a personal reserve at the Foreign Ministry, its intended purpose being to finance clandestine activities abroad.

' The value Ribbentrop's fund is put at seventy-two million Swiss francs. Part of this sum was remitted to Buenos Aires by Wehrli & Co. and other financial fences.

A U.S. State Department report of 1996 disclosed a curious Swiss practice. To save money when sending things overseas, the Swiss Foreign Ministry used to entrust the diplomatic bag to private individuals, such as trustees, bankers, and corporation lawyers going abroad on business. Whether traveling by sea or train, they enjoyed diplomatic immunity. Under the Vienna Convention, no customs or immigration officer had the right to search their baggage. However, an American secret agent broke the lock of one such privately transported diplomatic pouch. He found it to contain half a million U.S. dollars in bills, together with documentation showing that the money belonged to Ribbentrop and was being sent by a Swiss bank to its correspondent in Buenos Aires.

On Wednesday, December 11, 1996, the Banking Committee of the House of Representatives convened at Washington. At this public hearing on the subject of looted Nazi gold in Swiss banks and stolen assets transferred to South America in 1944 and 1945, the first witness was Senator Alfonse D'Amato of New York. With the aid of secret documents just unearthed from U.S. archives, he demonstrated the existence of another peculiar Swiss practice: one or two big German clients of Swiss financial institutions and trust companies were provided with papers and passports for the hazardous journey to South America.

Ribbentrop was the first to be hanged after the major war criminals were sentenced at Nuremberg. Göring committed suicide two hours before his scheduled execution. It is very probable that most of the loot amassed by those two is still lying in Swiss bank vaults or has long since found its way into the pockets of trustees, attorneys, and straw men based in Zurich, Basel, and Bern.

4. Neutrality

THE SWISS ARE NOT a people without a history. They possess a collective memory, a strong, centuries-old identity. Neutrality is the basis of that identity. No one can gain access to Switzerland's inhabitants' collective consciousness without previously analyzing the neutrality dogma. We shall undertake that analysis here.

The authorities at London's Ministry of Economic Warfare and the U.S. Board of Economic Warfare, striving to cripple the Swiss gold-laundering machine, put a stop to Switzerland's manifold exports of industrial goods and arms to the Third Reich, and terminate its compensation credits in Hitler's favor, sustained one defeat after another. They tried in vain, throughout those dark war years, to win the Swiss over. Diplomatic pressure achieved nothing, contractual agreements remained dead letters, warnings were disregarded—even the blacklisting of more than a thousand Swiss firms and the freezing of all Swiss bank accounts in the United States proved ineffective.

The Allies kept banging their heads against the wall of Swiss neutrality. Switzerland's plea could not but strike Allied negotiators as a lame excuse, but the neutrality dogma is an essential constituent of the national identity. In the name of neutrality the Swiss ruling class not only financed Hitler's wars of aggression; it also did much that was good—for instance, where

Switzerland's role as an international protecting power was concerned.

When wars break out, diplomatic relations between the belligerents are severed and many of their nationals are caught unawares on foreign soil. With their diplomatic representation in the host country suspended, they are at the mercy of that country's government. It was to remedy this undesirable state of affairs that the international community agreed, a century and a half ago, to create the institution of the protecting power.

From 1939 to 1945, Switzerland was the world's favorite protecting power. Although only minor when hostilities broke out, the importance of its role was quickly augmented by the Germans' onslaught in the West, their advance into the Balkans, and Italy's entry into the war. Switzerland eventually represented no fewer than thirty-five countries. Great faith was placed in Swiss diplomats, so much so that they were frequently entrusted with the protection of their national interests by countries at war with each other.[28]

A protecting power has three functions of special importance.

1. The repatriation of civilian internees. Belligerents often interned foreign civilians on the outbreak of war. Tedious negotiations were conducted by Switzerland with both countries, host and guest, about the exchange and repatriation of internees, tens of thousands of whom were swapped and provided with safe-conducts. Switzerland maintained a substantial staff for this purpose: more than 150 officials in Bern and more than 1,000 diplomats around the world.

The repatriation of internees—and, on occasion, badly wounded servicemen—tended to be a very expensive and complicated procedure. A total of 35,000 were repatriated. The biggest single operation concerned Eritrea and Abyssinia, from which 28,000 Italian men, women, and children were shipped back to Italy after the British marched into Asmara and Addis Ababa. Jews, too, were rescued: several hundred of them—initially from Germany, later from the Balkans—were exchanged for Germans resident in Palestine. In 1944 the Swiss protecting power managed to purchase the freedom of 1,870 Hungarian Jews with American money, at $100 apiece. They were brought to Switzerland.

The legal basis of Switzerland's activities as a protecting power was a bilateral mandate, but its representatives also operated by invoking the Geneva Conventions of the International Committee of the Red Cross, which enabled Swiss diplomats to visit prisoner-of-war camps. Only Stalin had failed to subscribe to the Geneva Conventions. Thus, Soviet prisoners of war were wholly at the mercy of their German captors, who murdered 2.5 million of them at Hitler's behest.

2. The transmission of grants-in-aid. Western countries paid Switzerland large sums of money to be passed on as grants-in-aid to their nationals interned on enemy soil. The Swiss transmitted a total of 245 million francs in this way, but such payments were far from easy to arrange. It was not, for instance, until 1944 that they obtained Japanese permission to transmit grants-in-aid to persons interned in the Philippines and Indonesia (then the Dutch East Indies).

3. Visits to prisoners. Edgar Bonjour describes the difficulties these presented:

> The protecting power's first duty was to visit prison camps. In violation of the agreement, inspectors were refused entry to the transit camps where prisoners often spent long periods. As a rule, representatives of the protecting power visited the living quarters and workplaces of prisoners of war every three months, identifying deficiencies, listening to complaints, and mediating between camp authorities and inmates. Unlike Red Cross delegates, representatives of the protecting power were entitled to converse with prisoners of war in private. In Germany in 1944, Swiss inspectors visited and wrote 350 reports on 150 camps, hospitals, and military prisons, as well as on 1,900 labor gangs attached to camps. Early in March 1945, officials of the Swiss protecting power traced some prominent British hostages, who were rescued

in the nick of time. In Japan it took over a hundred written applications before Switzerland received permission to inspect around one prison camp in three.[29]

Deserving of mention, although independent of protecting power activities, is the work performed by delegates of the International Committee of the Red Cross, who looked after seven million prisoners of war and 175,000 civilian internees. More than 3,000 people worked in the central agency for prisoners of war at Geneva, and more than 600,000 tracing requests were answered.

The Germans very seldom granted access to concentration camps. Their official attitude remained unchanged throughout the war: just like jails, prisons, and penitentiaries, concentration camps were state institutions of a domestic nature and, as such, not subject to the Geneva Conventions or the protecting power's mandate. Fifty-eight Swiss citizens died in German concentration camps and penitentiaries, seven of them in air raids and two by their own hand. Switzerland was unable to help any of them.

Switzerland's function as a protecting power and the activities of Red Cross delegates during World War II are deserving of great respect. This cannot, however, excuse or disguise the way in which Adolf Hitler was abetted by Switzerland's financial oligarchy and its visible government, the Bundesrat—hard though Swiss officialdom strove to bury that complicity after the war.

Switzerland's fictitious neutrality between 1939 and 1945 has a long history closely associated with the rise of capitalism but not entirely governed by it. The Confederation's neutrality was recognized by the European powers under the Peace of Westphalia in 1648 and subsequently renewed and confirmed by the countries attending the Congress of Vienna in 1815. It was there that the Genevese diplomat Pictet de Rochement managed to secure acceptance of the principle espoused by Switzerland to this day: that it is neutral not for its own sake but for that of others, because the existence of a neutral country in the heart of Europe accords with the special interests of every country on the European continent.

Etymologically derived from the Latin adjective *neuter* or the Vulgar Latin *neutralis,* the term "neutral" means, literally, "neither of two." According to Franz Blankart, onetime assistant to Karl Jaspers and now an undersecretary of state and Switzerland's most senior commercial diplomat, "neutrality is essentially a negative concept. If C is neutral, it is neither A nor B; or, more precisely, the definition of A and B is wholly independent of that of C. The definition of C, on the other hand, depends upon the form and inherent significance of the other two, A and B. In the first place, therefore, the neutral is neither one nor the other."[30]

So what *is* it?

"Switzerland does not exist." By this, André Gorz implies that a country which constantly avoids adopting an international position, which refuses to take sides and sometimes goes so far as to deny the existence of conflicts that are tearing people and nations apart, possesses no international existence.[31] This view of things is mistaken, as we have seen. Switzerland not only exists; but, in financial and economic terms, it is a great power.

That is why we must progress beyond semantics to a more meaningful level of discussion, one that concerns the self-interpretation of the banking oligarchy and of the government dependent on it. They both agree on one point: the positive evaluation of neutrality. What constitutes its positive aspect? The inventor of the requisite formula is a former federal president who later rose to become president of Nestlé: "Recent events, and the modest activities in which we were privileged to engage, seem to me to show that there is ample room in the world of today for a neutrality like that of our country, which is not a morally indifferent neutrality and has no connection with neutralism, which is not an escape from responsibility, which in no way signifies forbearing to pass judgment on events, and which does not shrink from taking action if it can further the cause of peace by so doing."[32]

But the positive value of neutrality is based, according to the official theory, on yet another consideration: implicit in the concept of neutrality are those of armed defense and independence. Being neutral, Switzerland is allied with none of the parties to a conflict. If that conflict spills over onto its territory, however, and threatens its neutral stance—in other words, its independence—Switzerland will defend itself by force of arms. As Franz Blankart rightly observes: "Neutrality is a kind of local pacifism that reserves the right of self-defense."[33]

Another idea associated with the concept of neutrality is that of "mediation." This mediator's vocation, to which the visible government of Switzerland lays claim, is in reality quite modest. It is construed, in essence, as an abstract opportunity for two enemies to meet on neutral territory and has more to do with geography than politics.

My hometown of Thun is situated on the important railroad line that links Basel with Domodossola by way of the Lötschberg and Simplon Tunnels. It possesses a big switchyard from which, every night during the years 1941–44, an almost incessant, muffled din used to carry to our house on the hillside. It came from the interminable German freight trains trundling south to Italy and from the Italian and German trains heading north to the Rhineland.

A big wall in the station concourse was adorned with all kinds of official posters. One of them showed a steel-helmeted, rifle-toting Swiss soldier in profile with his finger to his lips. The message beneath it was the Swiss equivalent of wartime Britain's "Careless talk costs lives!" Another poster was a "Wanted" notice concerning German saboteurs who had sneaked into Switzerland and tried to blow up some Swiss air force planes at Dübendorf. Other notices, signed "Air Raid Protection Commandant," warned people to black out their doors and windows after nightfall.

I have a particularly vivid memory of one public announcement. It explained the purpose and content of our government's agreement with Germany relating to "civilian freight traffic" through the Alpine tunnels. Signed by the federal president and the chancellor (the secretary to the cabinet), it solemnly declared that, pursuant to the "policy of strict neutrality," the government had permitted the railroad trains "of all belligerent powers" to pass through its territory, on condition that they carried nothing but "civilian freight" (clothing, foodstuffs, medical supplies).

Late one afternoon in December 1943, Thun was hit by an exceptionally violent snowstorm that swept down from the Aare Valley in the north. The blizzard vented most of its fury on the old quarter of the town, ripping off tiles and howling like a pack of wolves. The force of the wind was such that it snapped plane trees on the quayside and broke the metal rod on which the town church's rusty weathercock had perched for hundreds of years. The sky was black as pitch and the air filled with the smell of burning. Dead swans and panic-stricken ducks, rigid with terror, were washed up on the lakeshore.

Meantime, disaster struck the railroad station: dozens of freight cars bearing the black eagle and the initials DRB, for Deutsche Reichsbahn, toppled over like poleaxed cattle. The wind sent shreds of green tarpaulin fluttering through the air, wrenched off one of the main gates, and derailed some locomotives.

Startled by all the noise and heedless of my mother's prohibitions, I ran down to the station. My ears had not deceived me: strewn across the tracks like corpses on a battlefield lay antiaircraft guns and tank turrets, trucks with shattered windshields, and heavy machine guns. The bent gun barrel of one overturned tank resembled the trunk of a dying elephant. There were broken ammunition boxes everywhere, and some artillery shells had rolled out of a freight car that had damaged the tracks as it overturned.

Toward evening some Swiss army trucks drove into the station forecourt, followed by a convoy of black limousines bearing diplomatic license plates. The limousines disgorged some men in felt hats and leather overcoats.

A policeman told me that the men in leather coats were members of the German legation in Bern. They barked a series of curt orders at the Swiss soldiers and local gendarmes, who promptly and deferentially carried them out. A large crowd of curious spectators had gathered in the immediate vicinity of the tracks. On the Germans' instructions, the Swiss soldiers roughly thrust them back.

It started to snow again, heavily. I stood there in silence beside my father, who had joined me. He was a cultivated, intelligent, thoroughly honest man, the town's chief presiding judge and a colonel in the Swiss army. When I asked him where all the guns came from and to whom they belonged, he answered in a low, faltering voice: "Read the government poster in the station. That explains everything."

For the first and probably the only time in his life, my father had failed to tell me the truth. It was my first encounter with the Swiss neutrality lie—a trauma I took years to overcome.

PART FOUR

Vanquishing
the Victors

You made your own bed, so lump it,

don't expect to be tucked in too.

If anyone kicks, it's yours truly,

and if anyone's kicked, it's you!

BERTOLT BRECHT,

Rise and Fall of the City of Mahagonny

1. Settling Accounts

AFTER THE WAR CAME the reckoning. In 1946 the Western Allies summoned the gnomes to Washington for questioning. The Bern authorities had made prior attempts to prepare for this judgment day by making cosmetic corrections, prompted in part by what had happened early in December 1943. That was when Roosevelt, Churchill, and Stalin met at Tehran to draw up their preliminary plan for the reorganization of the postwar world. This provided for the unconditional surrender of the Axis powers, the dismemberment of Germany, the collection of reparations payments, and—of course—no mercy for Hitler's foreign fences.

The Swiss ruling class reacted swiftly. It reconstructed its government and sought a dialogue with the "Other Switzerland," the National Resistance Campaign headed by the Social Democrats under Hans Oprecht. On December 15, 1943, a Social Democrat was elected to the government for the first time in the history of the Swiss Confederation. Not, of course, the courageous Oprecht, but the mayor of Zurich, Ernst Nobs. One year later the regime sent its pro-Vichy foreign minister, Marcel Pilet-Golaz, into the political wilderness.

But Bern's ploy failed. The Allies were not deceived, especially as the Swiss gold-laundering machine remained in operation until April 6, 1945, three weeks before Hitler's suicide. Swiss supplies of arms, credit, and industrial goods were also maintained until Germany's final collapse.

The psychological climate in Washington was icy when the Swiss delegation, headed by Minister Walter Stucki and accompanied by William Rappard, a Genevese professor in international law, arrived there on March 11, 1946. The victorious Allies strongly suspected that the Swiss were hoarding, either in their vaults at home or in frozen accounts in the United States, large amounts of foreign exchange which the Germans could at any time use to finance a third world war. The Fourth Reich remained an Allied nightmare, especially since Martin Bormann and other leading Nazis had disappeared. At that stage even Hitler's death was still a source of some speculation.

The main aims of the Washington talks were reparations payments and the confiscation of German assets. They dragged on for sixty-eight arduous days.[1]

Although the Swiss had committed themselves to freezing German assets under the Currie Agreement, they were utterly opposed to handing them over. Switzerland had been neutral in the war and, like any neutral, had simply carried on business with all and sundry. We Swiss are "available," as Bernese political jargon still calls it. We have no political opinions, we merely offer our services.

Seated across the negotiating table from the victors of World War II were Hitler's receivers of stolen goods. These were the Swiss, who also represented the principality of Liechtenstein, with which Switzerland maintains a monetary union. The victors were a coalition of eighteen countries led by the United States, Great Britain, and France. The Soviet Union did not participate. In the Potsdam Agreement of August 2, 1945, Stalin had unilaterally waived all claims on German assets abroad, with the exception of those located in Finland, Hungary, Bulgaria, Austria, and Romania.

The Swiss, who had absolutely no sense of being in the wrong, behaved somewhat arrogantly. Chief delegate Stucki was annoyed when the Americans sat him opposite the young and brilliant Seymour J. Rubin—a "Jewboy," as the man from Bern so delicately put it.[2] As for his fellow delegate and adviser on international law, Rappard prided himself on his steadfast rejection of Allied claims.

I have personal memories of both men. Stucki, a lean, well-groomed man with piercing eyes, I saw as a child at my grandfather's house. Rappard, who tutored me at Geneva University, was a handsome man with a luxuriant mane of white hair, mocking eyes, and a huge American limousine. Stucki, onetime ambassador to Pétain at Vichy, and Rappard, likewise a former member of the National Council, were intelligent, personally likable men. But they, too, were "innkeepers" providing services.

Neither of them had the slightest sympathy for Nazism.[3] Rappard was on close terms with Hans Oprecht and August Lindt of the National Resistance Campaign. As for Stucki, he had cleverly and courageously mediated between Free French troops and Pétain's guard while head of the Swiss mission to Vichy in 1944.[4] When Vichy was liberated on August 26, the local hospital housed a number of badly wounded German soldiers who had been abandoned there by their officers. Stucki looked after their interests. Under extremely difficult circumstances, he arranged for the Red Cross to dispatch a consignment of medical supplies and food from Geneva. On the morning of August 27, Colonel Rounel, who commanded the Gaullist troops and the maquis of the Allier Department, paraded his maquisards in honor of Stucki, outside the Hôtel des Ambassadeurs, in which the Swiss mission was located.

———

The Washington negotiations concerned three related subjects: looted gold, especially that which had been stolen from Belgium's central bank, melted down in Berlin, and transferred to Switzerland; German nongovernmental assets; and the dormant accounts of persons murdered by the Nazis.

As regards the second subject—"Liquidation of German nongovernmental property in Switzerland"—the Allies were to get half as reparations. The Swiss government was permitted to keep the other half as a guarantee that the compensating credits extended to the Third Reich and still outstanding would ultimately be repaid. It was not until 1952 that the Allied Reparations Commission, the Adenauer government, and Switzerland managed to resolve the problem of confiscated German property. Thanks to Konrad Adenauer's generosity the settlement was extremely favorable to the Swiss.[5]

As for the third related subject, the "dormant" accounts, Israel did not yet exist in 1946. Jewish organizations were not represented at the negotiating table, and the question of dormant Jewish accounts at Swiss banks—and of assets belonging to other vanished Nazi victims—was mentioned only in passing.

A regular barrage of criticism descended on the Swiss government, the Swiss National Bank, and the Swiss delegation in Washington during the spring and summer of 1946. The American press adopted a particularly hostile attitude. Walter Stucki and his colleagues were daily bombarded with accusations, often of the most preposterous nature. It sometimes seemed as if the Swiss had personally robbed the central banks of Europe, wrenched gold teeth from the mouths of Jewish corpses, and organized Operation Odessa. The looted gold gave rise to some exceptionally complicated and often heated debates.

Why was such special importance attached to the Belgian gold? Hitler's Swiss fences had, after all, served the SS and the Reichsbank by hoarding and marketing looted gold from the central banks of all the occupied countries—not to mention gold from the extermination camps, gold stolen by the Einsatzkommandos, and gold from melted-down dental crowns, wedding rings, and coins of all kinds.

The Belgian gold received particular attention at Washington because of a particular historical circumstance: France, a powerful negotiator, was one of the victors represented there. Two years earlier the country had still been ruled by Marshal Pétain, Adolf Hitler's avowed and enthusiastic collaborator. The central bank of Belgium had entrusted the bulk of its gold reserves to the Banque de France, which, as we have seen, had done its best to protect them. Resisting German thievery by every means available, it had evacuated the bullion to Black Africa, raised legal objections before the Hemmen Committee, and so on, but to no avail: old Philippe Pétain knuckled under to Hitler.

General Leclerc's Free French armored division, supported by local résistants, liberated Paris on August 24, 1944. On October 1, General de Gaulle's provisional government sent a delegation to Brussels to conclude an agreement with the Belgian government. Under this, the Banque de France transferred from its own reserves a quantity of gold equivalent to the Belgian gold that had been taken by the Germans and laundered by the Swiss. In Washington, therefore, the head of the delegation representing de Gaulle's provisional government confronted the Swiss in the capacity of a direct creditor—and exerted pressure on them accordingly.

Some of the charges leveled at the Swiss by the Allies, and by the Americans in particular, were unjust. The Nazis had stolen the central bank gold reserves of eleven occupied countries, as well as countless millions in privately owned valuables. Every occupied country had been systematically despoiled by the "foreign exchange protection teams." Finally, there was the Totengold taken from slave laborers, gassed victims of the extermination camps, and murdered Gestapo detainees. The Reichsbank had laundered a large quantity of this gold in Bern.

Thanks to Operation Odessa, some of the looted gold had

been buried in the vaults of big Swiss banks and trust companies, deposited with corporation lawyers, or transferred via Swiss middlemen to Buenos Aires, Madrid, and Asunción. The Allied delegates rightly regarded themselves as the representatives of all these injured countries and individuals.

But Stucki and his colleagues could not, with the best will in the world, supply full particulars of the above transactions. They could not have come clean even had they wanted to—which is rather doubtful. They possessed no detailed list of all the Nazis' gold consignments and transactions.

Let us revert to the subject of Italy's looted gold. Mussolini was deposed in July 1943 by the Fascist Grand Council. On July 25 King Victor Emmanuel ordered Il Duce's arrest. On September 8 Italy concluded an armistice with the Allies.

Sicily and the south of Italy were already in Allied hands. Rome was proclaimed an open city. The Wehrmacht withdrew, together with the SS and the Gestapo. First, however, some SS trucks pulled up outside the headquarters of Italy's national bank on the Via Nazionale. The vaults were emptied not only of Italy's own gold reserves, but also of those which Mussolini had earlier stolen from Albania's national bank at Tirana. We now know that the haul amounted to 117 tons of gold bars and gold coins from all over the world. The convoy set off for Milan, where its cargo was stored for two months.

The Allies pushed north, threatening the German line, and partisan brigades waged a guerrilla war in Lombardy and Piedmont. At the end of November, fearing for the safety of their loot, the Germans transported it into the Alps. The new hiding place was La Fortezza, a fortress in South Tirol. Dating from World War I, it afforded excellent protection from attacks by Allied paratroopers and Italian partisans.

Mussolini was interned in an inhospitable building on Monte Sasso, 6,000 feet up in the Abruzzi. On September 12, 1943, he was rescued by a detachment of German paratroops under the command of SS Colonel Otto Skorzeny. Hitler installed Mussolini at Salò, a small town on the shores of Lake Garda, where he became a kind of Gauleiter of Northern Italy and proclaimed the Fascist Republic of Salò. Several of the Grand Council members who had voted against him in July were court-martialed and shot on his orders, among them his son-in-law and former foreign minister, Count Ciano.

In April 1945 Mussolini's protectors withdrew. On April 26, while on the run from the partisans with his mistress, Clara Petacci, the Fascist dictator was captured in a small village. The couple were shot by partisans during the night of April 27–28 and their bodies publicly displayed in Milan, dangling upside down from a beam.

As for the gold at La Fortezza, twenty-three tons of it were transported by road to the vaults of the Bank for International Settlements at Basel and ten tons to those of the Swiss National Bank during the brief existence of the Salò Republic. These consignments, which were delivered in settlement of outstanding debts, crossed the Swiss frontier at Chiasso.

Evidence exists that other consignments of gold were transported across the Swiss border, but only a fraction of it reached Berlin. American troops discovered Italian gold bars and coins in the salt mines at Merkers in Thuringia in April 1945. It is also on record that the Reich government transferred Italian gold coins worth millions to various German authorities, including the Foreign Ministry, "for special use."

The Allies returned twenty-three tons of stolen gold to Italy when the war ended, but fifty tons remain unaccounted for to this day. Walther Funk, war criminal and ex-president of the Reichsbank, stated under interrogation that the missing gold never reached Berlin. American investigators questioned hundreds of people in defeated Germany and liberated Italy, but without extracting any firm information. Most of the individuals questioned were Nazi members of the SS and Gestapo or Italian Fascists. They did not make credible witnesses, of course, but it is nonetheless remarkable that, despite the most intensive search, so little Italian and Albanian gold was discovered in Germany or identified in Operation Odessa's escape pipelines.

All the gold that left La Fortezza for Berlin passed through the Swiss canton of Ticino, either by rail or, more often, by road via the Gotthard Pass. No doubt many tons of gold seeped away, while in transit, into Switzerland's absorbent soil.... Dozens of heirs to wealthy trustees, corporation lawyers, and financial administrators are presently living in Canton Ticino.

The fact remains that the Americans were unjust. Stucki and the official Swiss delegation to the Washington conference could have known nothing about this seepage. Bank secrecy has been Switzerland's most sacrosanct law since 1934.

The Allies demanded that all German assets held by Swiss financial institutions be handed over and the "dormant" assets of the Nazis' victims paid out to the survivors or their heirs. The Swiss remained obdurate. Neutrality forbade them to hand over any German assets, let alone the looted gold. The Swiss demanded the abolition of the Allied blacklist and the unfreezing of all Swiss bank accounts in the United States. This blacklist enumerated all the neutral firms suspected of having dealt with the enemy—all whose turnover had increased during the war years. It identified them precisely: capital, responsible bodies, line of business, and so forth. Any commercial contact with such firms was prohibited and penalized.

The freezing of Swiss assets in the United States was a serious matter. They were valued at over five billion Swiss francs—an astronomical sum in 1946, worth more than fifteen billion dollars at current values.

Stucki made an extremely shrewd suggestion: the establishment of a compensatory system between German assets in Switzerland and frozen Swiss assets abroad. For the Nazi gold deposited in Switzerland he proposed to pay the Allies a lump sum of 100 million Swiss francs.

The Allies rejected this proposal as insulting. Stucki and his retinue made a haughty exit from the conference chamber.

It was a dangerous crisis. State Department officials were already drawing up a list of Swiss exports to be boycotted by the United States. Switzerland, the pariah, carried little weight in the post-Hitler world.

An incredible coincidence came to Switzerland's aid. The Swiss envoy to Washington, Carl Bruggmann, was married to Mary, née Wallace, sister of former Vice President Henry A. Wallace. In 1946 Wallace was Secretary of Commerce in Truman's cabinet. Mary Bruggmann sided with her husband's native land —and against common sense. Henry Wallace made representations to President Truman, who decreed that negotiations should be resumed.

The Swiss government of the time included Foreign Minister Max Petitpierre. A shrewd man, Petitpierre had not grown up in the Swiss Augean stables. A teacher of international law at Neuenburg University and a member of the federal parliament, and although a member of the liberal party, he did not belong to the inner circle of those who wielded power. Elected to ministerial office at the end of 1944, he had thus played no part in the worst of the government's aberrations between 1940 and 1943.

Petitpierre tried to inject a new spirit into Switzerland's foreign policy and escape from the straitjacket of passive neutrality. His contacts with Moscow were one instance of this novel approach. In 1946, despite Stalin's detestation of Switzerland, he succeeded in establishing diplomatic relations with the Soviet Union.

Having some idea of the disastrous impression Swiss self-righteousness was bound to make on victorious powers that had sacrificed millions of lives in the fight against Nazism, Petitpierre urged the Swiss representatives in Washington to adopt a more conciliatory attitude.

Rappard protested at Petitpierre's farsighted attempts to

change the delegates' minds. He eventually sent the foreign minister a letter containing the words: "You wanted it ... we've given in." The point at issue was the size of the sum to be paid by the Swiss in reparations. Rappard wanted to stick stubbornly to the 100 million Swiss francs Stucki had offered during the preliminary phase of the negotiations.

After battling against Swiss arrogance and intransigence for sixty-eight exhausting days and nights, the Allies gave up and accepted Stucki's new compromise proposal: Switzerland would pay them 250 million Swiss francs in full settlement of all claims relating to its gold transactions with the Reichsbank. Stucki made it clear, however, that this paltry sum did not constitute a form of reparation, still less the relinquishment of illegally accepted gold. Nobly, he stated that the 250 million were Switzerland's voluntary contribution to the reconstruction of Europe.

Discussion later turned to the dormant assets of victims of the Nazi reign of terror. Of the hundreds of millions of francs lying in dormant accounts, Switzerland shelled out just 20 million francs under the Washington Accord. These, Stucki declared, were a voluntary Swiss advance payable to the newly founded United Nations Organization.

The Washington Accord—technically speaking, an exchange of letters—was signed on May 25, 1946.

2. The Infuriated Hucksters

HITLER'S FENCES PULLED OFF an excellent deal in Washington. They paid only 250 million Swiss francs for the looted gold, yet the bullion from Belgium's central bank that was so adventurously stolen by the Nazis, melted down in Berlin, and shipped off to Switzerland was, alone, worth around one billion Swiss francs. To that must be added the looted gold from Holland (over half a billion Swiss francs' worth), Albania, Italy, Poland, and elsewhere.

Between 1939 and early 1945 the Reichsbank channeled gold worth 1.7 billion Swiss francs into the Bern gold-laundering machine. A great deal more was deposited in private accounts or transferred via Switzerland to South America and elsewhere. The Nazi loot naturally served to pay for Swiss consignments of arms and supplies and to settle Germany's outstanding debts. Nor did the gold that was laundered in Bern's washing machine simply lie fallow.

Switzerland was not the only neutral European country the victors invited to pay up after the war. No sooner had Stucki left Washington than another round of negotiations began. This time, Sweden was called to account.

Immediately after the signing of the Washington Accord the Swiss fences started quarreling among themselves. Having had to pay the victors 250 million Swiss francs for their transactions in looted gold, they looked around for a whipping boy and found one in the person of Alfred Hirs, one of the three board members of the Swiss National Bank, who was admirably suited to the role. Hirs was not a member of the Zurich financial oligarchy, but an ambitious apparatchik devoid of sound political connections. He was also an avowed anti-Semite, which made a rather embarrassing impression in 1946. Last but not least, he was on close terms with Emil Puhl, and Puhl was on trial for war crimes at Nuremberg in 1946. Hirs was held chiefly responsible for the Washington disaster.

The superficial reason was bizarre. The Swiss had become convinced that the U.S. Secret Service was tapping their phones, opening their mail, and bugging their conversations at the Swiss legation and in various hotels and restaurants. Stucki had consequently decreed that important conversations were to be conducted in whispers and imposed a total ban on correspondence. Hirs, however, had written home without enlisting the services of the legation's cipher experts. His letter, which he had simply dropped into a Washington mailbox, intimated that the Swiss would, if worst came to worst, be prepared to fork out 250 million.

The chilly psychological climate prevailing in the Bundeshaus and at National Bank headquarters during the summer of 1946 can be gauged from a letter addressed by Ernst Nobs, minister of finance and token socialist, to his fellow party member Johannes Huber:[6]

Bern, July 12, 1946
To: National Councilor Johannes Huber, St. Gallen

My dear fellow,
I proposed to give you, being a member of the banking council and banking committee, some information about conditions at the National Bank. President Weber will be retiring after the annual general meeting. It is presently being debated whether Hirs's conduct in Washington was so improper and so negligent as to justify his dismissal. The fact is that, although Minister Stucki had strictly enjoined all members of the delegation not to use the ordinary mails to apprise anyone of their confidential preliminary discussions or of the government's instructions as to the maximal sum to be paid in reparations, Hirs did communicate such information to Weber in Zurich. Instead of using the code or the courier service for the purpose, he flagrantly infringed these precautionary measures and may well have been responsible for the Allies' premature discovery that the delegation could go to a maximum of 250 million, whereas Stucki and the delegation were hoping—justifiably so —to get away with 150 million. This matter is presently under investigation. I have checked the relevant correspondence with Weber. It is true that in a letter of March 30, 1946, Hirs mentioned that the figure of 250 million was being discussed, not that the government had decided to go that high if necessary.

But this correspondence was extremely inappropriate and damaging nonetheless, and Hirs failed badly at Washington in other respects, never having come to terms there with his task and his role. The National Bank's Washington operations in the matter of the gold were clumsy in general. President Weber said, prior to Washington: "The gold question? As far as the National Bank is concerned, nothing of the kind exists!" The National Bank thereupon failed to supply the documentation requested by the delegation or its individual members. It was said, in answer to complaints, that Hirs himself was a member of the delegation. When Hirs was called upon at Washington to defend our position on the gold question, however, he talked his way out of it on the grounds that he had come to Washington as the delegation's expert adviser on banking matters. It was a very annoying business. It is uncertain what conclusions the government will come to. It appears meantime that President Rossy, too, has stated that he no longer wishes to work with Hirs, claiming that the latter has deliberately circulated false allegations about him. An investigation into this matter is being conducted, if my information is correct, by Herr Daguet. I learned only in recent months that personal relations between the three members of the directorate are not of the best. Weber will stay on until the annual general meeting next March. Then his days will be numbered.

Warmest regards to you and our highly esteemed Comrade Huber [Huber's wife].

Yours,

Ernst Nobs.[7]

Nevertheless, the 250 million payable by the Swiss in compensation for the looted gold represented a great triumph over the victors, a small fraction of the real figure, and a first-class piece of business.

The Swiss also pulled off an excellent deal in respect to the dormant assets of the Nazis' murdered victims. They did not enter

into any kind of definite, official commitment. Stucki's letter—
one of the negotiating documents on file—merely stated that the
Swiss government would favorably examine ways of making these
assets available to the Allies for humanitarian and reconstruction
purposes.

Switzerland ended by remitting 20 million Swiss francs to the
United Nations Organization, and bank secrecy was duly preserved.

That Stucki's written assurance remained a largely empty
promise is apparent from the dramatic events of 1996, when the
Swiss Bankers Association—fifty years late—yielded to pressure from the World Jewish Congress. The Memorandum of
Understanding of May 1996 set up the committee of inquiry that
is to unearth the dormant millions—now billions, in all probability—and transmit them to the descendants of the murdered
account holders.

But Stucki and his colleagues regarded the agreement to
liquidate German nongovernmental assets as a defeat. They found
it particularly galling that the Allies had managed to enforce a
novel legal proposition on them. Formulated by Seymour J.
Rubin, it held that private assets abroad are not truly private
because they enjoy a certain measure of governmental protection.

The Swiss still had more than a billion francs' worth of
German loans outstanding and hoped to reimburse themselves out
of the assets to be liquidated, it is true. But they were dissatisfied
nonetheless. They found it humiliating to have to negotiate under
constant, inescapable American pressure. The Swiss firms whose
trade with Germany and the Axis powers had increased during
the dark years of war were on the blacklist. Commercial dealings
with them were legally prohibited, and their accounts in the
United States—which amounted to the then horrendous sum of
five billion Swiss francs—were frozen. Despite opposition from
the British, who needed Swiss industrial goods, the blacklist remained in force until June 30, 1996.

One reason for the Americans' "cruelty" was psychological in nature: Randolph E. Paul, who headed the U.S. delegation, hailed from the Treasury Department, as did most of his colleagues. His mentor was Henry J. Morgenthau.[8]

Only one of the 1946 negotiators is still alive: Rubin, who joined the Allied delegation as a young Chicago attorney. He later left government service and opened a law office in Washington. Rubin never got over Stucki's arrogance—indeed, he has devoted the remainder of his life to a quest for justice and, more particularly, for the dormant assets in Swiss bank vaults and elsewhere in the world.

Now retired, Rubin confided his feelings of frustration to *Die Weltwoche*, the Zurich weekly, on November 7, 1996.[9] He remembered Stucki as a "competent, rather chilly, difficult person."

In spite of the form it took as an exchange of letters, the Washington Accord was an international treaty. Under the Swiss constitution, therefore, it had to be ratified by parliament before coming into force.

In June 1946 the Swiss government convened the two chambers of the parliament, the National and Cantonal Councils, for a hurried special session. The basis of the ratification debate was "the government's message of June 14, 1946, to the Bundesversammlung ['Federal Assembly'] regarding the acceptance of the financial agreement concluded in Washington."

To read the transcript of the Federal Assembly's extraordinary session of June 1946, the twelfth session of the thirty-second term, is enough to make one's hair stand on end. The right-wing press was beside itself in anger. "The right of the stronger" had prevailed at Washington. Switzerland had been compelled to "yield to the victors' power" and pay "reparations" like a defeated country. Parallels were drawn with the Battle of Marignano in 1515, where Swiss armies were annihilated by Francis I. In the Swiss collective memory, Marignano symbolizes the ignominy of defeat.

Three parliamentary blocs took shape. The Swiss German conservatives and a few Zurich liberals wanted nothing to do with the Washington diktat. Switzerland, they declared, must defend its neutrality and its rights against the arrogant Allies. The agreement was shameful and should not be ratified. Traugott Wahlen, the farmers' conscience, was eager to save the Confederation. It must, he said, remain "inflexible" amid the storms of the twentieth century.

Emil Anderegg, a liberal from Sankt Gallen, also voted against the disgraceful Washington treaty, which was characterized by "legal decadence, constraint, and brutalization."

National Councilor Paul Zigerli, a Zurich representative of the Protestant Party, displayed deathless courage. He branded the Washington Accord "the most profound humiliation" to which the Swiss Confederation had ever been subjected in the course of its existence and moved that it be rejected.

The agreement was defended by the Social Democrats and trade unionists. Paul Meierhans of Zurich was delighted because it expressed a "new conception of private property" and "personal responsibility, with all one's worldly possessions, for government conduct."

But all political parties have their fair share of stupidity. The Social Democrats, too, included some idiots, and one of them was Robert Grimm. Having led the general strike in 1918, Grimm later conformed to the prevailing ideology and became a docile member of the Bernese cantonal executive. As speaker of the National Council in 1946, he angrily, and erroneously, declared: "At Washington, might triumphed over right."

A realistic stance was adopted by the numerous financial administrators of big banks and industrial concerns who participated in the debate in their capacity as members of parliament. The Allies had won, period. Switzerland had lost, but not too badly. With an eye to future business dealings with these same Allies, the Swiss should accept the bitter pill and swallow it.

The Washington Accord was eventually ratified by majorities

of 142 to 29 in the National Council and 24 to 11 in the chamber of the Cantons.[10]

3. The Innocent Guilty

DENIZENS OF TWO DIFFERENT worlds confronted each other at Washington: on the one hand, the Allied democrats who had waged war against the Axis powers for more than five years and delivered our planet from the scourges of Nazism and Japanese militarism, sustaining immense human and material losses in the process; on the other, the money merchants of Switzerland. Total incomprehension reigned between the two worlds. The Swiss, in particular, failed to grasp why the victors refused to accept their "special position" as neutrals.

By their own lights, Walter Stucki, Charles Bruggmann, and William Rappard acted in good faith. They defended the interests of their neutral, geographically diminutive—and financially powerful—mercantile republic with tricks and dodges, half-truths and diplomatic lies—and, what is more, with a clear conscience.

The awesome, world-encompassing financial power wielded today by the major Swiss banks is founded on wartime profits. The bulk of the probable hundreds of millions of Swiss francs that reposed in ownerless Jewish and other accounts in 1946 was saved. The vast majority of that money has long since been absorbed—quite legally—into the undisclosed reserves of Swiss banks and trust, finance, and insurance companies.

Former Undersecretary Paul J. Jolles referred in 1996 to his compatriots' "shocking negligence,"[11] it is true—but that was a belated confession typical of many devout and upright Swiss Christians. It does not detract from the belief that the negotiators acted correctly in the interests of a small neutral country menaced on all sides.

In short, given Switzerland's very own selfish, short-term national interests, the Washington negotiators' achievement is definitely to be admired. Switzerland had financed Hitler's wars of aggression. Its leaders had become active, deliberate accomplices of one of the vilest mass murderers in human history. At Washington, the free world sat in judgment on them.

Stucki was determined not to vacillate in uncertain times. He steeled himself to deny everything. Guilty? Certainly not. Accomplices? Never heard of the word. Herr Hitler? A business associate like any other. The SS monsters? No concern of ours what they got up to. They ran amok in Poland and Russia, after all.

Stucki performed yet another feat. The Allied list of charges was based on intelligence reports, monitoring transcripts from Bletchley Park, confiscated Reichsbank records, depositions made by war criminals (Funk and Puhl, among others). Stucki covered his tracks by declining to comment on matters of fact and continually invoked bank secrecy. It was a strategy that called for strong nerves, and Stucki had them.

Complicated, protracted, interrupted by recurrent crises and then resumed, the Washington negotiations (and the subsequent diplomatic tussles with West Germany and the occupying powers in 1952) marked a watershed. Once a leprous neutral and Nazi accomplice, Switzerland contrived to transform itself—with the utmost difficulty—into a full and respected member of the Western democratic community of nations. The Swiss feat at Washington is worthy of admiration from this aspect too, even if it was performed with the aid of lies and half-truths.

The implementation of the handover of remaining private German assets under the provisions of the Washington Accord required the approval of the Allied authorities in occupied Germany, who supervised all German transactions with foreign countries, Switzerland included.

The laborious step across the threshold from complicity with Hitler to respected membership of the free world is documented by numerous secondary sources, most of them doctoral dissertations.[12] They make interesting and informative reading, because they shed light on what primarily interests us here: the mentality of Switzerland's rulers.

What really happened at Washington was that Switzerland compelled the Western Allies to give ground. *The Swiss vanquished the victors of World War II.* It was a victory attributable in large measure to the incredible self-righteousness of the Swiss, backed by the fiction of their neutrality. Those who emerged triumphant were the leading Swiss negotiators, notably Stucki, Rappard, and Bruggmann, their aides from the National Bank, and the handful of gnomes who lurked in the corridors.

Here is a confidential letter from Walter Stucki to Max Petitpierre dated May 28, 1948:

> The whole point is that, pursuant to the Federal Act of September 14, 1945, and in full accordance with the discussions held with the governmental economic delegation prior to negotiations in Washington, every effort was made to prevent the assets of the Reich and the Reichsbank from being subject to the agreement. By arguing that these resources should be reserved for the financing of German interests, we achieved that aim. Were these funds now to be employed, contrary to the explanations we gave, to satisfy Swiss creditors, the Allies could not, admittedly, charge us with breaching the agreement, but they could accuse us of having deceived them at Washington.[13]

The Swiss envoy in Washington, Charles Bruggmann, crowed about having hoodwinked the Allies. On December 27, 1948, he wrote as follows to Jean Hotz, who headed the Commercial Section of the Federal Ministry of Economic Affairs:

> Above all, I should like to thank you for your generously appreciative words on the subject of deliberate noncooperation. I naturally find it a great source of satisfaction to be assured of your approval. It wasn't certain that the Americans wouldn't bear us a grudge, but there are, to date, no signs whatsoever of disapprobation. In view of forthcoming discussions, we shall, I believe, be exceptionally happy to have acted as we did. The only thing

is, the press ought not to speak of success on similar occasions in the future.[14]

In 1946 Paul J. Jolles, a former undersecretary and a great commercial diplomat, was then a young attaché in Washington. He attended the negotiations without any personal jurisdiction but kept his eyes and ears open. In the *Neue Zürcher Zeitung* of October 30, 1996, he looked back on the agreement with satisfaction and pronounced it excellent because "[our] policy of neutrality" had been reconciled with "the right of the victorious belligerents to the spoils of war." Jolles regards the Bern gold-laundering machine as an institution born of Swiss neutrality. That neutrality, he declares, is ever "dependable"—and he's right.

Throughout the sixty-eight days of diplomatic warfare in Washington, Stucki displayed an astonishing degree of arrogance and self-righteousness. Utterly convinced that he was in the right, he constantly put Hitler and the Allies on a par. To him, Switzerland was the land of the sanctified. That it could have done something wrong or might even be guilty of some crime was an idea that never crossed his mind.

He negotiated under extreme pressure, and his outbursts against the Allies were correspondingly violent. One of these occurred on a day when Allied war aims were under discussion. Randolph E. Paul had just endeavored to make it clear to the Swiss that, in waging war and making vast sacrifices for more than five years, the Western democracies had been fighting for the freedom of everyone on the face of the earth, not merely to preserve their selfish national interests.

Stucki contemptuously brushed this argument aside: "Hitler and Goebbels would not have shrunk from basing their demands on the need to make Europe big and united, and to preserve it from Bolshevism. Even if we readily grant that this end was bad and that the end you mention is good in itself, we must emphatically remind you that there is no distinction in law between ends. The old Jesuitical principle 'the end justifies the means' is just as inadmissible in individual countries as it is under international law."[15]

Stucki was not only hypocritical but also cunning. He silenced Paul by quoting Roosevelt at him: "You certainly have the capacity to force us to our knees, as Hitler could have done during the war. But we cannot believe that one of your late, great president's finest and most important declarations should be forgotten. He said at Christmas 1943: 'The rights of every nation, whether large or small, must be respected and preserved as carefully as the rights of every individual in our own republic. The doctrine that the strong shall dominate the weak is the doctrine of our enemies, and we reject it.' "[16]

The most interesting man in the Swiss delegation, without doubt, was William E. Rappard of Geneva. He was a member neither of Switzerland's visible government, the political elite of Bern, nor of its invisible government, the banking oligarchy of Zurich. His life belonged to the university.

The League of Nations installed itself in Geneva shortly after World War I. Rappard, the young Genevese who had studied at Harvard, became a prophetic advocate of collective security, the settlement of international disputes by international arbitration, and national self-determination. His historical model was Jean-Jacques Rousseau, and he was devoted to President Woodrow Wilson, founder of the League of Nations.

Rappard was an ardent pacifist who abominated militarism and political expediency. Having been a student of his, I shall never forget him. An impressive speaker even in old age, he would lecture us on international understanding and worldwide disarmament. His funeral took place on May 2, 1958, at Geneva's Saint-Pierre Cathedral. It was attended by the Bernese political elite and the money merchants, but also by hundreds of ordinary citizens and, more particularly, of grateful students.

As a young man Rappard had founded the Institut des Hautes Études Internationales, a private, internationally funded university on the right bank of the Lake of Geneva. This institution was his life's work. The principal subjects were, and still are, international law, modern history, international economics, and the law of international organizations. Rappard's aim was to train cadres of young people for employment in international organizations and imbue them with a spirit of toleration. He was an admirer of Aristide Briand, the French foreign minister and advocate of a united Europe, who had written: "Never again must the long black mourning veils wave in the sky over Europe." Just as Rappard admired Briand, so he detested and fought against Heinrich Rothmund, the federal police chief noted for his anti-refugee policy during World War I.

Although Rappard personified the Calvinist Genevese aristocracy, he opposed the entente cordiale, or Genevese bankers' political cartel, in 1941. The Communist Party and the Socialist Federation were banned and their two national councilors, Léon Nicole and Jacques Dicker, debarred from parliamentary attendance. In the election that followed their dismissal Rappard was elected to the National Council on September 28, 1941. The Genevese bankers were furious, and even Rappard felt rather uneasy about his election. "As of [sic] my poor old self," he wrote in English to Jacob Viner, "I am afraid that I am getting truly senile. Not only have I published articles, but I have, even almost against my will, been elected to the federal parliament."

In short, Rappard was a splendid person whose intellectual brilliance went hand in hand with an agreeable lack of self-importance. Yet even he fell prey in Washington to the Swiss mania for self-righteousness, guiltlessness, and perpetual purity. Here he is, writing to his friend Max Petitpierre on May 27, 1946:

I don't know how future historians will judge our negotiations, which we have conducted in conformity with your instructions. I have a feeling that they will be tempted to congratulate us for having come so well out of the affair as regards the gold. Against this, I believe they will be less indulgent toward us in the matter of the German assets, which we have declared ourselves ready to share with the victors. To justify such a violation of our traditional neutrality and such a disregard for existing principles of international law, they should take account of the material and moral upheavals that have been provoked in the world by Hitler.

In another letter to Petitpierre he actually degrades himself into the bankers' mouthpiece:

In hunting for the German assets in Switzerland, the Americans are sometimes animated by a spirit that has nothing to do with their desire to pocket reparations, with their fear of the military potential of a resurrected foe, with their aversion to the neutrals, with their professional pride, or even with their sportsmanlike ambition to have the last word in their dispute with the Swiss Arsène Lupin. What do they really want? Don't they simply want to weaken or even eliminate and replace an inconvenient competitor? They pretend to be seeking the deaths of the German sinner and his Swiss accomplice because of their past misdeeds. In reality, however, they wish to discover their secret and pocket their inheritance.[17]

How could such a shrewd, self-assured, and ironical man be so blind and, on occasion, so subservient? How could two such sophisticated and internationally experienced operators as Rappard and Stucki so badly misjudge Switzerland's international position? How can a man like Jolles be so obdurate to this day?

It is, of course, true that the scales were tipped afresh by the Cold War, which ushered in a new international ice age soon after the Washington Accord. Hitler's gold-launderers and suppliers of arms and industrial goods were suddenly transmuted into staunch allies of the free West. Switzerland, so recently the Nazis' thieves' den and loot depository, had become a financial center essential to the fight against Communism.

But Stucki and Rappard should surely have noticed what Petitpierre suspected: that nations possess a collective memory, and that Switzerland would some day be called to account for its crimes in World War II. As so often where Swiss dealings are concerned, the answer to questions of national blindness is very much more banal than one would expect.

I recall one recent winter's night in the Bundeshaus at Bern. I was working late in the lobby. Chandeliers were sparkling overhead and snow falling outside when Franz Blankart came in. Currently an undersecretary and Switzerland's most senior commercial diplomat, Blankart is an influential man. His office is situated in the east wing of the parliament building and on the same floor as the chamber itself. We fell to discussing the latest Bern scandal (not the Washington Accord). Although technically very competent, the government had once more behaved in a humanly unconscionable manner.

Having spent some time seeking an explanation, Blankart eventually found one: "In this house, the highest compliment one can pay a government minister, civil servant, or politician is to say he 'disposed of the matter.' We always want to dispose of everything—quickly, thoroughly, conclusively. That's the supreme ambition in this house. The methods we employ and the ensuing consequences are unimportant."

Blankart's analysis fits the Washington negotiations to a tee. There was this annoying file relating to the German gold. It had to be disposed of, and it was. To our immense surprise, the Allies agreed to our proposal for a minimal, lump-sum payment. It was accepted, disposed of, placed on file.

A final question remains. Why did the victorious powers, nations that had overthrown the Nazi monster at enormous human and material cost to themselves, yield to the Swiss just like that, quite suddenly, and almost—where the second round of negotiations was concerned—without demur? The Cold War had not yet begun, and the American, British, and French delegates rightly felt no sympathy at all for the Swiss and their dealings in looted gold. Why, then, were they so lenient?

One hypothesis: the Allied camp was subject to influences that militated against the desire for complete elucidation. Financial groups and individuals in the United States, Great Britain, and other Allied countries had done business with the Nazis via third countries during the years 1939–45.

Also to be borne in mind is the thoroughly dubious role of the Bank for International Settlements (BIS), in which Nazi and Allied bankers worked together throughout the war. Deputy Managing Director Paul Hechler's letters from Basel to Emil Puhl, vice president of the Reichsbank, always concluded with the words, "Heil Hitler!"

Gian Trepp has shed light on the BIS's singular activities during the war.[18] An American, Thomas H. McKittrick, served as its president from January 1940 to May 1946. Secretary of the Treasury Morgenthau tried to have him relieved of his post for collaborating with the Nazis, but without success. Morgenthau was not the only American to criticize the conduct of certain Allied financial groups during the War. Wilfred G. Burchett, an Australian special correspondent of Britain's *Daily Express*, quotes a statement made by Russell Nixon, U.S. Control Commission representative, to a Senate committee:

I further charge certain elements in the foreign ministries of the United States, Britain, and France with deliberately attempting to obstruct the participation of all four Powers in the inquiries into German assets in neutral countries, because the fascist or reactionary nature of the governments of countries like Spain, Portugal, Switzerland, Sweden and Argentina would emerge, and because full details of collaboration with those governments by certain interest groups in Allied countries would come to light. An operation in which all four Powers genuinely participated would destroy the compromise plans in regard to German assets abroad that are intended to safeguard certain business interests and prevent the development of overly radical systems.[19]

Another hypothesis: the looted Nazi gold whose relinquishment was under discussion in Washington did not come solely from the central bank reserves of countries occupied by the Wehrmacht, but included gold taken from the dead. The Reichsbank melted down and stamped gold from its SS deposit account as well as some of the stolen central bank caches. Most was sent to Switzerland, but no one could subsequently ascertain its varied sources.

The chief negotiators on the Allied side were Randolph E. Paul (United States), Francis W. McCombe (Great Britain), and Paul-Henri Chargueraud (France). All three were thoroughly decent, caring men. They must have felt more than a little uneasy at the thought that their own central bank reserves would incorporate bars reconstituted from gold teeth, wedding rings, and articles of jewelry taken from millions of murdered concentration camp victims. Our second hypothesis suggests that their lenient treatment of the Swiss gold-launderers stemmed from a bad conscience, and that their unexpected signing of an agreement so advantageous to Switzerland was prompted by a half-perceived sense of shame.

The Swiss are now being overtaken by their murky past. It has not, after all, been "put to rest."

In 1996 the chairman of the U.S. Senate Banking Committee demanded that negotiations be reopened. Under international law, agreements based on deceit, lies, and subterfuges are invalid. Stucki, Rappard, Bruggmann, and company had lied their heads off at Washington in 1946. The chairman's call for fresh negotiations is not entirely unfounded.

The Holocaust Haul

Oh, you miserable wretches!

Your brother is maltreated and you shut your eyes!

The victim cries aloud, and you keep mum?

The bully goes around, selects his victim,

and you say: He'll spare us because we hide our disapproval.

BERTOLT BRECHT, *The Good Person of Szechwan*

1. The Kind Soul of Europe

NACHT UND NEBEL . . . FOR half a century, those three words, "night and fog," have conjured up the darkness and destruction that engulfed millions of people in the extermination camps. They come from Wagner's opera *Das Rheingold,* in which Alberich the dwarf, ruler of the subterranean realm, renders himself invisible in order to torment his slaves and rebels against Wotan, the lord of Valhalla. Anyone who utters the magic spell and dons the helmet of invisibility cannot be seen by others and disappears into thin air. No one can see or touch him. His identity is destroyed. He dissolves and becomes transparent. He no longer exists.[1]

Richard Wagner was a brilliant composer—and a fanatical anti-Semite. The Nazis took over Alberich's magic spell, but with a difference: they rendered their victims invisible, not themselves.

On January 20, 1942, a number of SS officers, lawyers, and civil servants gathered at a villa beside the Wannsee, a lake on the outskirts of Berlin. There they decided on the Final Solution: the systematic, industrially organized murder of all the Jewish men, women, and children within their orbit. The Jews were to disappear from the continent of Europe—rendered invisible and dissolved into thin air, singled out and expelled from the world of the living.

Shoah, meaning "devastation," is the Hebrew word Jews have given to the industrial cremation of millions of people in the middle of the twentieth century and the middle of Europe. Elie Wiesel: "Night engulfed these communities, to spit them out at a sky on fire."² Shoah, the destruction of a people by fire, was preceded by a long period of humiliation and discrimination.

Both before and immediately after Hitler came to power, Jewish families, firms, and communities conveyed a proportion of their assets to putative safety in Switzerland. As war became imminent, more and more Jews from all over Europe attempted to salvage some of their endangered assets by transferring them to Swiss bank accounts or bank vaults or placing them in the hands of Swiss trustees, business partners, attorneys, and notaries.

Part Five of this book is devoted to the fate of those assets.

However, no one can understand the present and past policy adopted toward their Jewish creditors by Swiss bankers, trustees, corporation lawyers, gallery owners, and private persons or firms without knowledge of Switzerland's official refugee policy in the years 1933–45.

Not only Jews, but many tens of thousands of other oppressed, intimidated people—escaped Ukrainian and Polish slave laborers, resistance fighters on the run, and others—were turned back at the Swiss frontier. I for one refuse to forget their tragedy.

All over Europe, Hitler's reign of terror transformed millions of people into refugees, expelled them from their homes, robbed them of their possessions and their private lives, and drove them into exile. Caught up in this terrifying exodus, the Jews underwent a tragedy that was even worse than that to which the refugees of other groups were subjected. The Jews were outcasts of a special kind. Hannah Arendt wrote:

They are persecuted not because they have done or thought this or that, but because of what they are, unalterably, at birth: born into the wrong race.... The modern [Jewish] refugee is that which a refugee may never be by nature: he is innocent even in the minds of the powers that persecute him.... All at once there was nowhere on earth where wanderers could go without being subject to the most severe restrictions; no country that would assimilate them, no territory on which they could establish a new community.... What emerged was that the human race, which had for so long been conceived of as a family of nations, had actually reached that stage—with the result that all who were excluded from one of these closed political communities found themselves excluded from the entire family of nations, and, thus, from humanity itself.[3]

Switzerland is one of the least known, most mysterious countries in the world—as mysterious and wrapped in myths as Outer Mongolia. One of the most influential myths imparted to foreigners by the Swiss oligarchy is that of Switzerland the Sister of Mercy, the comforter of the oppressed, the cradle of humanity, international solidarity, and universal compassion: Helvetia, "the kind soul of Europe," as Yves Fricker puts it.[4] Hundreds of thousands of Jewish men, women, and children believed in that myth, and many people throughout the world continue to cherish the same misapprehension.

How many refugees, victims of persecution, emigrants in transit, internees did Switzerland shelter, temporarily or permanently, in the years 1939–45? The figures vary in accordance with the tide of war. Alfred Häsler gives the following statistics. When war broke out in September 1939 there were around 7,100 refugees in Switzerland. To these, by July 31, 1942, had been added some 1,200 more. By December 31, 1942, the number of civilian refugees had risen to some 18,000. Between January and July 1943, 4,733 refugees were taken in; between August and December, 8,719. Then there was a big influx of military refugees. By the end of 1943 Switzerland housed 39,713 internees, escaped prisoners of war, military refugees from Italy (more than 20,000 of them after the Fascist regime collapsed), hospitalized Frenchmen and Finns, and 34,232 civilians. Total by the end of 1943: 73,944. In the first half of 1944 all told, 5,763 civilian refugees were taken in, and on December 1 of that year the number of refugees, military and civilian, totaled 103,162. By the war's end on May 8, 1945, Switzerland harbored 115,000 refugees, all of whom were consigned to camps.[5]

Twenty-eight thousand Jews were taken in while the Nazi regime lasted, of whom 7,000 arrived before 1939.

The Swiss government resolved from the very start, quite illegally, that the cost of accommodating Jewish victims of persecution and sending them on to other countries should be borne by Switzerland's Jews. This form of discrimination was entirely devoid of constitutional validity. Jacques Picard, who rightly states that the Swiss Jews were subjected to "financial extortion," gives an idea of the immense financial burden that had to be carried between 1933 and 1945 by the Jews of Switzerland, some 5,000 of whom were gainfully employed. The following is an extract from his account:

Between 1933 and the end of 1937, the Swiss Jewish Welfare Association (VSJF) had spent around 680,000 Swiss francs on the 6,000-plus refugees in its care: the SIG [Swiss Federation of Jewish Communities] had thus accumulated, in the course of its refugee collection campaigns, a total of 1,044,000 Swiss francs in five years. At the beginning of 1938 the SIG forecast that its expenditure on refugee relief would amount to 80,000 Swiss francs, a sum which the delegates' assembly in March was informed was probably too low. That actual expenditure proved to be twenty-five times higher than the scheduled budget resulted from the repercussions of notorious political developments and the Nazi expulsion of Jews from Germany, by whom the association found itself, in the short term, "taken completely unawares" and compelled to resort to rapid improvisation. The VSJF's annual report ascribed this to the annexation of Austria, the Munich Agreement, ongoing expropriations, and the professional disqualification and social ostracism of Jews in Germany, the November pogroms, racist legislation in Italy, and the "systematic expulsion of Jews from Austria and Germany cunningly and forcibly initiated in July-August, after the Evian Conference." After enumerating individual relief operations, which "have long since gone beyond association work, so called" and entailed a permanent commitment, the annual report spoke of the resulting financial burdens: "It transpired from a preliminary conference at the Bundeshaus that the authorities expected Swiss Jewry to realize that it devolved primarily on the Jews of Switzerland to care for Jewish refugees, undertake their further travel arrangements, and bear the financial consequences."[6]

This government ruling was taken lying down, both by Swiss Jews and by American Jewish organizations. Switzerland footed the bill for all refugees except victims of ethnic persecution. Between 1933 and 1953 Jewish relief organizations in the United States and other countries sent the hard-pressed VSJF a total of 44 million Swiss francs. The Swiss Jews themselves made immense financial sacrifices: the 5,000 gainfully employed members of the SIG paid out 10 million Swiss francs for the benefit of their persecuted coreligionists.

But extortion was not enough. Bern also imposed a special tax on well-to-do Jews who had settled in Switzerland or were waiting to emigrate. This special levy, which yielded the Swiss exchequer a handsome 1.6 million, was also devoid of legal validity in a constitutional state like the Swiss Confederation. The funds thus extorted were euphemistically termed a "solidarity sacrifice." They were doubly scandalous because Jewish refugees were denied work permits and precluded from gainful employment.

In the same context, children from various European countries came to Switzerland for holidays. These "vacation trains" were arranged by the children's welfare organization attached to the

Red Cross. Jewish children were excluded, however. The reason: "One doesn't know if they can be sent back." Peter Surava published a vehement protest in *Die Nation*. The newspaper was censored and Surava placed under police surveillance.[7]

No one knows the precise number of people turned away. No records of those refused entry were kept until August 13, 1942. Moreover, it is highly probable that the civil and military authorities destroyed many such lists after the war. The *Neue Zürcher Zeitung* for December 5, 1996, stated that these lists were "largely" destroyed. Most of those refused entry were Jews.

It is uncertain how many rejection lists were removed from the files. What is clear is that these documentary records were destroyed without any legal justification. Their removal was wholly illegal and dictated by panic. The government was smitten with fear in 1945—panic fear of being called to account. For half a century it has clung to the figure repeatedly publicized by official sources: the refugees turned away numbered "only" 10,000.

The year is 1996. The Swiss parliament convenes for its winter session. In Washington, hearings open before the Banking Committee of the House of Representatives. Senior Swiss diplomats and representatives of the Swiss Bankers Association are, willy-nilly, called to account by the Congress of the United States. The subject under discussion: the Nazi looted gold in Swiss bank vaults and the "vanished" Holocaust funds that lie beneath Zurich's Paradeplatz.

Then something unprecedented occurs: a volume of documentary evidence is published by Christoph Graf, the courageous director of the Swiss Federal Archive, and his colleagues. Entitled "Die Schweiz und die Flüchtlinge 1933–1945" ("Switzerland and the Refugees 1933–1945"),[8] it contains an evaluation of 45,000 refugee files. The upshot: Switzerland rejected not 10,000 refugees but at least 30,000. Of these, 24,400 men, women, and children, mostly Jewish, were turned back at the frontier itself, many of them straight into the hands of the SS waiting on the other side.

A further 14,500 asylum seekers had vainly applied for entry permits abroad.

To repeat: this volume is based on the evaluation of 45,000 files dating from the years 1933–45. To them should be added the files that were destroyed, so the number of those refused entry is, in all probability, very much higher. Future research will shed light on this question, but current estimates already exceed 100,000.

2. Deterrence on the Frontier

"THE MURDERED CANNOT RECOUNT their fate," writes the historian Stefan Mächler.[9] The fate of some, however, is well documented. Recounted below are four quite different refugee tragedies.

Saul Friedländer, one of Israel's most distinguished historians,[10] was born into a Jewish family resident in Prague. The family fled to France, and Saul survived the war in a Catholic boarding school. In the fall of 1942 his parents, Jan and Elli Friedländer, left Montluçon and attempted to cross the Swiss frontier at the eastern end of the Lake of Geneva.

The Friedländers were in a party that had assembled at Lyon. Their aim was to get across the mountains into the canton of Valais at a point near Saint-Gingolph, a picturesque little town that straddles the Valais–Haute-Savoie border. The frontier is marked by a mountain torrent called the Morges. Above Saint-Gingolph lies the village of Novel, and higher still the Mont Grammont massif.

The refugees made their way, unobserved, up the tree-clad mountainside and down into the valley of the Morges. They were in Switzerland! Then, as ill luck would have it, they were caught unawares by a patrol made up of Swiss soldiers and policemen, who arrested them and handed them over to the French militia at Saint-Gingolph.

Jan and Elli Friedländer were sent to the camp at Rivesaltes, near the Spanish frontier. From there they were deported to a death camp in the east.

Decades later Saul Friedländer, by then teaching at Geneva's Institut des Hautes Études Internationales, visited Novel and Saint-Gingolph. At Novel he obtained an account of what happened from Frau Franken, an eyewitness:

> We never learned what became of the couple. Deported, no doubt. They were young—two Czech Jews. The infamous Sergeant Arrettaz of Saint-Gingolph always handed over refugees with sadistic pleasure. His colleague the customs officer, on the other hand, always walked off and made himself scarce so as not to have to see the terrible expressions on the faces of the people who were handed straight over to the militiamen at the frontier.[11]

A letter from Saul's mother dated September 30, 1942, and evidently addressed to her son's foster mother, reads like a cry for help:

> Having reached Switzerland after a very tiring journey, we were sent back. We had been misinformed. We're now awaiting our transfer to the camp at Rivesaltes, where our fate will be decided in a manner doubtless known to you. No words can describe our misery and despair. We have no baggage of any kind. Can you imagine our physical and mental state?...Perhaps a word at Vichy could save us from the worst. It isn't the camp we're afraid of, you know that. If there is the smallest chance of your helping us, do so, we implore you. Act quickly. It should surely be possible to find a solution at Vichy that would be less disastrous for us. Don't forget the boy![12]

On October 3 came a final telegram from the camp at Rivesaltes: "Without intervention Interior Ministry our impending removal inevitable. Jan Friedländer, 3548 Rivesaltes, Block K."

Men and women of the Society of Friends waited at railroad stations and beside the tracks along which trainloads of deportees traveled, ready to gather up any last messages they threw from the cars. One such communication, dated October 5, came into Saul's possession. It reads:

> Madame, I write to you from the train that is taking us to Germany. Thanks to a Quaker representative I have sent you 6000 French francs, together with a bracelet and—thanks to a lady—a stamp album. Keep them all for the boy and accept, for the last time, our infinite gratitude and our warmest regards to you and your entire family. Look after the boy! May God thank you for it and bless you, you and all your family. Elli and Jan Friedländer.[13]

It was the deportees' last sign of life.

Alfred Häsler pioneered critical research into Swiss refugee policy at the time of the Third Reich. His 1967 book, *Das Boot ist voll* ("The Boat Is Full"), now a classic, opens with an account of another refugee tragedy:

> Early one morning the gardener of the Jewish cemetery in Bern discovered a couple who had spent the night among the rows of graves there. They identified themselves as a young Belgian married couple of Jewish origin who, to evade deportation to the East, had sneaked across the Swiss frontier and reached Bern after a dramatic escape from Belgium through occupied France. The couple had promptly reported to the Belgian legation, where they were given some money and referred to the refugee relief organizations. For fear that these would lend them no effective assistance, the two refugees had first spent the night in the Jewish cemetery. It was to be their last night of freedom.
>
> The cemetery gardener informed the refugee relief people, whose organizations at once took charge of the couple and, intent on doing the right thing, immediately notified the police.
>
> The police, who took pity on the young people and put them up at the police station in a thoroughly helpful and sympathetic

manner, awaited relevant instructions. The order from the Federal Police Department ran as follows: the refugees were to be expelled into the occupied territory whence they had come. A campaign was thereupon launched by the refugee relief representatives, who, with the backing of respected individuals extraneous to the Jewish community, did their utmost to save the two refugees from deportation and, consequently, separation and disaster. We shall have occasion to discuss the details of this two-day struggle later on; suffice it here to state the bitter truth, which was that every démarche failed and that the Federal Police Department issued its fateful edict.

The Bern [cantonal] police were instructed and ordered to carry out the expulsion forthwith, via Pruntrut. The refugee relief organizations have had no further news of these refugees, who were thrust back into the great sea of misery.[14]

Thirty years later, thanks to documents from Israel's Yad Vashem, the historian Guido Koller managed to identify the young deportees and ascertain their subsequent fate.[15]

Céline and Simon Zagiel were deported into occupied France—a further act of cruelty. France south of the Loire was not occupied by the Germans in August 1942. The deportees could easily have been transported to the border at Geneva by road or rail. The Wehrmacht was not stationed all along the Swiss frontier. Until France was occupied in its entirety at the end of 1942, a narrow strip of Switzerland abutted on the unoccupied zone. Trains ran from Geneva/Eaux Vives to Annemasse, La-Roche-sur-Furon, and Annecy. This line was open. Although the Vichy regime was detaining Jews at the time, there would have been a chance of going underground in unoccupied France.

The young couple were, in fact, arrested by an enemy patrol as soon as they crossed the frontier in the Ajoie, taken to Belfort, and then sent to the camp at Drancy, on the northern outskirts of Paris. On August 24, 1942, they were herded aboard

Transportation Train No. 23 and deported to Auschwitz. Céline was sent straight from the selection ramp to the gas chamber. Simon was singled out for forced labor. He survived.

The third case history concerns the Sonabend family, whose fate has been reconstructed by Stefan Mächler.[16]

Simon Sonabend was a Brussels-based dealer in clocks and watches. The active and often friendly business relations he maintained with Swiss watch manufacturers, especially those at Biel, were of seventeen years' standing. Respected and valued for his commercial acumen in Biel and Brussels alike, he gave the Swiss a lot of business. His purchases of Swiss watches, which had since 1925 averaged 125,000 Swiss francs a year, made a substantial contribution to the prestige of the Swiss watchmaking industry.

In 1942 Simon Sonabend was forty-three years old and his wife Laja thirty-eight. They had two children, fifteen-year-old Sabine and eleven-year-old Charles. The children miraculously survived. The parents were gassed at Auschwitz.

Charles, Mächler's source of information, recalls that by the summer of 1942 every member of the Jewish community in Brussels knew that deportation to the east spelled certain death. The Nazis had occupied Belgium in May 1940. Tidings of the horrors that awaited deportees in the death camps reached there—from Poland especially—in April 1942. Charles Sonabend:

> They killed them all with gas. That means it was no secret in Brussels: if you were sent to Auschwitz you were sentenced to death, practically on arrival. The Germans started deporting people via Malines. They sent the family or an individual a ticket with instructions to turn up at Malines with a suitcase.

Malines is the town near Brussels where the Jews were assembled. They were sent a "work order" (usually through the Association des Juifs de Belgique) and summoned to report there. In August 1942 the Sonabends, too, received an order of this kind.

They resolved to escape—to Switzerland, naturally, in view of the close and friendly relations, both business and personal, which Simon had maintained with that country over the years.

Simon Sonabend was a wealthy man, so their escape preparations were completed quite quickly. Forged passports and papers were purchased, guides for the hazardous journey through occupied Europe contacted and paid. Mächler estimates that the Sonabends' expenditure amounted to ten times a Belgian worker's annual wage. Two highly paid guides smuggled the family as far as the Jura forests, or, more precisely, the mountain ranges that separate the Franche-Comté from the Jura of Canton Vaud. Although terribly frightened, they got through the German checkpoints by virtue of their well-forged papers.

Their journey by rail ended at Besançon, where they waited at a small hotel before moving on. A truck picked them up and delivered them to a French village near the border. There another guide took charge of them. Heavily laden and on foot, they crossed the Mont Risoux, a wooded Jura range that now boasts some of the loveliest cross-country skiing tracks in Europe.

At four in the morning the Sonabend family entered Switzerland by way of the idyllic Vallée de Joux, with its lake and two traditional watchmaking villages of Le Sentier and Le Pont. For two days they stayed at a chalet in the woods. Charles Sonabend recalls: "We all felt sure that, having reached Switzerland, we were safe."

It was Friday, August 14, 1942. Their escape had taken six days. Accompanied by his wife and children, Simon Sonabend set off to see his friends at Biel. They went first to Ernst Schneeberger, who ran the Freco watchmaking factory. Parents and children were accommodated separately. Simon and his wife stayed with Fernand Lob, the children with Jacques Wollmann. Arrangements had to be made for the refugees to stay in Switzerland, so the authorities were notified the next morning. Fernand Lob, one of Schneeberger's employees, was a Jew. In view of the anti-Semitism rife among officialdom, he advised Schneeberger—who was not Jewish—to contact the cantonal police at Biel. This he did by phone. Within hours, Cantonal Policeman Muhl turned up at Lob's home accompanied by some other police officers. He arrested the elder Sonabends and escorted them by train to Pruntrut in the Ajoie, former summer residence of the bishops of Basel. In those days the little town of Pruntrut, now situated in Canton Jura, was in Bernese territory. Simon Sonabend was locked up in the local jail, which was situated in the old castle. His wife also ended up behind bars, in the Ursuline convent.

That same Saturday afternoon, two plainclothes detectives rang Wollmann's doorbell and announced that they had come to take Charles and his sister to the station. Charles protested that Saturday was the Sabbath and that they weren't allowed travel by train, but to no avail. Wollmann helped the children to pack their things with the policemen looking on. They were escorted to the railroad station in silence and closely guarded throughout the journey to Pruntrut—"even when we went to the toilet."

The children were taken to join their mother at the Ursuline convent and locked up. It was the feast of the Assumption of the Virgin. Peering through a barred window, little Charles could see the procession wind past in the street below.

It was nuns—people of whom you would expect a little more humanity—who lacked the compassion to try to comfort us and give us a modicum of hope that we might not be deported. Nothing of the kind, though—they were very cold. It was if they did their work without thinking.... I wasn't insensitive, but I couldn't understand how people could act that way—as if they'd entirely failed to see what was happening, even though they'd been told why we had left, why we were in danger, and that we were being sent to certain death. It was as if they'd completely detached themselves because they didn't want to know what was happening. Such is the impression I've retained for fifty years of the Swiss who didn't want to know, as if this were a different world to them.

Simon Sonabend's Biel business associates had been compelled to look on, powerless to intervene, as the parents and children were carted off to Pruntrut. Once the cantonal policemen had disappeared, however, they got busy and mobilized their personal connections.

Expulsions of Jewish asylum seekers in the French-Swiss frontier district of Ajoie were generally carried out by military police in conjunction with the Bernese cantonal police. In this connection, Stefan Mächler cites two individuals in particular: Choffat, the Bernese cantonal police chief, and Corbaz of the military police.

The Sonabend family's enforced deportation to France was scheduled to take place near the Swiss village of Boncourt at ten o'clock on Saturday night. At nine o'clock a police car pulled up in front of the jail at Pruntrut. Simon Sonabend resisted fiercely, but in vain: he was manhandled into the car, which then drove to the Ursuline convent. We owe our knowledge of what happened outside the convent to an official report that Police Chief Choffat sent to cantonal police headquarters in Bern the next day:

> Frau Sonabend was invited to join her husband in the car. She refused, succumbed to a fit of despair, and fell to the floor in a faint. The children screamed for help. Assisted by the nuns, she recovered consciousness. She called for help, despairingly cried out that she was being taken to her death. These persons' cries could naturally be heard outside, and it was not long before fifty people gathered in the square. The public were overcome with sympathy and protested against the police measures. They even abused Military Police Officer Corbaz, who was keen to see his orders respected at all costs. In view of this opposition, and the more so because a woman and two children were involved, it was decided to refrain from using force rather than provoke a free-for-all.

A second report, addressed by Military Police Officer Corbaz to Major Hatt, his superior at Biel, described the situation thus:

We did all that was necessary to get them out, but it proved impossible to take them away despite the assistance of Pruntrut's cantonal police. Sonabend and his wife and children shouted and refused to budge. They claimed that they would be shot by the Germans if they entered occupied France. Frau Sonabend even tore her clothes and lay down on the ground, and it was useless to insist because some fifty passersby, who had been alerted by the cries, protested and shouted that no such action should be taken. In view of the impossibility of getting these people into the car and sending them back, we were obliged to confine them in Pruntrut jail.

But ordinary folk—the passersby who took pity on the harassed family and fumed at the brutality of their own authorities—were not alone in protesting. Similarly outraged were local dignitaries and persons loyal to the state and government. They included Alfred Ribeaud, the local district court judge, who belonged to the Catholic Conservative Party, and Colonel Ali Rébétez, in civilian life a teacher at Pruntrut high school and a member of the Liberal Party.

Both men were influential political figures. Although personally on bad terms, they approached the police chief and vehemently demanded to know why the authorities should deport a Jewish family with close connections in Switzerland and ample financial assets. Paul Graber, a Social Democratic national councilor and editor of *La Sentinelle,* the official organ of the Socialists of western Switzerland, telephoned from La Chaux-de-Fonds and demanded that the deportation order be suspended at once. Dr. Edouard Gressot, another influential figure in Ajoie, quickly provided Frau Sonabend with a medical certificate stating that her condition urgently necessitated rest and precluded deportation.

Heinrich Rothmund, chief of the Federal Police Department, was consulted at Bern. Neither he nor his deputy showed any compassion.

According to the record of an interrogation kept by Military

Police Officer Corbaz, Simon Sonabend stated: "I cannot return to Belgium because I and my family are threatened with deportation. On the other hand, it is almost impossible for me to enter unoccupied France because similar measures against Jews are being taken there."

Frau Sonabend fought to save her children, begging the policemen to spare them. (Swiss families in Pruntrut had offered to take them in.) The deportation order was confirmed. In view of the many representations that had been made on the maltreated family's behalf, however, a legally cogent reason for doing so had to be found. The officials in Bern found it: illegal entry.

When darkness fell on Monday evening, military policemen in civilian clothes drove up to the gates of Pruntrut's district prison in a taxi. The elder Sonabends offered no resistance, possibly in the belief that they were going to be deported to unoccupied France. They were mistaken. The military policemen took them to Boncourt, where they handed them over to the cantonal police, who drove the family, parents and children alike, to a spot near the village of Saint-Dizier. A hundred yards west of there lay French territory controlled by the Wehrmacht, SS, and Gestapo. The next day, Cantonal Policeman Choffat wrote the following report to headquarters in Bern:

> The border crossing went off well. Once the German patrol had passed by, all members of the Sonabend family crossed the frontier with the intention of returning to their home in Brussels. The cost of the taxi and escort was borne by the persons concerned. They made no trouble. The allegedly sick wife agreed, in the end, to accompany her husband.

Charles recounted his subsequent experiences to Mächler half a century later:

> We had no road map and no instructions on where and which way to go. When we reached the track we didn't know whether to turn left or right. There was a wood in the distance in one

direction and a track in the other. And, while we were deciding which direction to take, we heard a dog barking in the distance.... We hid behind a small clump of bushes. There was, in fact, another German patrol coming. They had a dog that had spotted us and tugged at its leash. The Germans found us right away.

The German soldiers took the family to Belfort, where they were detained. The parents were carted off to Paris and confined in the camp at Drancy. On August 24, Laja and Simon Sonabend were deported straight to Auschwitz, where they were murdered. The children miraculously survived. The camp at Drancy was overcrowded in August 1942 because Adolf Eichmann lacked sufficient trains to transport all Jews to the gas chambers on time. He gave orders that some of the children under the age of sixteen were to be temporarily entrusted to the care of the Union Générale des Israélites de France.

Tens of thousands of Jewish refugees who had vainly sought asylum in Switzerland shared the fate of Laja and Simon Sonabend. Here is one last example.

In the Federal Archive is a letter to National Councilor Paul Graber from Max Feingold, a German Jewish member of the German Social Democratic Party (SPD).[17]

Feingold and his wife had been detained as "stateless persons" in the French internment camp at Gurs. They managed to escape, got to the Rhône Valley, and tried to enter Switzerland by way of the Valais Alps. They were turned away.

Things could have been worse, however, because the Swiss frontier guards expelled them into that part of France which the Germans had not yet occupied. From there Max Feingold wrote to Paul Graber. A Social Democratic national councilor of international repute, Graber was a gifted public speaker, a well-known journalist, and one of the Socialist International's most prominent figures. Feingold gave him a detailed account of his predicament:

Lyon, October 27, 1942

Dear Comrade Graber,

Permit me, esteemed Comrade, to acquaint you with the following circumstances:

At 7 o'clock on the evening of Tuesday, October 13, 1942, I and my wife (who is in her fourth month) attempted to enter Switzerland via the Col de Balme, Canton Valais. My wife being utterly exhausted, we decided to spend the night in a chalet on Swiss soil about one kilometer from the frontier. Shortly afterward a Swiss customs officer appeared. He showered us with the foulest abuse, including remarks such as "You're Jews. We've got enough of that trash here already, we don't need filth like you." When I asked him to examine my papers because I was a journalist and political refugee who requested the right of asylum, the customs officer replied: "You'll have to get out of here just the same." We were taken to the frontier post, where there were about a dozen soldiers. The customs officer left us there and asked the corporal in charge to expel us from Switzerland the next day.

I explained my position afresh to the corporal, who, after examining my papers, said that he would see I was brought before the relevant committee. At noon on Wednesday, October 14, another customs officer turned up. He refused to listen to any explanations and addressed the assembled soldiers as follows:

"Why are you here, men? Because of these filthy Jews. Why do we get only 225 grams of bread a day? Because of these Jewish swine. I haven't had any lunch yet, and all because I'm having to deal with these damned Jews. They've got to die and be exterminated, the whole bunch." Turning to my wife, who had dissolved into tears, he said: "If you don't go, I'll smash your husband's head in with a rifle butt." To me he said: "Take one step back, and I'll shoot you like a dog."

Twelve Swiss soldiers stood there with tears in their eyes. Three corporals and nine men stood there, powerless to intervene, and were compelled to listen to a Swiss customs officer threatening a defenseless married couple in the direst manner.

Since I am not personally acquainted with the twelve Swiss soldiers, their names can be ascertained from the daily report. They included a corporal who had lived in France many years before and whose sister is married to a Frenchman at Cannes. He was visiting the frontier post on October 14 and witnessed my expulsion. All the soldiers were very kind to us. They tried to ease our sufferings in every conceivable respect. "Our hands are tied," they told us innumerable times. "The customs officer's word is law—we have to obey."

I had produced the following papers: certification that I am stateless; my SPD membership card; my press card; my birth certificate; a certificate from the Camp de Gurs covering evacuation to Germany; a refugee card issued by the Préfecture du Rhône at Lyon; an internee's identity card from the Camp de Gurs.

Being politically sophisticated, Feingold was familiar with Switzerland's idiosyncrasies:

I cannot forbear to tell you, dear comrade, how well aware I am of the unique sacrifices Switzerland is making on behalf of refugees. I know that many, many thousands of persons in mortal danger have found at least a temporary refuge in your country. I know how sympathetic the Swiss people are toward those unfortunates. Switzerland certainly cannot and should not be reproached because a few customs officers hold views dissimilar to those of the bulk of the Swiss people.

If I now, despite this, lay stress on my personal fate and turn to you, it is because I am fighting for my life. From the purely legal aspect, I was entitled to request the right of asylum. I should at least have been taken before the committee competent to decide my fate. Surely it cannot be left to a junior official, who also happens to be anti-Semitic, to pass judgment on so serious a matter.

When expelled on October 14, I was detained on the return

journey by some French gendarmes. How I and my wife managed to escape is another story, but undoubtedly more tragic than what had happened to me in Switzerland a few hours before.

Feingold's letter ends on a note of despair:

I address to you today, dear comrade, the polite but heartfelt plea: Help us. Save our lives.

Grant us a chance of bare survival in your country. Take pity on us and champion our cause. It would be humane to show us compassion. I place my fate in your hands and appeal to you in utter despair: for God's sake, save us.

I have not heard from my eighty-year-old mother, who used to live in Nuremberg, since November 1938. I have had no news of my brother, who was at Dachau and later at Oranienburg, since April 1939. My parents-in-law and three of their children were sent in November 1938 to Zbanzyn (the Grynszpan affair).[18] A cousin resident in Paris was sent to Drancy and later deported to Poland. I have been trying to trace them all for years through the International Red Cross (Mademoiselle Bordier), so far without success. My wife and I were interned in France for months. We are staying here illegally. With deepest gratitude, and assuring you of my very greatest esteem, I am your comrade

Max Feingold.

Court historian Edgar Bonjour and his colleague Christoph Graf are at one in their basic evaluation of Switzerland's asylum policy.

Bonjour: "The egoism and latent anti-Semitism harbored by every citizen prompts him to shut his eyes to the inhumanity of many aspects of official policy relating to the right of asylum."[19]

Graf: "Just as the domestic political truce (and its relativizations) were influenced by political developments abroad and by Switzerland's flexible foreign policy, so foreign policy, too, was naturally founded on adjustment to internal conditions inherent in the system. By this we mean that Switzerland's restrictive refugee policy was additionally governed by a narrow-minded basic attitude within the country, and that its realpolitik-inspired accommodation with the Axis powers was also based on ideological, social, and economic affinities."[20]

The "ideological affinity with the Axis powers" detected by Graf in official refugee directives trickled down the ladder of officialdom. Border guards, the men who actually expelled refugees, were often infected with it. Here is an extract from a report submitted by the guard post at Riehen, near Basel: "Increasing numbers of refugees from Germany, too, are trying to enter Switzerland. All races and types of European countries are being detained by our border guards and at once forced back across the frontier or handed over to the police, whichever standing orders prescribe."[21]

But the Swiss authorities were fork-tongued. On the one hand they discriminated against Jews seeking help; on the other, they verbally celebrated their own (lost) virtue of universal solidarity. Gerhart Riegner, Geneva representative of the World Jewish Congress, puts it this way: "While Switzerland proudly described itself as the land of asylum and often stressed the important role it had played, especially in the nineteenth century, as a country where many European revolutionaries and victims of autocratic oppression had found a safe refuge from persecution, its post-1933 behavior toward the Jews of Germany, and, later on, of Austria and Czechoslovakia, was exceptionally cautious and hesitant. This cautious and hesitant behavior on the part of the Swiss authorities was undoubtedly attributable to the deep-rooted anti-Semitic prejudice entertained by a substantial proportion of the population and, at the same time, to a grave economic and social situation that did little to encourage a more liberal attitude."[22]

Yet Edgar Bonjour is wrong in one respect: not all the citizens of the Swiss Confederation harbored "latent anti-Semitism" and shut their eyes to the official inhumanity of turning away those seeking help at the Swiss frontier. Quite the contrary. While voices in parliament, frontier posts, and the army general staff were tirelessly warning against the "Judaization" of Switzerland and invoking its social and economic straits, thousands of the country's inhabitants—notably Swiss Jews, trade unionists, democrats, and Christians—displayed active and steadfast sympathy for the victims of persecution.[23]

The large Jewish communities in the United States were already playing an important role in the mid-1930s. More than 50,000 Jewish men, women, and children from Germany had managed to escape to America by 1938. They brought tidings of the Brownshirt reign of terror in the streets, of the first concentration camps and the enforced Aryanization of Jewish businesses—in short, of the lawlessness and psychological intimidation to which Jews in German cities were daily subjected. These reports were published in the American press and struck a chord with the public. They stirred consciences and generated political pressure.

In the summer of 1938 President Roosevelt urged the Europeans to find a solution to the problem of enforced emigration. The relevant conference should by rights have been held at the Palais des Nations in Geneva, headquarters of the League of Nations, whose high commissioner for refugees was James McDonald, an American of great persuasive power and unflagging energy. But the Swiss government resisted American pressure and refused to allow the World Refugee Conference to take place on Swiss soil. It was held instead at Evian, a small French spa situated on the south bank of the Lake of Geneva, some thirty miles from the city of Geneva itself.

The Evian conference took place in July 1938. Hitler had just annexed Austria, and the "Czechoslovak problem" was to be resolved without bloodshed. Ribbentrop's diplomats were working overtime. Hitler roamed around in sheep's clothing, preached peace in Europe and security for all, claiming that stability was the aim of German foreign policy. The premiers of Britain and France, Neville Chamberlain and Edouard Daladier, one naïve and the other crafty, were destined to attend the Munich "peace conference" in two and a half months' time.

Goebbels feared for the Third Reich's good name. The emigration of German, Moravian, and Austrian Jews was obstructing his propaganda machine. Reports of atrocities from Germany and Austria were undesirable. The Nazis brought pressure to bear on their Swiss business associates. The Swiss defended themselves, pointing out that it was traditional for their country to shelter political refugees and that such people couldn't be turned away. The German response: "The Jews aren't political refugees at all; they're running away simply because they're Jews." To which the Swiss countered: "True, but how can our border guards tell the difference between politically motivated German emigrants and German Jewish asylum seekers?"

In August 1938 Berlin stepped up the pressure. Visas had not been required for travel between Switzerland and Germany since 1926. The Germans threatened to reintroduce them, thereby hampering business relations between Switzerland and the Third Reich.

Then the Swiss had an idea: German Jewish passport holders must be identified in some way.[24] Two Swiss suggestions were discussed: (a) underlining the names of Jews in red ink as opposed to black; and (b) stamping the front page of their passports in the top left corner, the stamp to consist of a circle approximately two centimeters in diameter and the letter J or some other symbol. Berlin chose the stamp. From then on, and throughout the war years, Swiss refugee policy was based on this form of discrimination between political refugees and victims of ethnic persecution.

When Europe went up in flames a short while later, Jewish escapees and deserters from various armies occasionally made for the Swiss frontier in the belief that it offered safety. All countries are obliged, under international law, to grant asylum to foreign deserters. Switzerland took in all but the Jewish kind. Where

Austrian Jews were concerned, it imposed a de facto entry ban in September 1938.[25]

Although complex international developments should not be personalized, one man played a special part in devising the Swiss refugee policy. Heinrich Rothmund (1888–1961) was versed in all the professional stratagems of which a cunning and astute lawyer is capable. He does, in fact, look quite personable in one or two of his archive photographs, which show us a man with a lofty brow, neatly parted graying hair, gray mustache, long nose, and pale, deep-set, rather melancholy-looking eyes. A man of principle, Rothmund was altogether devoid of vanity and the desire for personal gain. He never wavered in his views, not even after the war, when it was common practice for Swiss civil servants to plead extenuating circumstances and claim that they were acting under orders.

Rothmund spent the whole of his energetic life in the public service. During World War I he served as secretary first to the War Materials Administration and then to the Industrial War Economy Office. In 1919 he became head of the aliens branch of the police force. Ten years later he attained the highest rung on his professional ladder: head of the Police Department of the Federal Ministry of Justice and Police. He did not retire until 1954.

The historian Heinz Roschewski paints a subtle pen portrait of this man:

Dr. Heinrich Rothmund was . . . a split personality. His attitude toward Jews was correspondingly ambivalent and discriminatory. It was typical of Rothmund that he always invoked his good relations with one or two prominent and particularly patriotic Swiss Jews. Typical, too, was his hostility to foreigners and his oft-avowed fear that Switzerland would become Judaized. Also characteristic of him was the distinction between good, readily assimilable Swiss and Western Jews in general, and Eastern Jews, who were either not assimilable or would take many long years to become so, and whose business methods, customs, and habits were disreputable and suspect. Equally characteristic was Rothmund's arrogance: the non-Jewish, Christian Swiss was the exemplary person and good citizen to whose status "good," assimilable Jews had if possible to be "raised," whereas all other Jews, being unassimilable, were to be either removed from Switzerland as swiftly as possible or not admitted at all. In Rothmund's view, the Jews were largely to blame for anti-Semitism; this was also—and especially—the case in Germany, whereas Switzerland had been preserved therefrom by the aliens police.[26]

The Swiss Federation of Jewish Communities (SIG), headed by Saly Mayer, had no less than seventeen subsidiary organizations for which many hundreds of Swiss Jews of both sexes toiled to the point of exhaustion, day and night. They made representations on behalf of their persecuted coreligionists, kept the public regularly informed, and combated Switzerland's inhumane refugee policy in company with Social Democratic and Liberal legislators, journalists, Protestant and Catholic clergy, and thousands of men and women from all parts of the country, every social class, and every political color.

Rothmund enjoyed the special protection of his immediate superior, the head of the Federal Ministry of Justice and Police, Eduard von Steiger, a Bernese aristocrat of limited mental outlook. That Rothmund cherished a perverse admiration for the Jews emerges from a letter he wrote to Alexandre Girardet, a Swiss diplomat stationed in London:

> If I can elicit something favorable, I intend to bring it to the attention of the gentlemen [of the SIG] with whom I have been most faithfully cooperating on emigration issues for the past five years. I am doing my utmost, especially in such matters, to combat unworthy and harmful anti-Semitism in Switzerland. For their part, the influential members of Swiss Jewry are countering all the improprieties committed by Swiss Jews that come to their

notice, their primary aim being to eliminate every vulnerable spot. There will probably be many more matters to correct.[27]

Rothmann displayed incredible naïveté toward the German authorities, with whom he was also in regular professional and personal contact. From October 12 to November 6, 1942, for instance, he attended a series of official discussions in Berlin accompanied by the Swiss minister, Hans Frölicher. The charming gentlemen from the Central State Security Bureau had arranged a little excursion for their Swiss guests: a conducted tour of Sachsenhausen (Oranienburg) concentration camp, near Berlin. Sachsenhausen, whose huts and barbed wire fences were situated in the immediate vicinity of a residential district, was one of the first camps constructed by Himmler. Most of its inmates were German Communists, Social Democrats, Christian opponents of the regime, homosexuals, and Jews. Although it was not initially an extermination camp, SS sadism developed a momentum of its own, and it was not long before Sachsenhauen acquired a place of execution and a gas chamber. Hundreds of people were killed there, usually by being shot in the back of the neck, and many others died under the scalpels of SS doctors engaged in so-called medical experiments.

Heinrich Rothmund, ever the punctilious civil servant, described his visit to the camp in a report to his minister at Bern:

> I was shown the hutted hospital, which is equipped with every essential including an operating room. X-rays are made available to all with lung diseases and chairs to those prescribed rest cures, who receive additional food. Food in general seems unavoidably limited to the minimum required by someone engaged in physical labor. I was also informed that the withholding of food is no longer employed as a punishment because anyone punished in that way would not be fit for work the next day. For those doing strenuous work, substantial extra rations of good bread and tasty sausage are brought to their places of work.[28]

The guests from Berlin and Bern were also entertained with lunch at Sachsenhausen by the camp commandant. Rothmund took advantage of the occasion to lecture the nice SS officers on one or two of their shortcomings.

> I endeavored to explain to them that, in Switzerland, the public and the authorities had long ago recognized the danger of Judaization, and had always combated it in such a way that the disadvantages of the Jewish inhabitants were offset by their advantages, whereas in Germany that did not apply. That danger can be countered only if a nation defends itself against all forms of Jewish exclusivity and renders it impossible from the outset. The Jew is then a useful member of the national community and can, in time, adapt. I added that I had seen some excellent people among the Jews who had fled to us from Germany. The Jewish race has stood the test of history, is tough and proof against persecution. It has so far withstood all attempts to annihilate it, and has always emerged stronger than before. I concluded my remarks by saying that, in the light of these considerations, German methods struck me as mistaken and dangerous to us all because they ultimately brought the Jews down on our heads.[29]

The federal police chief ended his report to von Steiger on a complacent note: while not concurring with his remarks, the SS officers had nonetheless listened to him with polite attention. Rothmund's visit to Sachsenhausen was political dynamite. Red Cross delegates and protecting power diplomats were not in general granted access to concentration camps. The head of Switzerland's Federal Police Department clearly enjoyed a special relationship with the SS.

Rothmund was not alone. His every pronouncement, decree, and action was backed by the government. And that government, and his minister and immediate superior, Eduard von Steiger, pursued a criminal policy in regard to turning away Jews.

Rothmund's deputy, Robert Jezler, addressed an appeal to his boss in 1942: "Consistent and reliable reports about the manner in which deportations are being carried out, and about conditions prevailing in Jewish areas in the East, are so terrible that one cannot fail to sympathize with the desperate attempts of refugees to escape such a fate, and can no longer assume responsibility for expelling them."[30]

Heinrich Rothmund rejected this plea. "In my opinion, Article 9 should now be applied." Article 9 of the Federal Act of October 7, 1939, provided for the forcible expulsion of all victims of persecution who had entered Switzerland illegally. An illegal entrant was one who crossed the Swiss frontier without a visa.

Rothmund did not reveal precisely where in Europe legal entry visas could be obtained by Jewish men, women, and children hunted by the Gestapo, the SS, and the Central State Security Bureau.

Switzerland's frontiers were completely sealed off during the winter of 1942–43.

Commenting on Rothmund's decision, Alfred Cattani, historian and editor of the *Neue Zürcher Zeitung*, wrote in 1986:

> In full cognizance that terrible things awaited the Jews in the East, the head of the Federal Police Department recommended the government bar Switzerland to refugees. Rothmund cannot be absolved of responsibility for initiating that measure. But the government assumed an equal or even greater burden of responsibility when it approved the proposal and expressly stated that Jews were not to be regarded as political refugees.[31]

Cattani described Rothmund's decision as "an enormity" colored by "brazen cynicism," and he was right. Government directives in 1942 and 1943 were expressly targeted at Jewish refugees, who were debarred from acceptance by Switzerland, though exceptions were occasionally made for the old, the sick, and young children. The directives were widely publicized, the government's intention being to deter West European Jews threatened with deportation from making for the putative safety of Switzerland. Gerhart Riegner rightly states that the officially rejected—and registered—refugees constituted only a small fraction of the people whom Switzerland sent to their deaths.

Once it became known that the Swiss frontier had been closed, hundreds of thousands of persecuted Jews abandoned all hope of reaching it from Belgium, France, and elsewhere. Despite the existence of smugglers' networks, traversing occupied Europe was an exceptionally dangerous business.

What exactly did the Swiss authorities know about the fate of the Jews? How much were they in a position to know? Jacques Picard describes their state of knowledge in the spring of 1942:

> The first photographs of the Nazis' atrocities in the Warsaw ghetto were brought back to Switzerland in the spring of 1942 by members of the official Swiss medical mission. The pictures and items of evidence did not, however, get into the "wrong" hands because of the *absolute confidentiality* to which members of the medical mission were pledged. The only one who refused to keep silent was Rudolf Bucher, chief physician of the army's blood donor service, who made no secret of the atrocities committed by the Nazis and was subjected to intense pressure by the federal authorities. The federal prosecutor's office possessed proof in the form of pictorial material as early as the spring of 1942. Another member of the medical mission, Franz Blättler, alias Max Mawick, had secretly photographed the atrocities in the Warsaw ghetto but was subject at home to a ban on publication. At almost the same time, Franz-Rudolph von Weiss, Swiss consul in Cologne, sent a series of photographs from the Eastern Front to Roger Masson, director of Swiss military intelligence, showing gassed Jews being unloaded from cattle cars. All this material remained under lock and key.[32]

At 3 P.M. on October 14, 1942, the members of the International Committee of the Red Cross assembled in the spacious conference room on the ground floor of Geneva's Hôtel Métropole. Mellow fall sunlight was streaming through the lofty windows and dancing on the surface of the nearby lake. For months now Gerhart Riegner and other witnesses of Nazi genocide had been supplying the ICRC with photographs, firsthand accounts, and German documents attesting the Einsatzkommandos' atrocities, repression in the ghettos, horrific conditions aboard the deportation trains, mass murder in the extermination camps. Shocked to the core, the ICRC members proposed to break with their organization's time-honored tradition and issue an international appeal on behalf of the victims. Also present was Minister of the Interior Philippe Etter, who had come to Geneva from the Bundeshaus at Bern.

The minutes of the meeting contain the following passage:

> Herr Etter said that this appeal was a very noble idea. Herr Etter had certain misgivings, however. The belligerent powers are becoming more sensitive as the war goes on. They will, therefore, construe the appeal as a judgment, and its effect will be lost from the outset if it upsets them. We should bear in mind that quite different interpretations might be placed on the appeal depending on its time of publication, and that it could thus be accused of lacking impartiality. A further danger: whether published or not, it may be misused for propaganda purposes. One could be in favor of it if there were the smallest hope of its exerting a positive effect, which the speaker doubted. Methods of warfare have changed to such an extent that an entire country can now, on occasion, become a fighting front. Another danger: one of the powers might say that it would, for example, discontinue air raids if the enemy stopped deporting civilians.[33]

So Auschwitz had become an aid to modern warfare, and the Allies might misuse the Jews' salvation in order to blackmail the Third Reich...

The appeal was dropped.

Archival photographs show some well-fed Swiss officers in glossy boots standing, hands on hips, beside a group of steel-helmeted Swiss soldiers with fixed bayonets. The scene is a snowy clearing in the Jura mountains. Affixed to a tree trunk is a poster inscribed in German and French: "Halt! Swiss territory. It is forbidden to cross the frontier. Anyone disregarding this order will be fired on." The clouds are low. The clearing is traversed by a barbed wire fence. Thronging the other side of the fence are ragged, emaciated figures: men with stubbly chins and fear-haunted eyes, little children clinging to their mothers' hands, shivering women in threadbare overcoats and worn-out shoes.

For how many days and nights had those families made their way across occupied Europe to seek sanctuary in Switzerland, running the gauntlet of SS patrols and dogs, dodging the searchlights that probed the forest tracks? They had gotten to within a few feet of safety, only to be shooed away by smiling men in uniform.

Many Jews committed suicide at the frontier fence.

Der Zyschtigsclub ("The Tuesday Club") is by far the most popular talk show on German-language television in Switzerland. On Tuesday, January 14, 1997, the guests were discussing our refugee policy during World War II. The chairman of the panel looked perceptibly uncomfortable when reference was made to some terrible wartime incidents. "I know our refugee policy was anti-Semitic," he broke in, "but wasn't it a *moderate* form of anti-Semitism?"

From late 1942 onward Swiss guards stationed at the Genevese frontier village of Moillesullaz would drive Jews back across the border with fixed bayonets, straight into the clutches of waiting SS men. The SS trucks had already started up by the time the columns of deportees from Le Bout du Monde reception camp approached the frontier under cantonal police escort. Most of the refugees deported via Moillesullaz, Saint-Gingolph, Pruntrut were sent to the death camps. They were not "moderately" murdered at Auschwitz; they were gassed to death.

To recapitulate: Heinrich Rothmund and his superiors in the government, as well as many anti-Semitic officers, border guards, soldiers, and military and cantonal policemen, behaved like Hitler's stooges during the dark days of the Nazi regime in Europe, a disgrace to Switzerland for all time.

Even so, the "other Switzerland" to which this book makes only incomplete and fragmentary references—the Switzerland dedicated to human dignity, solidarity, and resistance—numbered many thousands of courageous men and women. Jews, Protestants, and Catholics, young and old, representatives of all four linguistic groups, French and Italian, German and Rhaeto-Romanic, they hailed from every profession and occupation, every social category and political party.

I should like to single out one of the less prominent figures among them for special mention: Police Superintendent Paul Grüninger (1891–1972), who commanded the cantonal police of Sankt Gallen. When Hitler marched into Vienna, the Swiss government made it compulsory for Austrian Jews to obtain entry visas. In practice, this rendered it impossible for them to seek refuge in Switzerland. The terror, despair, and entreaties of these rejects were more than Grüninger could endure. Between the fall of 1938 and the spring of 1939 he allowed more than 3,000 Jewish men, women, and children to enter Switzerland illegally by way of the Rhine and the Vorarlberg. He also solicited donations from private individuals to enable these victims of persecution to be housed and fed. This infuriated Rothmund, and on March 31, 1939, Grüninger was hounded out of office by Sankt Gallen's cantonal government. Convicted by the district court of "persistent malfeasance" in the fall of 1940, he lost all his pension rights and remained an outcast thereafter. Paul Grüninger died a poverty-stricken and forgotten man in 1972, but those who owed him their lives refused to let the matter rest. In 1993, with the help of Stefan Keller, Paul Rechsteiner, Richard Dindo, and other Swiss citizens, they pressured the Sankt Gallen executive into "politically rehabilitating" him.[34]

3. Misappropriation

JACOB AND MARGITA FRIEDMAN, an elderly couple, live in a run-down neighborhood in Brooklyn. Their mother tongue is Yiddish. Jacob, originally from Satu-Mare in Romania, comes of an Orthodox and once extremely prosperous family. His father, a businessman, was not only well-informed but farsighted. When Jacob was seventeen he sent him off to Zurich with gold and valuables sewn into his overcoat. Jacob made a total of seven trips to Switzerland, where he deposited assets to the value of more than 200,000 Swiss francs. When interviewed by the journalist Anne-Frédérique Widmann, he stated: "Today that would be two million, plus four percent interest over fifty-eight years. The assets were deposited with the Union Bank of Switzerland and the Swiss Bank Corporation."[35]

In the spring of 1944, while young Jacob was away on a business trip to Budapest, all the Jews in Satu-Mare were detained, herded into cattle cars, and deported. The SS murdered Jacob's parents and his seven brothers and sisters in Auschwitz.

Jacob has made several attempts, notably during the 1970s, to persuade the big Zurich banks to return his family money. To no avail. Although he is the sole heir, he cannot prove it by producing the requisite death certificates. He also lacks other items of information. Account number? Code name? Credit balance?

The banks are protected by bank secrecy.

Estelle Sapir inhabits one small room in Rockaway Park, New York, with only her cat for company. An old woman who scrapes by on a small pension, she has never married and devotes herself entirely to her father's memory. Estelle hoards all her mementos of him—every letter, photograph, and document, bank statements and bank correspondence included—like sacred relics.

Born in 1926, she first saw the light in an elegant town house in the middle of Warsaw. Her father, a successful private banker, had business interests all over Europe. He managed to spirit his family away to Paris when the Germans invaded Poland, complete with a great deal of baggage and all his financial papers. In May 1940, when the Wehrmacht was nearing Paris, the family caught the last train to Avignon. From there they planned to travel on to Spain, only to be betrayed by the smuggler they had hired to guide them across the Pyrenees. Detained by the French police, they were consigned to a camp in the South of France.

In 1942 came the Jewish deportations to the East. Sixteen-year-old Estelle and her mother, who were temporarily spared, succeeded in escaping later on. Not so Father Jozef. Estelle preserves a vivid recollection of their parting: through the barbed wire fence, her father recited the names of the banks, their location, and the accounts they held on his behalf. She had to memorize all these particulars and repeat them to him. Concerned for his wife and child's financial future, Jozef wanted to ensure that they could get at the money essential to their survival. Then the guards hustled him away from the wire. He was murdered by the SS in Maidanek.

Estelle has undergone all manner of experiences during her long search for Jozef's estate. The money he had deposited in British and French banks was handed over to her after the war in a cooperative and unbureaucratic manner, but it ran out long ago. The largest sums are held by Swiss banks, Crédit Suisse in particular.

The putative sums must be substantial, because Estelle received preferential treatment: instead of a questionnaire and the customary, computerized letter of rejection, she was sent a personal invitation to meet with representatives of Crédit Suisse at the bank's New York office. It goes without saying that they, too, demanded to see Jozef Sapir's death certificate from Maidanek extermination camp. It also goes without saying that they declined to pay his daughter a cent. The same old story: insufficient information, bank secrecy. Still, Estelle Sapir was at least accorded a personal interview. The old lady's comment: "The Swiss banks have cheated me in an inhuman manner."[36]

Gizella Weisshaus is an Orthodox Jew who lives with her husband in Brooklyn and has spent her days as a seamstress in a clothing factory. Her children are long grown up. She comes from Sighet, the small town in Transylvanian Romania where Elie Wiesel, too, was born. Her father, Eugen Stern, was a foreign currency dealer as farsighted as Jozef Sapir. Anxious to provide for his wife Sarah, née Halpert, and their children, he not only secreted dollars and articles of jewelry in the walls of his house, but also opened accounts at various Swiss banks. Unlike most of his fellow Jews from Sighet, Eugen Stern was apprehensive about the future.

In the summer of 1944, when Gizella was a carefree girl of fourteen, the Jews of Sighet were detained, cooped up in camps, and deported. Being young and strong, Gizella was selected on arrival at Auschwitz to do forced labor in a German munitions factory at Gelsenkirchen. Her parents, her brothers and sisters, and fifty-six of her relations met their end in the SS gas chambers. Gizella survived, made her way back to Sighet after the war, and recovered the jewelry and handful of banknotes concealed in the walls of the family home. She married and became pregnant. The money was just enough to pay for a guide, bribe some officials, and engineer her escape from the Communist dictatorship.

The young Weisshaus family emigrated to New York. By the end of the 1960s Gizella had finally saved enough money for a preliminary trip to Switzerland. Fischl Halpert, an uncle resident in Zurich, telephoned the big banks and accompanied his niece to the counter. It was a waste of time. Gizella paid two subsequent and equally fruitless visits to Switzerland. She eventually received one of Ombudsman Häni's celebrated questionnaires, together with a bill for 300 Swiss francs, payable in advance, to cover outstanding expenses. She threw the questionnaire and the bill into the wastebasket. Like hundreds of other injured parties she joined the class action suit being conducted by the New York attorney Edward Fagan directed against three big Swiss banks—Crédit Suisse, Swiss Bank Corporation, and Union Bank of Switzerland—with damage claims amounting to $20 billion.

Gizella Weisshaus sums up: "The Swiss banks have cheated me out of the estate of my father, who was murdered at Auschwitz."[37]

The Swiss drove foreign Jews back across the frontier and refused asylum to those who sought it, but they hoarded their assets, jewelry, gold, and art treasures. The latent but seldom publicly professed anti-Semitism of the Swiss ruling class manifested itself in another, surprising form: private property. "The protection of property is at the heart of our civic system," comments Roger de Weck. "Clearly, the property of many Jews was a little less worthy of protection."[38]

Under the terms of the May 1996 Memorandum of Understanding between the World Jewish Congress and the Swiss Bankers Association, Swiss financial institutions are obliged to cooperate fully with the committee of inquiry on which both parties are equally represented. Appointed to trace dormant Jewish bank accounts in Switzerland, the committee is chaired by Paul J. Volcker, former chairman of the Federal Reserve Board, who has an army of investigators available to him: accountants, examiners, auditors, and computer analysts belonging to the international firms of Arthur Andersen, Price Waterhouse, and KPMG Peat Marwick. It remains to be seen how much they will unearth.

From the legal aspect, dormant assets fall into two categories:

1. Assets for which creditors exist (articles of value deposited in safes; art treasures; pieces of jewelry; money in deposit accounts; portfolios of securities; sleeping partnerships in industrial

concerns; real estate and immovables, possibly purchased under cover names).

The search is on for pecuniary and material assets conveyed to "safety" in Switzerland by Jewish and other creditors, either before the war or during its early stages. These assets reached the banks either directly or by way of attorneys, trustees, financial administrators, or straw men. The creditors of the first instance (more precisely, the depositors) then became victims of Hitler's mass murders. Their descendants are now the rightful heirs to the money.

The banks, trust companies and other such institutions include these accounts in their balance sheets, but the creditors either fail to get in touch or their heirs present themselves at the counter without the requisite documentation. In consequence, such accounts have remained untouched for years: no transfers, no withdrawals, nothing. No money has been paid out and none deposited, so the accounts are—in the strictest sense of the term —dormant.

2. Other Jewish estates for which no identifiable heirs exist. Whole families—grandparents, parents, children, cousins, uncles, and aunts—were gassed, shot, or murdered by other means. The tracing of "heirless assets" is a task that also devolves upon the investigators of Price Waterhouse, Arthur Andersen, and Peat Marwick.

Under a Federal Act of December 13, 1996, bank secrecy has been lifted in respect to all dormant and heirless accounts belonging to victims of the Nazis.

Notwithstanding all this, the Holocaust accounts continue to be shrouded in obscurity. Why? Instead of helping creditors to search for and identify these accounts, Swiss bank officials adopt a legally irreproachable but humanly ridiculous stance: they demand proof of inheritance—in practical terms, the deceased creditor's death certificate. Even if a descendant manages to produce a death certificate (or a declaration of presumptive death), the chicanery continues unabated: "I shall also require proof that you're the sole heir."

That ends any hope of receiving help. At Auschwitz and Maidanek, Treblinka and Belsen, the SS gassed whole families and communities, often wiping out the population of entire towns. More than six million people—infants and adolescents, men and women, young and old—were consumed by fire. In the East, very few survived the *Shoah*.

For over half a century, Swiss banks displayed an inhumane and abhorrent attitude toward Jewish clients in search of Holocaust funds, yet bank secrecy was instituted in 1934 primarily for the protection of foreign clients.

Although flights of capital to Switzerland were far from easy to arrange during the 1930s and early 1940s, tens if not hundreds of thousands of individuals, families, and firms were so afraid of having their property "Aryanized," and so intimidated by the Nazi thieves who coveted it, that they sent their financial reserves—in whole or in part—to that country. An additional incentive to do so was the exceptional competence of Swiss bankers and the integrity for which they were universally—and sometimes mistakenly—renowned. But their choice of Switzerland was based first and foremost on Swiss bank secrecy, an institution whose concrete development rendered it the only one of its kind in the world.

In what does Swiss bank secrecy consist? Its statutory basis, Article 47 of the Federal Law Relating to Banks and Savings Banks, lays it down that:

1. Anyone who divulges a secret entrusted to him in his capacity as an organ, employee, authorized representative, liquidator, or commissioner of a bank, or as an organ or employee of a recognized audit office, or which he has perceived in that capacity, and anyone who seeks to instigate such a breach of professional secrecy, shall be liable to imprisonment for a term not exceeding six months or a fine not exceeding 50,000 francs.

2. If the perpetrator acts out of negligence, the penalty shall be a fine not exceeding 30,000 francs.

3. Breaches of professional secrecy are also punishable after the perpetrator has terminated his official status or ceased to practice his profession.

The list of potential authors of indiscretions is a long one:
- members of an organ (directorial board or committee) and private bankers, stockholders in a collective or limited partnership;
- authorized representatives, meaning all persons to whom a bank has entrusted a task within the context of its business activities;
- the liquidators of a bank that has gone bankrupt and the administrators of an estate;
- experts dispatched by the Banking Committee to act as observers at banks whose creditors are in danger of being harmed by grave irregularities; and
- employees of a recognized audit office and members of the organs of such an institution.[39]

The management of money possesses a quasi-sacramental character in Switzerland. Taking charge of it, counting it, hoarding it, speculating with it, laundering it—all these are activities that have been invested with positively ontological nobility ever since the arrival of the first wave of refugees: the Huguenots who fled France to Geneva in 1685. No aspersions must be cast on such an exalted occupation. It is pursued with mute reverence.

In order to understand the present ideology of secrecy, we must make a brief excursion into history. Having been reared in the spirit of Protestantism by his mother, Jeanne d'Albret, Queen of Navarre, King Henry IV of France proclaimed in 1598 the Edict of Nantes in the city of that name. Although an act of toleration, the edict was far from being a law granting complete religious freedom. Only the French Revolution and the First Republic of 1792 would legally guarantee the freedom of religion and conscience previously postulated by the Declaration of the Rights of Man. Nonetheless, Henry IV—himself a survivor of the St. Bartholomew's Day massacre—brought a long period of religious and civil peace to a country rent by religious strife and mass murder. He paid a high price for his tolerant attitude: in 1610 he was assassinated in the middle of Paris by François Ravaillac, a Roman Catholic fanatic.

Louis XIV, the Sun King, pursued quite a different policy generations later. He regarded the Catholic faith as a political tool, a unifying ideology that would secure his kingdom against the centrifugal forces that threatened it. In 1685 he revoked the Edict of Nantes.

Henry IV had granted the Protestants some hundred places de sûreté, or fortified towns and castles, as sanctuaries recognized by the king. These were now besieged by the royal armies. They were looted and razed to the ground and their inhabitants banished to the galleys. Louis XIV had all the religious ministers arrested, suppressed Protestant worship, and abolished all the other rights enjoyed by Protestants. Despite this, most of the upwardly mobile bourgeoisie had by now adopted the Protestant faith. Two hundred thousand of them, the so-called Huguenots, fled to Prussia, Holland, and, more especially, the Protestant strongholds of Geneva, Zurich, and Basel. Geneva supported the beleaguered Protestant towns of France and administered the fortunes of the Huguenot refugees, most of whom were well-to-do, within its walls. The maintenance of absolute secrecy in respect to all transactions was not only an essential precaution (Louis XIV's spies were everywhere) but, above all, an act of fraternal solidarity—in short, a duty ordained by God.

Although deprived of its raison d'être and perverted, this ideology exerts an influence in Switzerland to this day. The architecture of Swiss banks reflects the sacrosanctity that continues to characterize the handling of money in the Confederation's various cantons: majestic marble temples with columns and porticos for the big banks; smaller, less ostentatious "chapels" for the family-owned private banks, with their somber, paneled boardroom walls. Opacity, discretion, and confidentiality are the Swiss banker's supreme virtues. Anyone who commits the sin of disclosure profanes those virtues, and his sacrilege is punishable by law. Silence and reverence attain their culmination in the Calvinist doctrine of predestination, according to which personal affluence is an outward sign of divine grace. Only the elect acquire material riches.

A bank's legal obligations are crystal clear. If a creditor cancels a custodial agreement, the bank is legally at liberty to destroy the relevant documents after ten years. If the creditor is unknown—in other words, has not closed the account—the bank may not destroy any records. Other laws prevail in other countries. In New York State, for example, banks are empowered to liquidate dormant accounts five years after a creditor's last recorded sign of life, but they must first advertise for him to come forward. If he does not, the money in the account (or assets in a safe-deposit box) must be remitted to the State of New York. No such law exists in Switzerland.

If putative creditors present themselves at their counters, Swiss banks must afford them every possible assistance. They are obliged to comb their records for clues to the existence of an account. If an account is orphaned—in other words, if the account holder must be presumed dead—the bank is duty-bound to inform his or her heirs and successors in title. Indeed, it is legally obliged to seek them out. Yet Swiss banks do no such thing. They shake off Jewish creditors and make no attempt to trace the heirs to supposedly orphaned accounts. Here is just one example:

In December 1996, on behalf of the Swiss government, the historians Marc Perrenoud and Peter Hug submitted their report on "Assets of Nazi victims held in Switzerland and compensation agreements with Eastern countries." They listed the names of 1,048 missing account holders whose heirs had never been informed.

During the late 1930s and for some time thereafter, Hans Ulrich Kellerhals headed the department that handled current account deposits at the headquarters of the Schweizerische Volksbank in Bern. He recalls: "Before and during the war it was virtually impossible to buy dollars, let alone gold, in any European country. It was simply unobtainable."[40]

Foreign exchange controls were in force everywhere. Exports of private funds were prohibited, not only in Central and Eastern Europe but in the Third Reich as well. Private individuals could not buy gold except in very rare instances. Central banks had a monopoly on gold everywhere save in Switzerland.

Kellerhals: "In Europe, those seeking substantial amounts of gold, dollars, or [Swiss] francs had to go to the central bank—and that, of course, identified them." International communications, too, were defective. Kellerhals again: "Telegraphic contacts were uncommon almost everywhere—except, perhaps, between the headquarters of one or two big banks. Telegraphic remittances to Switzerland were almost impossible to effect."

Telephoning presented problems too. Conversations were relayed by the central telephone exchanges only, and Swiss banks followed a cautious procedure. Before embarking on a conversation with a client, a bank official would call back—to the foreign telephone exchange, of course. This meant that the police could immediately identify every client of a Swiss bank by consulting the record kept by the exchange.

The flight of capital to Switzerland was massive nonetheless. Polish, Hungarian, Romanian, and other businessmen delivered goods to Switzerland. They either deposited the proceeds at a bank or invoiced the goods they delivered at a price below the sum actually paid for them. Swiss purchasers would then pay the difference into the foreign supplier's Swiss deposit account.

The opposite method was employed by those who imported

spare parts, optical instruments, pharmaceutical products, agricultural chemicals, medicines, or dyes into Warsaw, Budapest, Vienna, or Hamburg: they arranged to be overinvoiced. Foreign importers would pay their Swiss suppliers a sum higher than the actual price, and the difference, once again, ended up in their Swiss deposit accounts.

Many other methods of transferring funds to Switzerland could be mentioned. Foreign clients might bring foreign currency with them in cash and pay it straight over the counter on Zurich's Bahnhofstrasse. They might also travel with checks, drafts, or letters of credit in their briefcases.

Exchange controls notwithstanding, foreign clients could always rent a personal safe-deposit box in which to keep any amount of jewelry, gold, silver, watches, and securities.

Swiss art galleries acted as depositories for sculptures, paintings, drawings, valuable books and manuscripts, and other material assets. The insurers had a field day, as did corporation lawyers who set up so-called sociétés immobilières at Geneva in particular. These were joint-stock companies with bearer stock that enabled foreign investors to acquire whole blocks of real estate anonymously.

Flights of capital were also effected by means of compensatory transactions. Foreigners would sell goods or services in Switzerland and purchase goods or services from Switzerland. The two transactions were calculated so as to produce a pecuniary surplus that was paid into their Swiss accounts. Compensatory deals could be engineered on any scale, between any number of participants, and in many different ways.

The assets of thousands of the Nazis' murdered victims are safely preserved in Swiss bank vaults today. The World Jewish Congress estimates that, allowing for compound interest, the moneys on deposit amount to many billions of dollars. In November 1996 the Swiss Bankers Association conceded a figure of 32 million Swiss francs—repeat, million.

Some of these assets have undoubtedly been stolen. Like their counterparts in other countries, not all Swiss bankers are saints. Hans Ulrich Kellerhals speaks of "skulduggery," and he should know. In the case of numbered accounts, for example, the name of the rightful account holder never appears. (Numbered accounts have long been one of the gnomes' specialties. They do not exist in the United States or Britain, Germany or France.) Clients ride up in the elevator directly to the boardroom, identify themselves, and deposit their money (by signing a custodial agreement). In spite of universal bank secrecy, they demand additional anonymity. Within the bank, and in all its correspondence with them, the account they have just opened is designated by a number alone. The account holder's name never appears again, whether on bank statements, authorizations, or letters.

Only the bank's director knows to whom the numbered account really belongs.[41] If a client visits the bank to withdraw money, he remains seated upstairs in the boardroom. The director goes to the cashier in person and withdraws the requisite sum himself. If numbered accounts remain dormant for decades, and if heirs to them can be turned away with little difficulty, a director or manager will be severely tempted to misappropriate the account. The temptation may someday prove irresistible. . . .

Swiss bankers, like others of their breed, are extraordinarily ingenious. Another method of looting accounts presupposes that a foreign, Jewish client deposits some money with instructions to use it to finance a portfolio. This gives the mandatory representative—the board—a pretty free hand. He buys and sells according to the state of the market. If he wants to enrich himself, he can, without much risk, palm off a series of losses on the absent client and pocket the profits himself.

Until 1990 there existed a document—unique to Switzerland and Liechtenstein—known as Form B. Acting in a fiduciary capacity, an attorney could sign a custodial agreement on behalf of a client he was not obliged to name. Many Jews, especially those from Germany and Austria, chose this method because they knew of the latent anti-Semitism that prevailed in Swiss banks. By so doing they placed themselves at the attorney's mercy. If they failed to get in touch for years, or if their heirs presumptive could be shaken off without much trouble, the temptation to misappropriate these accounts, too, became almost overwhelming. . . .

During the early postwar years, a great deal of money from dormant accounts was initially transferred to so-called collective accounts. The same applied to individual safe-deposit boxes. Their contents were placed in collective safes.

Then came the day when these assets disappeared into the bank's "undisclosed reserves."

A bank has three different balance sheets. The first is the published balance sheet accessible to its stockholders. Discussed at the annual general meeting and released to the press, this is the bank's public report and account. Then there is the balance sheet drawn up for the fiscal authorities. "Undisclosed reserves" are contingency funds set aside to cover losses and bad debts that might, if worst came to worst, endanger the bank's survival. The third and only "true" balance sheet is known only to the board of directors—in the case of some large banks, to the chairman and his inner circle alone. It is plausible to assume that dormant Holocaust assets worth many millions of francs were buried in Swiss banks' undisclosed reserves immediately after the war.

Bankers read newspapers, after all. They, too, must have learned that Hitler was sending whole populations up in smoke.

In March 1966 the federal parliament debated a question submitted by a Social Democratic representative. The government confirmed the World Jewish Congress's supposition. The parliamentary question ran as follows:

> Relying on detailed evidence, the World Jewish Congress has preferred charges against various Swiss banks (February 1996) that appear to have deliberately destroyed records of bank accounts opened by the Nazis with stolen Jewish funds. Can the government confirm that these documents were destroyed? In addition,

what urgent steps does it propose to take to ensure the preservation of the remaining documents?

An extract from the government's response: "It is indisputable that Swiss banks destroyed documents dating from the time of the Second World War. The data which have been published by the World Jewish Congress, and on which the question is based, indicate as much."

The Federal Act of December 13, 1996, has finally and expressly prohibited the destruction of bank records relating to the circumstances mentioned in the said piece of legislation. These documents must, on pain of punishment, be made available to the Volcker committee and the government-appointed historians' committee. Where they are concerned, bank secrecy is regarded as having been lifted.

Has this law prevented the banks from destroying documents? Not at all—quite the contrary, one is tempted to say. The two committees of inquiry started work in March 1997, and the prospect of auditors' inspecting bank records must have frayed the nerves of many executives on Paradeplatz and elsewhere.

During the night of January 8, 1997, Christoph Meili, a thirty-year-old father of two employed by Wache AG, a private security firm, was making the rounds of the Zurich offices of the Union Bank of Switzerland at No. 45, Bahnhofstrasse. Standing in the shredding room were two huge wheeled containers overflowing with papers. His curiosity aroused, he took a look: they were ledger sheets, bills of sale, and similar papers. They dated from the years of the Nazi regime and related to transactions between Union Bank and the Third Reich.

Although a devout Christian and entirely apolitical, Meili had shared his fellow countrymen's intense interest in the public debate of recent months regarding the putative complicity of the big Swiss banks with Hitler. He made off with two bound ledgers and forty pages from a third. They dealt with the Nazis' com-

pulsory auctioning of Aryanized properties in Berlin and the acquisition of those buildings by the Swiss. Going to the Israelische
Kulturgemeinde Zürich (ICZ), he handed the documents to
Werner Rom, the organization's chairman. Rom promptly laid
charges against the Union Bank of Switzerland for violating the
federal law of December 13, 1996.

At a press conference held by the ICZ, Meili declared that he
had felt "duty-bound to help the Jewish people." On January 15,
1997, the *Neue Zürcher Zeitung* carried the politely restrained
headline: "Incomprehensible Destruction of Records by Union
Bank." The management spoke of a "regrettable error." Christoph Meili was promptly dismissed by his employer and is, at the
time of this writing, under investigation by examining magistrate
Peter Cosandrey for "stealing documents and breaching bank secrecy." The *New York Times* of January 18, 1997, sarcastically
commented: "No one espouses the theory that Swiss bankers
robbed the accounts of Jewish Holocaust victims better than the
bankers themselves."

Swiss banks are reliable. So is the administration of justice in
Zurich. The informant is being penalized, not the bank.

For more than fifty years, the descendants and legitimate heirs
of victims of the Nazis have been pursuing a lonely, arduous, and
usually unsuccessful quest for the assets to which they are entitled.
The search for Holocaust funds in Swiss bank vaults goes back a
long way. An account of its history was prepared for the BBC by
Jacques Picard. His expert opinion dealt with the Swiss-based
assets of victims of ethnic, religious, and political persecution and
their repayment between 1946 and 1993.[42]

In Washington on May 25, 1946, acting on behalf of the Swiss
Confederation and the Principality of Liechtenstein, Walter Stucki
signed the reparations agreement with eighteen victorious Allied
nations. The terms of the Washington Accord were carried out at
varying speeds. The gold problem was swiftly resolved, as was
the lifting of Allied economic sanctions. But not so the problem

of German assets. The Swiss delayed its settlement and kept demanding fresh negotiations. At subsequent talks in London they managed to get the Third Reich's outstanding debts to Switzerland included in the equation. A final settlement was reached in 1952: the Allies waived their claims to German assets in Switzerland in return for a lump-sum payment of 121.5 million Swiss francs. The German Federal Republic assumed legal succession to the Third Reich, and Chancellor Adenauer paid the Swiss 650 million Swiss francs in settlement of outstanding debts. East Germany was not represented at the negotiating table. The Swiss money men had every reason to feel content: their paramount objective—the restoration of foreign creditors' confidence—had been attained.[43]

Hardly anyone took an interest in the dormant assets belonging to victims of Nazi mass murder. No Jewish organizations were represented at the negotiating table in Washington. The Jewish people had yet to found their state and were consequently unable to lodge any specific claims for restitution. Stucki assured the Allies in a letter that the Bern government would submit the troublesome matter of the "dormant accounts of murder victims" to benevolent scrutiny.

Pressure was exerted by the International Refugee Organization (IRO) and the Swiss Federation of Jewish Communities (SIG). In June 1947 the IRO requested the victorious powers to open negotiations with Switzerland regarding the return of Holocaust loot. It further requested that bank secrecy be lifted in respect to the accounts in question. The SIG published preliminary estimates amounting to several million Swiss francs and gave some specific examples: real estate, bank deposits, current accounts.

News articles began appearing in the international press. Becoming concerned, the Swiss Foreign Ministry circulated an inquiry among banks and other potential holders of Holocaust accounts. The Swiss Notaries Association, the Swiss Bar Association, the Federation of Swiss Life Insurance Companies, the Association of Swiss Bookkeeping Experts—all these bodies flatly refused to reply. Their argument: bank secrecy.

The Swiss Bankers Association maneuvered with greater subtlety. Of course it would transmit all individual claims by potential heirs to the relevant banks. Unfortunately, however, the majority of such claimants were not in a position to prove their right of inheritance. Another snag was that these dormant funds were held largely under false or fanciful names or in numbered accounts, which rendered identification almost impossible. Furthermore, any dormant or heirless Jewish accounts held in Switzerland were likely to be very few in number.

The Foreign Ministry wanted some figures nonetheless. On October 7, 1947, the Bankers Association reported as follows: "A total of 208,000 Swiss francs may belong to persons assumed to have succumbed to German acts of violence."[44]

Then came 1949 and the major deal with the Communist countries. We have already analyzed Switzerland's agreement with the Poles, but Stalin had established satellite states throughout Eastern Europe. These countries nationalized domestic and foreign private property, thereby inflicting substantial losses on many Swiss firms, banks, and private individuals. The countries of Eastern Europe, having been ravaged first by Hitler and then by the Red Army, were in need of development loans, access to world financial markets, and imports. The Swiss—quite rightly—demanded to be indemnified for their expropriated real estate, industrial concerns, and business enterprises. Although only too willing to grant this request, Stalin's puppets did not possess the requisite foreign exchange. That's not a problem, replied the gentlemen from Bern, and they negotiated an agreement, complete with secret protocols, with Hungary, Yugoslavia, and other Communist countries. The Swiss government requested the private banks—altogether illegally—to liquidate the accounts belonging to missing citizens of the country concerned and transfer them to the East.

Being victims of Communist expropriation themselves, the

private banks complied. They arranged the transfer without any legal justification and in flagrant violation of bank secrecy. Stalin's stooges then made due restitution to the expropriated Swiss—in hard foreign currency.

The ratification debate in parliament concerning the agreement with Poland (October 1949) was a heated proceeding, though not to be compared with the debate on the Washington reparation agreement three years earlier.

The SIG and other Jewish organizations inveighed against this "cold nationalization." The agreement with the Poles infuriated the Jews, who drew attention to their anti-Semitism. Poland had witnessed a recurrence of pogroms immediately after the war, their victims being the little band of Jewish survivors.

Once the U.S. Senate's Banking Committee had published in October 1996 the secret protocols of the Polish agreement, the Swiss government swiftly appointed a special committee to investigate and publish all Switzerland's agreements with East European countries. Peter Hug and Marc Perrenoud submitted their report on December 19, 1996, but questions about the Holocaust accounts continued to be raised. The nightmare was never-ending, and outside pressure persisted.

In the fall of 1956, the federal Ministry of Justice and Police had sent another questionnaire to the Bankers Association and the members of the Swiss Insurance Companies Association. It asked: (a) Do you hold any dormant accounts belonging to victims of the Nazis? (b) If so, what does the putative sum amount to?

Twenty-one banks admitted to definite knowledge of accounts totaling 36,580 Swiss francs and surmised that they were holding other accounts amounting in all to 825,000 Swiss francs. The insurance companies, on the other hand, had nothing definite to report, though they listed eight doubtful cases. These eight policies were worth a total of 29,000 Swiss francs.

The ministry's lawyers in Bern felt uneasy. There seemed to be something fishy about the bankers' and insurers' replies. Being civil servants they did what civil servants invariably do in such situations. Instead of pursuing their inquiries and getting to the bottom of the matter, they published a report but adorned it with a prophylactic preamble: "We would point out that substantial assets that have become heirless are located in safe-deposit boxes that were rented for long periods and have not, therefore, been opened to date, or are being administered and/or held by trust companies, notaries, attorneys, business associates of the missing depositors, or by other individual persons."[45]

In March 1957 Harald Huber, a national councilor from Sankt Gallen, acting on behalf of the Social Democratic group in the Federal Assembly, moved that the government immediately enact a law of disclosure to which banks, insurance companies, and all other financial administrators would be subject. For the benefit of creditors, the procedure governing declarations of presumptive death would be simplified. Heirless assets belonging to untraceable victims of Nazi genocide were to be paid into a public fund devoted to humanitarian purposes.

The bankers cried bloody murder, protesting that bank secrecy—that holy of holies—was being desecrated. But times had changed. Israel was by then an almost universally recognized nation-state, and the Jewish communities of the United States girded themselves for the fray.

On December 20, 1962, the Swiss government initiated a federal act relating to "the assets, presently in Switzerland, of foreign or stateless victims of racial, religious or political persecution." This typically Swiss law required bankers, insurers, trustees, and others to inform a central registration office of all such assets in their keeping. They were to do so voluntarily, not subject to any form of government supervision, within a statutory term of ten years.[46]

How large a sum did the gentlemen from the Bahnhofstrasse deign to report? It amounted in all to 9,469,881 Swiss francs. The breakdown was as follows:

Banks	6,068,123
Swiss Clearinghouse	2,471,900
Government authorities, trust companies, private individuals	670,053
Insurers	259,805[47]

Recently Edgar Bronfman, chairman of the World Jewish Congress, Elan Steinberg, executive director of the Jewish Agency, and even Stuart Eizenstat, whom President Clinton appointed to oversee the Holocaust file, were largely vilified by Swiss newspapers as extremist zealots. No such charge can be leveled at Michaël Kohn, Jean Halpérin, or Gerhart Riegner, all of whom look back with abhorrence on the "voluntary duty of disclosure" instituted in 1962.

Michaël Kohn is a dominant figure in the Swiss Federation of Jewish Communities and one of Switzerland's leading industrialists. The Jews of Switzerland were not consulted about the federal act of 1962, nor were they represented in parliament. In the late fall of 1996 the SIG issued a public statement: "The use of Swiss Jewry must not be permitted to recur."[48]

Professor Jean Halpérin is one of the most cultured, refined, and sweet-tempered men I know. He heads the Center for Jewish Studies at Geneva and teaches philosophy at Fribourg University. His verdict:

> The banks employ bank secrecy, whose original purpose was to protect their clients, to protect themselves. . . . I have discovered that the banks entertained not the smallest moral scruples nor the most elementary decency toward their clients. The demand for death certificates in respect to account holders who perished in the crematoria of the extermination camps is based on entirely false logic.[49]

Gerhart Riegner, lawyer and honorary vice chairman of the World Jewish Congress, says of the Swiss banks' ostensible search for Holocaust funds: "It horrifies me that we were lied to throughout our negotiations in the early 1960's.... The banks were completely uncooperative.... I just don't know what to believe, not now, they served us up with so many lies."[50]

The tragedy persisted when the term of the federal act expired in 1972. Whenever they were threatened with renewed attacks from abroad, the gentlemen from Paradeplatz examined their books again. And, wonder of wonders, they contrived to unearth more dormant accounts belonging to victims of the Nazis. In early 1997 Swiss banks turned up "new" Holocaust moneys amounting to approximately 40 million Swiss francs. In January Avraham Burg, chairman of the Jewish Agency, branded the disappearance of the bulk of the Holocaust assets the biggest bank-organized theft in history. The Swiss Bankers Association defended itself against this wholesale, and premature, condemnation. Burg was, after all, a member of the Volcker committee scheduled to begin its investigations two months later.

What can, however, be said at this stage is that a very strong suspicion of embezzlement exists. Roger de Weck is more explicit: "After the war, so the experts say, some of the ownerless assets were *misappropriated*."[51]

Over the past fifty years Switzerland's bankers have made the transition from hypocrisy to cynicism: immediately after the war they denied the existence of dormant assets; now they acknowledge their existence but claim they cannot find them.

In February 1997 Peter Vallone, speaker of the New York City Council, proposed a bill prohibiting transactions between Swiss banks and institutions and authorities dependent on the city administration. Most of the city council members are Democrats like Vallone, but Rudolph Giuliani, the Republican mayor, also supported the proposal. The state legislatures of New York, New Jersey, and Rhode Island also scheduled hearings and demanded that Swiss banks at once restore Holocaust moneys to their lawful owners on pain of being forbidden to conduct business within their state boundaries. On Thursday, February 6, Governor George Pataki of New York resolved to institute an inquiry into "the activities of Swiss banks between 1939 and 1945" and dispatched a fact-finding committee to Zurich.

Panic broke out on Bahnhofstrasse. The major Swiss banks earn a sizable proportion of their profits on the East Coast, notably on the two New York stock exchanges and as financial administrators of American pension funds.

The reaction by Switzerland's big three—Union Bank, Crédit Suisse, and Swiss Bank Corporation—was instantaneous. They created a fund of 100 million Swiss francs "for the benefit of the *Shoah* victims." They announced that they were prepared to pay out a (small) part of the money they owed—on the condition that New York's city council members, state legislators, the mayor, and the governor withdrew their horrific legislative proposals.

A front-page article in the *New York Times* on February 6, 1997, put the banks' generosity in the right light: "The gesture was apparently intended to head off threats from Jewish groups and from New York state and city institutions of sanctions against Swiss banks—a pillar of the Swiss economy—that would further harm their battered reputation." The Swiss money merchants have failed to understand, even now, that the survivors of the Holocaust and their heirs are not after charity. What they demand is theirs by right. Their obsession is with justice, not money.

EPILOGUE

Hope

———

Living means remembering.

JOSÉ MARTÍ

NATIONAL HISTORY IS THE product of collective ideas and myths, just as all historical writing is fraught with ideologies that render it a political weapon. To quote Herbert Lüthy, former professor at Basel University, "The science of history is indissolubly related to the awareness of history on which we base our historical—that is to say, political—thoughts and actions."[1]

The conception of history presently entertained by Switzerland's rulers is illustrated by two events: the so-called Diamond Jubilee of 1989 and the extraordinary session of the Combined National Assembly held on May 7, 1995.

The Diamond Jubilee commemorated the fiftieth anniversary of Hitler's attack on Poland, an event that, the world over, conjured up unspeakable horrors in people's minds and inclined them to sorrow and contemplation. In Switzerland, however, the federal Ministry of Defense took advantage of the occasion to revitalize the myth of Swiss resistance, commemorate general mobilization, and celebrate the heroic combat-readiness of the ever invincible—because ever neutral—Swiss army. At this nationwide festival, surviving veterans of active wartime service were regaled with food and drink. In addition to gorging themselves on sausage and receiving commemorative medals (financed by the taxpayer), they were treated to smugly patriotic speeches in which they were thanked for having preserved their native land and praised for their heroic fortitude. These festivities took their title from a poem by Gottfried Keller, one of Switzerland's great literary figures, who had likened the Confederation to an indestructible diamond.

Peter Bodenmann, chairman of the Swiss Social Democrats, irreverently calls the army a Trachtenverein, that is, a society for the preservation of traditional and/or national costume. In 1989 this Trachtenverein, which has a membership of more than 400,000 and swallows up billions of francs a year, mounted a touring exhibition and sent it around the cantons on an egotistical parade of triumph. According to Colonel Corps Commander Rolf Binder, the army's director of training, more than 500,000 people turned out to witness this bizarre display—the only festival on earth to celebrate the outbreak of World War II.

The man in charge of preparations for the Diamond Jubilee, Colonel Friedrich Nyffenegger, has since turned out to be a corrupt public servant. In 1996, Federal Prosecutor Carla del Ponte arrested him on suspicion of having misappropriated money and medals.

The second event: In May 1995, the fiftieth anniversary of the armistice, nations throughout the world planned to celebrate the downfall of the Third Reich and civilization's victory over Nazi tyranny. Not so in Switzerland. The government felt that, having been neutral during World War II, the Confederation had no need to celebrate its end. Indignant legislators rebelled under the leadership of National Councilors Helmut Hubacher, Andreas Gross, and Judith Stamm, and the government was compelled, after all, to commemorate the victory over Hitler's Reich. On Sunday, May 7, the Federal Assembly convened for an extraordinary session at the Bundeshaus in Bern. Kaspar Villiger, federal president and minister of defense, delivered the commemorative address in German, Italian, and French.

Our country was spared the Second World War. That is cause for gratitude. Other countries liberated Europe, preserved European civilization, and enabled us, too, to enjoy a future in freedom. That is cause for humility. In an extremely menacing situation, our country did all that was humanly possible to preserve its independence, its values, and its integrity. That is cause for respecting the achievements of the wartime generation. Our nation, too, had to make sacrifices, albeit far fewer sacrifices than those that were embroiled in the war. That is cause for restraint. And Switzerland, too, did not by any means act in keeping with her ideals. That is cause for reflection. Gratitude, humility, respect, restraint, reflection: let those be the values that characterize today's commemoration.

Villiger courageously acknowledged Switzerland's war guilt in respect to the tens of thousands of Jewish people who were turned away at the frontier:

I refer to the many Jews for whom rejection at the Swiss border spelled certain death. Was the boat really full? Would Switzerland have been threatened with extinction had it been more definitely receptive to victims of persecution more than it was? Was this question, too, affected by anti-Semitic sentiments in our country? Did we always do our utmost for the persecuted and disfranchised? I have no doubt whatever that we incurred this guilt by adopting this very policy toward the persecuted Jews. Fear of Germany, fear of foreignization by mass immigration, and concern lest the anti-Semitism that also existed here receive a political fillip—these sometimes outweighed our tradition of asylum, our humanitarian ideals. We were also prompted by excessive timidity to resolve difficult conflicts of interest at the expense of humanity. In introducing the so-called Jewish stamp, the Germans were acceding to a Swiss request. That stamp was approved by Switzerland in 1938. An unduly narrow conception of the national interest led us to make the wrong choice. The government profoundly regrets this. It apologizes for it in the knowledge that such a lapse is ultimately unpardonable.

Did Villiger's speech represent a break with fideism? Unfortunately not. Fifty years after the then government's "lapse," the federal president came to its defense:

All who then bore responsibility for our country framed their actions solely and exclusively in the interests of the country's welfare as they perceived and saw it. To castigate them today would be unjust, and, no doubt, self-righteous. Let us not, therefore, set ourselves up as judges.

The executive board of the Swiss National Bank laundered Hitler's looted gold and changed it into foreign currency for use in the world market on which he depended for his strategic raw materials. The Swiss financed his wars of conquest and aided the Third Reich's survival. But for them, World War II would have ended sooner and hundreds of thousands of lives would have been saved.

The gold from wedding rings and dental crowns, the hard metals from artificial limbs and spectacle frames, and the jewelry taken from their victims by the Einsatzkommandos in Eastern Europe and by the Gestapo and SS in the ghettos and death camps—these stolen goods were seldom deposited in the Reichsbank or in the accounts of Göring's institution, the Trusteeship Office East. Usually offered for direct sale in Zurich, Basel, Bern, Lugano, or Geneva, they were bought up by local financial administrators, corporation lawyers, trustees, and private bankers.

In 1944, when the Third Reich was nearing its Götterdammerung, the big Swiss banks helped Nazi dignitaries to convey many of their stolen treasures to safety across the Atlantic. The looted gold crossed the frontier at Basel by rail or road, while refugees from the Nazis, most of them Jewish men, women, and children, were sent back at Pruntrut by the Swiss police—often enough, from 1940 onward, straight into the hands of the SS. In 1942 the Swiss government sealed off the frontier, despite its already detailed knowledge of the death camps and execution squads, the reign of terror in the Eastern ghettos, and the mass deportation of West European Jews to Poland.[2] Swiss soldiers and border guards were compelled to abet the persecution of the Jews. The government protected Heinrich Rothmund, the desk perpetrator.

Kaspar Villiger claims that the authorities acted in good faith, in Switzerland's best interests, and that we should not sit in judgment on them. If he is right, then the Nuremberg War Crimes Tribunal acted illegally in trying and convicting the major war criminals in 1945–46. Their Swiss and other accomplices were mentioned only in passing, yet complicity is a penal offense.

Villiger's clumsy denials cannot alter the facts. Crimes against humanity never become outdated.

A question remains: What would have happened in 1940 if the Swiss financial oligarchs and their visible government in Bern had chosen to ally themselves with the Western democracies? What if they had—as the Allies urgently requested—rejected Hitler's looted gold instead of Jewish refugees and refrained from providing the Third Reich with massive amounts of foreign currency, financial aid in the form of compensating credits, and exports of arms and industrial goods?

In my view, Switzerland would very probably have suffered the same fate as Austria or Czechoslovakia.

There is no doubt that certain sections of the Swiss population would have gone underground and resisted the invader. The Gestapo would then have wreaked as much havoc in Switzerland as it did in Germany and all the occupied territories. In view of this, shouldn't I be grateful to our compliant wartime government, our industrious launderers of gold and arms racketeers?

I venture no answer to that question.

———

Had the Swiss ruling class evinced any remorse and discernment at the close of the war—had its members apologized for their transgressions and quietly left the stage—I should never have written this book. But the Swiss powers-that-be have learned no such lessons. Far from apologizing and quitting the stage, they have converted their wartime derelictions into a monumental lie that clouds the horizon of Swiss history to this day. Since 1945, the Swiss ruling class has passed judgment on world events from the summit of its Alpine massif—that "undulating sea congealed at Yahweh's behest," as Victor Hugo described it. Arrogant, overweening, self-righteous, and ever ready to dispense moral advice to others, it regards Switzerland as a special case and its inhabitants as the simon-pure elect.

Walter Stucki defied the victorious powers at Washington in the Spring of 1946. Shortly thereafter the world split into two blocs. Stalin's threat to Europe ushered in a political ice age. The Cold War preserved the Swiss ruling class from its nemesis because it was the country's good fortune to be located in the western hemisphere. From then on no one demanded that Hitler's accomplices be called to account. Zurich, Basel, and Geneva were financial centers of vital importance to the West. Loans were floated there by foreign governments and banks, both national and commercial, and capital flowed into Swiss bank vaults from all five continents. The result: no retribution. No discernment, either.

Throughout Europe, the attitude of local authorities to Hitler and his fellow accomplices has been intensively discussed for more than fifty years. The Third Reich's accomplices have been pilloried—punished, too, in many cases—everywhere save in Switzerland. No denazification has ever taken place there, or only, as Jakob Tanner puts it, in the most "selective" manner.[3]

Jean-François Bergier, chairman of the government-appointed historians' committee, knows why this is so: "People are afraid of ruthlessly reassessing history. Switzerland has hitherto idealized its past and suppressed unseemly aspects of history. . . . Historians are often hard put to it to obtain full information."[4] The result: a collective memory that reeks of putrescence.

World War II was not just another of the many wars that have ravaged our continent in the past two thousand years, but a crime that will haunt the world's conscience forever. It was while that crime was being committed that the Swiss banks laid the foundations of their current world-power status.

The earth is presently inhabited by 5.2 billion people, 3.8 billion of whom live in the 122 so-called developing countries of the Third World. Vast amounts of capital from those countries are forever pouring into Swiss bank vaults: fugitive funds, the proceeds of corruption, dictators' loot, spoils that have been systematically wrested from some of the poorest nations on earth. At the time of this writing, children in Zaire are dying of epidemic diseases and starvation while the personal, Swiss-administered fortune of Joseph Mobutu, the country's former dictator, is estimated at four billion dollars.

For eight years now, the government of the Philippines has been vainly trying by means of litigation to recover the looted billions deposited in Switzerland by Ferdinand Marcos, the late dictator, and his accomplices. The governments of Haiti, Mali, and Ethiopia have also hitherto failed to recover the public funds transferred to Switzerland by their erstwhile autocrats (Duvalier, Traore, Haile Selassie). Many other examples could be cited. In spite of the reform of the penal code in 1990, Switzerland remains one of the most efficient international laundries for billions in drug money and the profits of worldwide organized crime. Also worthy of mention are the proceeds of tax evasion from European countries.

The "other Switzerland" is continuing its efforts to remedy this situation. In parliament, National Councilor Rudolf Strahm is proposing concrete structural reforms on behalf of the Social Democratic group. These envisage that economic, monetary, and fiscal offenses be expressly excluded from protection by the federal law denying legal assistance to foreign countries. Where the law relating to money-laundering is concerned, those who collaborate through negligence must also be liable to prosecution. Within the context of the double taxation agreement among all members of the Organization for Economic Cooperation and Development that possess a legal system similar to Switzerland's, administrative assistance must be granted in fiscal matters, in order that evidence may be obtained about taxpayers in those countries. Bank secrecy—more precisely, Article 47 of the federal law relating to banks and savings banks—should be abolished. Once liberated from time-worn lies, bank hypocrisy, and governmental cynicism, the Swiss Confederation will be able to join a united Europe and the United Nations. Switzerland is the product of seven centuries of fascinating history of cooperation between four different cultures, four different languages, and three religions: a unique experiment in the history of Europe. The overwhelming majority of its people harbor but one ambition, that of fulfilling in the world an active role characterized by humanity and solidarity with other nations.

The Babylonian Talmud says: "The future has a long past." And until we Swiss clear up our own past, our nation will have no future.

Afterword

———

Anti-Semitism

MUCH HAS CHANGED IN Europe and Switzerland since the first edition of this book appeared in March 1997. For months now new documents have been emerging in a steady stream from American, Swiss, and other archives. Witnesses are coming forward and government representatives retracting earlier lies: Switzerland's wartime past is becoming ever more manifest and shocking. These disclosures are involving my country in a profound and dangerous crisis of identity. Anti-Semitism is more rampant there than at any time since the late 1930s, as witness this report by Frank A. Meyer:

> Last Tuesday afternoon on the Limmatquai, Zurich. I board Streetcar No. 4. The young man who gets in with me is wearing a dark suit, a white shirt, and a black hat: he's a Swiss of the Jewish Orthodox persuasion. I make my way up front, he remains at the rear. The streetcar has only just moved off when a voice rings out over the passengers' heads: "Hey, Jew, get lost! You've no business here. We don't need your kind."
>
> The young Jew evades his abuser and makes his way forward. The other passengers have gotten the picture at once, thanks to

the religious associations of his everyday garb. They look at him and look away. Meantime, the avid voice continues to abuse our Jewish fellow citizen. I go to the rear of the car and stand beside its owner. A young man himself, he's sitting there with *Focus* magazine on his lap. So he's neither drunk nor crazy, just a well-dressed youngster in a peaked cap: a young Swiss brimming with hatred.

"You must stop that now," I tell him in a low voice. "What's your problem?" he yells back. "These Jews are robbing our country blind. I'm a Swiss, I have to work for every franc. If you don't like what I'm saying, you can emigrate."

The young man stands up and threatens me. The other passengers look on impassively. Then one of them comes to my assistance. The aggressor resumes his seat, gets out a few stops down the line. So much for what happened in Zurich's Streetcar No. 4 last Tuesday afternoon."[1]

Other incidents bear witness to the rapid spread of racist poison.

In August 1997 a British rabbi and his family wanted to take a vacation at Arosa, the celebrated mountain resort in Graubünden. There was a chalet to rent. The rabbi applied, the owner refused. His grounds: "These Jews give us nothing but trouble." The story received worldwide publicity, whereupon Arosa's tourist authority presented its excuses and offered the Jewish family a villa for two weeks, all expenses paid.

Nearly all the heads of Switzerland's Jewish organizations can testify that their mailboxes are inundated with anti-Semitic missives. What is more, this hate mail displays a radically new feature: anonymous no longer, it bears the senders' names and addresses. In Switzerland, it seems almost as if anti-Semitism has become socially acceptable once more.

Switzerland is a very ancient, lively democracy and a thoroughly civilized country. Racist venom is under vigorous attack by its parliament, its government, and almost every section of its press, but these efforts are being undermined by the numerous contradictions inherent in Swiss government strategy.

Stuart Eizenstat is the U.S. Under Secretary of State for International Trade and special representative for reparations in Central and Eastern Europe. On May 8, 1997, acting on President Clinton's instructions, he submitted his investigative report. The original version comprises 210 pages, 16 of which are devoted to the foreword. The remaining 194 pages are a historico-critical analysis of the documents available in American and foreign archives. This historical section, which was drafted under the supervision of William Z. Slany, the State Department's senior historian, was accepted without demur by the Swiss government. Eizenstat's foreword, on the other hand, was vehemently rejected. Why? Because in May 1997 Eizenstat had come to the same conclusion as the book I published in March: by laundering Hitler's gold and converting it into foreign currency disposable on the world market, Swiss banks helped to prolong the Second World War. They share responsibility for the deaths of millions of people during the years 1944–45.

Hans-Ulrich Jost, who teaches history at Lausanne University, writes: "I am shocked by the reaction to American criticism in Switzerland."[2] Eizenstat's conclusions in regard to Swiss war guilt are dismissed in Bern as "ideologically based." Although the Swiss government states—in all good faith—that it wishes to make every effort to get to the bottom of our country's distasteful past, it is simultaneously spending vast sums of taxpayers' money on a worldwide propaganda campaign designed to silence the criticisms voiced by foreign, mainly American, historians. In the United States the Swiss propaganda war is being waged by Ruder Finn, the New York public relations firm, and the Washington lobbying agency Barbour, Griffith and Rogers.

Nazi Accounts with Major Swiss Banks

THE AMERICAN LAWYERS ENGAGED by Holocaust victims are stepping up the pressure. In August the first class action submitted by attorney Edward Fagan was pronounced formally valid by a New York court. Lodged on behalf of 4,000 plaintiffs, it claims compensation to the tune of $20 billion from Switzerland's three leading banks.

The Swiss Bankers Association committed an embarrassing blunder. To counter the dangerous loss of prestige inflicted by the class actions where American public opinion was concerned, the bankers voluntarily published a preliminary list of holders of so-called dormant accounts. Their method was as follows: each member of the association was asked to contribute some names to the list. The Association collated their reports, and its New York public relations firm arranged for the first to appear on July 23, 1997. Published in 19 languages, 73 newspapers, and 27 countries, it comprised the names of 1,872 "untraceable" foreigners who had opened private accounts in Switzerland, either immediately before or during the war. The only trouble was, neither the banks nor their association nor their public relations people had thought to "expurgate" the list prior to its publication. The result was disastrous. Readers of the morning papers in London, New York, Paris, and Berlin found the list to contain the names of notorious war criminals. Holders of dormant accounts with one leading Swiss bank included Willy Bauer, deputy commandant of the concentration camp at Theresienstadt; the widow of Gestapo boss Ernst Kaltenbrunner; Heinrich Hoffmann, Hitler's court photographer; Karl Jäger, responsible as an SS commandant for the murders of 130,000 Jews in Lithuania; and Vojtěch Tuka, the Nazis' puppet premier of Slovakia, who had 107,000 Jews deported to Auschwitz and Treblinka.

Georg Krayer, a private banker from Basel and the astute president of the Bankers Association, called this "a terrible mistake." It was indeed, and it presents the gnomes with some new and

almost insurmountable problems. The law entitles a bank to refuse to accept deposits—in other words, to let someone open an
account or pay in money subsequently—whereas an existing account and the sums it contains create an irrevocable title. The
result: the descendants of mass murderers can quite legitimately
lay claim to the once dormant accounts whose existence has just
become known. That these represent blood money extorted from
victims of the Nazi reign of terror is morally disquieting, to be
sure, but Swiss banks are legally obliged to pay out such money
to the executioners' heirs.

A similar disaster threatens to overtake the relief fund for
needy survivors of the Shoah that banks, industrial firms, and
insurance companies have set up in response to the publication
of American secret documents. This fund contains 170 million
Swiss francs, and to date (January 1998) several thousands of
requests for aid have been submitted. On September 29, 1997, the
board of the Swiss National Bank made Parliament a seemingly
generous proposal: that 100 million Swiss francs be diverted from
Switzerland's gold reserves for the benefit of Shoah victims. Fine,
except that a large proportion of the Swiss National Bank's gold
reserves still consists, even today, of looted Nazi gold, including
dental gold from the extermination camps. Thus the fund's governing body finds itself in an awkward position: survivors of the
Holocaust are receiving grants financed with the proceeds of laundering services performed by the Swiss National Bank for Nazi
extermination camps.

The Children of La Martellière

THE LATTER HALF OF 1997 has seen the publication at Bern of
Volume 14 of *Swiss Diplomatic Documents*. For the first time this
proves beyond doubt that the Swiss government knew all about
the extermination of the Jews by the late fall of 1941. The volume
contains a long telegram from the Swiss consul in Cologne dated
November 21 and describing the transportation of Jews to

Poland. Writing from Rome on November 24, Minister Ruegger presented Foreign Minister Pilet-Golaz with a detailed account, obtained from Vatican sources, of the sufferings undergone by Ukrainian and Polish Jews. Yet the Bern government decided to seal off our national frontiers to the Jews.

Recently discovered documents illustrate the tragic effects on Jews of this policy of rejection. To cite only one example, a report in the Paris daily *Le Monde* states that, while examining the records of the Alliance Israélite in Paris during August 1997, a student of political science came across a list of twenty-one Jewish children and young people aged between seven and twenty-one. In 1943, under the aegis of the Oeuvre du Secours aux Enfants, a welfare organization devoted to the care of children of parents imprisoned or deported during the war, these youngsters were moved from the department of Gers to La Martellière, a small village near the Swiss frontier. There, hidden away on an isolated farm, they spent months waiting for permission to enter Switzerland. Permission was refused. On the night of March 23–24 a Gestapo squad raided the farm, detained the children, and deported them to Drancy. They were gassed in a Polish concentration camp soon afterward.

Even senior churchmen were powerless to alter Switzerland's anti-Semitic refugee policy. Edith Stein, a Jewish intellectual from Breslau, had converted to Christianity and become a Carmelite nun in the convent at Cologne. In 1938 she transferred to the Carmelite convent at Echt in Holland. In 1940 Hitler invaded the Low Countries. Meantime, Edith's sister Rosa had also moved to Echt. The two sisters applied for admission to the Carmelite convent at Fribourg, Switzerland. Monsignor Besson, the bishop of Fribourg and Geneva, endorsed their request at the very highest level in Bern. On August 3, 1942, Police Chief Rothmund turned it down. Edith and Rosa Stein were arrested by the Gestapo and deported to the East. Both were murdered in Auschwitz on August 8.

The Slave Trains

IN THE WAKE OF my book and the debate it unleashed, the BBC aired an impressive and carefully researched documentary entitled *Nazi Gold*. Directed by Christoph Olgiatti and produced by David Marks, this film documented the existence of the Nazi slave trains that passed through Switzerland from the fall of 1943 onward, uusually by night and in the strictest secrecy. Bound for the Third Reich from northern Italy, they undoubtedly contained Italian conscripts whom the German authorities had rounded up in Milan, Turin, Verona, and elsewhere, and sent off to do forced labor in Germany's munitions factories. Were Italian Jews also deported to extermination camps in the East by way of the St. Gotthard and Simplon tunnels? A woman interviewed in the BBC film told of volunteers from Zurich's Jewish community who had contrived to give water to some Jewish deportees at Enge, a suburban railroad station on the outskirts of the city.

The Swiss government lodged an official and extremely vigorous protest with the BBC's London complaints department, claiming that no such slave or deportation trains had ever existed. After carefully examining this protest in the light of witnesses' statements and available documentary evidence, the BBC rejected it as wholly unfounded.

In Switzerland the BBC film provoked a series of unforeseen reactions. Witnesses—principled individuals from all parts of the country and all classes of society—suddenly took their courage in both hands. Having held their peace for over fifty years, they now spoke out.

Bruno Savio, a retired businessman aged eighty-one, preserves a vivid recollection of one morning in the fall of 1943. He lived in St. Fiden, a suburb of St. Gallen, and was getting ready to board the early train to St. Margrethen, where he worked. Alongside Platform 1 at St. Fiden station he spotted a train made up of closed cattle cars. Heartrending cries were issuing from the interior. He also saw hands clutching the bars over the little windows of some of the cars and heard terrified voices calling in Italian, *Lasciate mi fuori!* ("Let me out!"). Some military policemen promptly surrounded the train and shoved Savio back. Later in 1943 and throughout 1944 he saw many such trains standing in the frontier station at St. Margrethen. The locomotives were switched in a secluded siding, Swiss locomotives being exchanged for German.[3]

Jakob Barandun, eighty-three, who served in the Swiss military police from 1943 to 1945, recalls one of his assignments in particular. At Chiasso he and his comrades had to take delivery of a Swiss Federal Railroad train—he himself calls it a "slave train"—and escort it through Switzerland to Basel. The third-class cars, which were hermetically sealed, contained some 500 Italian girls and 200 elderly men, all without baggage and all beside themselves with fear. There was a lone German nurse in the rearmost car. "During one unscheduled stop," Baradun recalls, "the hungry Italians sighted a large cannery with large quantities of sausages.... We jumped out of the train with drawn revolvers so that no one could escape." At Basel's Baden Station, on German territory, the Swiss MPs handed over the train to a German officer. Barandun feels ashamed to this day. "We handed over the train...and went away at once. We didn't want anything to do with those *Sauschwaben* (lousy Germans)."[4]

Another piece of testimony comes from Americo Ferrari, seventy-three, who was deputy stationmaster at Bellinzona in 1944. "Some freight trains were directed past the station into sidings. We had orders from the management not to worry about them. I heard after the war that Italian Jews were deported via the St. Gotthard to concentration camps."[5]

The Swiss railroad network was militarily important to Hitler from 1943 on.[6] More than a million German soldiers were stationed in northern Italy, and their supplies of arms, ammunition, gasoline, spares, etc., came partly by way of Switzerland. The other potential transalpine route, the Munich-Brenner-Bolzano line, was often unusable from 1943 on because of Allied air raids.

From the fall of 1943 until the spring of 1945, northbound and southbound German freight trains passed through Switzerland at ten-minute intervals. The transalpine route that carried the heaviest traffic was the one from Zurich to Chiasso via the St. Gotthard Tunnel. The other Swiss transalpine route (Basel-Lötschberg-Simplon) was not used after January 1945 because Italian partisan units were in control of Domodossola. They not only sabotaged the 130 kilometers of track between Iselle and Milan in many places but threatened to blow up the Simplon Tunnel itself.

The Allied advance had come to a halt on the Ravenna-Pisa line, and German tanks were inflicting terrible losses on the American troops holding the central sector of the front around Bologna. President Roosevelt addressed an urgent request to Federal President Eduard von Steiger: Would he at least prohibit the transportation of gasoline through Switzerland, thereby immobilizing the German armor. Von Steiger refused on the ground that only civilian goods and coal were transported through the Gotthard and Simplon, not arms or ammunition. This was a brazen lie.

Hitler's southbound military supply trains did not return empty. From the fall of 1943 he had been transferring substantial parts of his munitions industry, notably facilities for the manufacture of fighter planes and other heavy weapons, to industrial centers in the Po Valley and the Piedmont. His own armaments factories in Germany were being subjected to incessant air raids.

On their return journey, therefore, German trains brought back dismantled aircraft, tank gun barrels, and other heavy weapons manufactured in Italy under German supervision. This they did with the full knowledge of the Swiss government. Numerous American and British secret agents were operating in Bern and Zurich. For that reason, Germany's foreign trade committee and the Swiss authorities agreed upon certain forms of words designed to mislead the Allied secret services. Heavy weapons were generally registered as *Eisenwaren* (hardware in the nonmilitary sense). The term *Rohre* (pipes or tubes) also occurs in the records. If quesitoned by the Allies, the Bern authorities could claim that these were civilian conduits. They were, in fact, gun barrels. Railroad manifests dating from 1943–45 were subsequently destroyed.

Italian labor conscripts deported via Switzerland and employed in German armaments factories were subjected to even harsher treatment than Soviet forced laborers and prisoners of war. Nicknamed "Badoglios" after Marshal Badoglio, who had signed the armistice with the Allies in 1943, they were made to pay for the "treachery" committed by Germany's former ally.

Between 1943 and 1945 Switzerland earned many millions of francs from the railroad traffic that plied its two transalpine routes in both directions, that is to say, from the transportation of German munitions, Italian labor conscripts and, possibly, Jewish detainees. By making its railroad network available—and leasing its rolling stock—to the Wehrmacht, the SS, the Central State Security Bureau, and the Ministry of Munitions, the Bern government substantially helped to prolong the war.[7]

The All-powerful Union Bank of Switzerland

EARLY IN OCTOBER 1997, District Attorney Peter Consandey of Zurich finally dropped his investgation of Christoph Meili. To recapitulate: during the night of January 8, 1997, Meili, a security guard at the Union Bank of Switzerland, had saved some highly compromising documents from being shredded by the bank and handed them over to the Israelische Kulturgemeinde. Zurich's judiciary charged him with violating bank secrecy. He lost his job and was ostracized. Anonymous callers threatened his life and that of his family. Together with his wife and their two young children, Meili fled to the United States, where President Clinton granted him an open-ended resident's permit by special decree.

Meili's courageous act bears witness to two facts. First, that leading Swiss banks are still, although forbidden to do so by law, destroying important evidence of their complicity with the Third

Reich, and, in particular, of their appropriation of Aryanized Jewish property. And, second, that Switzerland does possess persons of integrity who, even when charged with penal offenses and threatened by anonymous callers, are prepared to fight for justice and openness.

On home soil the Union Bank of Switzerland appears to be all-powerful. Its archivist and director Erwin Haggenmüller clearly contravened the federal act of December 13, 1996 (a strict ban on the destruction of records) by proposing to shred the documents salvaged by Meili, but District Attorney Consandey declined to indict him.

New York City comptroller Alan G. Hevesi reacted more robustly in October 1997. The city is floating a public loan worth $1 billion. At the time of this writing, various bank syndicates are competing for the offer, one of them being headed by the Union Bank of Switzerland. Hevesi has vetoed the bank's participation. His reasons: "The UBS is the bank which, notwithstanding a legal prohibition, destroyed documents relating to the expropriation of Jewish assets during the Nazi period; which persecuted the security guard who discovered this; and which took no action when its honorary president, Robert Holzach, declared that activities connected with the Holocaust are the product of a Jewish conspiracy.... The UBS must be made to realize that, if it wishes to operate on a global scale and do business with the world at large, it has to conform to the standards of the world community. On the threshold of the next century, anti-Semitism and racism are unacceptable in an international concern."[8]

Censorship

THE CONTINENT OF EUROPE and its islands are inhabited by the citizens of forty-two countries, of which the Swiss Confederation, which controls the principal Alpine passes, is the wealthiest in terms of per capita income and the second wealthiest in the world. Today the ghosts of the past are rearing their heads throughout that continent. In the fall of 1997 even the mighty Roman Catholic Church, in the person of Cardinal Archbishop Jean-Marie Lustiger of Paris, sought the forgiveness of France's Jewish community because the French Church steadfastly refused to speak out against the racial decrees of 1940, the incipient detention of stateless or foreign Jews in 1941, and the deportation of tens of thousands of French Jews from 1942 on. The Church's conscience—like that of many other social groups in Europe—is now awakening. The Swiss government alone makes every effort to conceal its active and highly profitable collaboration with the Third Reich. No Swiss banker to the Nazis, no railroad executive or officer responsible for turning away Jews at the frontier has ever acknowledged his guilt.

My book has been torn to shreds by many sectors of the Swiss press. Writing in the *Neue Zürcher Zeitung*, Wolfgang Bauer characterized it as a *Lügenepos* ("epic pack of lies").[9] The foreign minister instructed all our embassies to persuade "friendly" journalists to denigrate the book in the foreign press. The federal cultural authority has published an official bibliography for schools that lists the fifty most important books on the Swiss Holocaust controversy. Mine was excluded for being "too extreme." Although this act of censorship was fiercely contested in Parliament,[10] the government backed the censors.

Light on the Horizon

FORTUNATELY, MY COUNTRY is more than the sum of its government authorities, ruling class, and bankers. It is also inhabited by a cultured, diverse people shaped by 700 years of democratic existence. A private foundation established for the benefit of needy Holocaut survivors is enjoying the support of tens of thousands of ordinary Swiss citizens. Erstwhile frontier guards, military policemen, and railroad personnel are volunteering fresh evidence every week. The horizon is brighter than it was. Cracks are appearing in the official wall of silence; sooner or later it will collapse.

The nation's desire for truth is combating official amnesia, refusal to acknowledge guilt, and suppression of the past. The Swiss people are in a ferment. They want to burst the bonds of their isolation. The most recent opinion poll (October 1997) yielded a clear majority in favor of Switzerland's joining the European Union. The Social Democrats and the trade unions are currently at work on a constitutional initiative proposing Swiss membership of the United Nations. Profound and painful though the present crisis of identity may be, I am convinced that the Swiss Confederation is on the verge of a revolt: a rebellion of conscience.

Jean Ziegler
Geneva, November 1997

Appendix

Switzerland's Political System

THE FOLLOWING BRIEF NOTE may help the foreign reader to resolve certain problems of political terminology.

The Swiss Confederation is governed by a seven-member Bundesrat (Federal Council), which combines the functions of a government with those of a collective head of state. Federal councilors are elected to become federal president in annual rotation, depending on their date of election. Each federal councilor is in charge of a department of the federal administration, or ministry.

The Bundesrat is elected by the Bundesversammlung (Federal Assembly), which consists of the Nationalrat (National Council) and the Ständerat (Council of the Cantons). The Nationalrat is a house of representatives, directly elected by the people every four years. The Ständerat, elected by procedures that vary from canton to canton, represents the twenty-six cantons that make up the Confederation.

The Swiss Confederation is a direct democracy. Thus, 50,000 citizens may request that a law be submitted to referendum, and 100,000 can at any time launch a "Constitutional initiative" aimed at the partial or total revision of the federal constitution (introduction of a new article, amendment or repeal of existing articles).

The first federal pact between the three original cantons—Uri,

Schwyz, and Unterwalden—came into being in 1291. The present constitution dates from 1848.

J. Z.

Document 1

MEMORANDUM OF UNDERSTANDING
BETWEEN
THE WORLD JEWISH RESTITUTION ORGANIZATION
and
THE WORLD JEWISH CONGRESS
representing also the
JEWISH AGENCY and ALLIED ORGANIZATIONS
and
THE SWISS BANKERS ASSOCIATION

(1) An Independent Committee of Eminent Persons will be appointed. Three persons will be appointed by the World Jewish Restitution Organization (WJRO) and three persons will be appointed by the Swiss Bankers Association (SBA). The Committee of six will jointly appoint an additional member as Chairperson. Furthermore, each side will nominate two alternates.

(2) The Chairperson will administer the budget of the Committee which will be funded by the SBA.

(3) The Committee of Eminent Persons will appoint an international auditing company; this company must be licensed by the Federal Banking Commission (FBC) to operate in Switzerland. The SBA will assure the auditors unfettered access to all relevant files in banking institutions regarding dormant accounts and other assets and financial instruments deposited before, during and immediately after the Second World War.

(4) The Committee of Eminent Persons will instruct the auditing company as to the scope of its duties. It will examine the methodology of the individual banks, the Swiss Bankers Association and the Office of the Ombudsman as regards the search for accounts and assets in question. The Independent Committee will also be authorized to retain the

services of other experts, as necessary. The Independent Committee will publish progress reports from time to time.

(5) The parties of the agreement will cooperate to assure that the Swiss Government will deal with the question of looted assets in Swiss banks or other institutions which were not reported or returned under the relevant laws during the years before, during and immediately after the Second World War.

(6) All negotiations will be handled in an environment of absolute discretion with a view to reaching an amicable resolution of all issues.

(7) As soon as the contents of this Memorandum are agreed upon, there will be a summit meeting of the presidents and their delegations to affix their signatures and to announce the names of the members of the Committee and the scope of its task to the public.

Signed and agreed:

New York, New York, May 2, 1996

Edgar M. Bronfman   Zvi Barak
Dr. Georg F. Krayer   Hans J. Baer
Avraham Burg   Israel Singer
Dr. Josef Ackermann

Members of the Independent Committee of Eminent Persons for the clarification of dormant assets in Swiss banks dating from the Second World War:

Switzerland

Prof. Dr. Curt Gasteyger
Professor of International Politics at the Institut Universitaire des Hautes Etudes Internationales, Geneva

René Rhinow
Councellor of the Council of Cantons

Prof. Dr. Klaus Jacobi
Former Undersecretary in the Foreign Ministry

Jewish Organizations

Mr. Shevah Weiss
Speaker, Israel Knesset

Mr. Avraham Burg
Chairman, Jewish Agency

Mr. Reuben Beraja
Chairman, Latin America Jewish Congress

Document 2

Federal Act concerning the historical and legal inquiry into the fate of assets that came to Switzerland in consequence of the National Socialist regime

December 13, 1996

The Federal Assembly of the Swiss Confederation
pursuant to Articles 64 and 64a of the Federal Constitution, after examining the report dated August 26, 1996,[1] of the National Council's Legal Affairs Committee and the government statement of September 16, 1996,[2] *resolves that:*

Art. 1 Object
[1]There be investigated the extent and fate of assets of all kinds acquired by banks, insurance companies, attorneys, notaries, financial administrators, or other natural or juristic persons domiciled or resident in Switzerland, entrusted to the same for safekeeping, investment, or transmission to third parties, or received from the Swiss National Bank which
a. belonged to persons who became victims of the National Socialist regime, or of whom reliable information is lacking in consequence of that regime and whose assets have not since been claimed by legitimate persons;
b. were taken from their rightful owners in consequence of the racial

---

[1] BB1   1996   IV   1165
[2] BB1   1996   IV   1184

laws or other discriminatory measures prevailing in the sphere of influence of the National Socialist German Reich; or

c. derive from members of the National Socialist German Labor Party, the National Socialist German Reich, its institutions or representatives, as well as natural or juristic persons closely associated therewith, including all financial transactions effected with the said assets.

[2]The inquiry shall likewise embrace those government measures taken by Switzerland since 1945 relating to assets as defined in Paragraph 1. [3]The government may, either at the request of the experts' committee or on its own initiative, adjust the object of the inquiry to accord with fresh information or to the work of other investigative committees. (96.434)

Art. 2 Implementation of the Inquiry

[1]The government shall appoint an independent committee of experts to investigate, historically and legally, the extent and fate of the assets defined in Article 1. The committee shall consist of experts from various fields of study.

[2]The committee of experts shall keep the government regularly informed of its progress, notably if there emerge definite pointers to assets claims as defined in Aricle 1.

Art. 3 Confidentiality of the Inquiry

Those persons entrusted with carrying out the inquiry, together with their associates, shall be subject to official secrecy. The government shall determine details in its investigative instructions.

Art. 4 The Obligation to Preserve Documents

Documents that could assist the inquiry as defined in Article 1 may not be destroyed, conveyed abroad, or rendered less accessible in any other manner.

Art. 5 The Obligation to Grant Access to Documents

[1]The persons and institutions referred to in Article 1, their legal successors, and government authorities and public agencies, shall be obliged to grant the government-appointed members of the experts' committee, as well as the investigators enlisted by them, access to all documents that could assist the inquiry.

[2]This obligation shall take precedence over any legal and contractual duty of secrecy.

Art. 6 Disposal of Investigative Material
Right of disposal of all investigative material shall be vested in the government alone.

Art. 7 Publication of the Inquiry's Findings
[1]The government shall publish the inquiry's findings in full.
[2]Personal particulars shall be rendered anonymous for publication wherever this may be required by the legitimate interests of living persons.

Art. 8 Legal Protection
[1]Should disputes arise over the obligation to preserve documents and grant access to the same, the ministry shall settle these at the experts' request.
[2]An administrative court appeal against the ministry's decision may be lodged with the federal court within ten days.
[3]The ministry and the federal court shall render a decision without delay.
[4]The federal law of June 19, 1992,[1] relating to data protection shall not apply.

Art. 9 Penal Provisions
[1]Anyone who deliberately contravenes Article 4 or a regulation based on Article 5, Paragraph 1, shall be liable to imprisonment or to a fine not exceeding 50,000 francs. Where the offender has acted out of negligence, the penalty shall be a fine not exceeding 10,000 francs.
[2]The penality of breaches of official secrecy under Article 320 of the Penal Code[2] shall stand.
[3]Articles 6 and 7 of the administrative penal law[3] shall be applicable to contraventions within commercial concerns.
[4]Criminal proceedings shall be a matter for the cantons.

Art. 10 Funding
The Federal Assembly shall grant a loan of several years' duration for the implementation of the inquiry as defined in Article 1.

Art. 11 Final Provisions

[1]This act is universally binding.

[2]It is declared urgent in accordance with Article 89a Paragraph 1 of the Federal Constitution, and shall come into force one day after its passage.

[3]It is subject to the facultative referendum in accordance with Article 89a Paragraph 2 of the Federal Constitution and shall remain in force until December 31, 2001.

Document 3

FEDERAL DEPARTMENT OF FOREIGN AFFAIRS
FEDERAL DEPARTMENT OF THE INTERIOR

Bern, December 19, 1996

Appointment of the independent committee of experts and government instructions thereto

Historical and legal investigation of the fate of assets that came to Switzerland in consequence of the National Socialist regime

Pursuant to the Federal Act passed unanimously by both Houses relating to the historical and legal investigation of the fate of assets that came to Switzerland in consequence of the National Socialist regime, the government today unanimously appointed the members of the independent committee of experts. This is charged with investigating the role of Switzerland, and of its financial center, within the context of the Second World War.[. . .]

The government has chosen Jean-François BERGIER of Zug, professor at the Federal University of Technology, Zurich, to be its chairman.

The other members are:

Wladyslaw BARTOSZEWSKI, Warsaw
Saul FRIEDLAENDER, Jerusalem

---

[1] SR 235.1
[2] SR 311.0
[3] SR 313.0

Harold JAMES, Princeton (USA)
Georg KREIS, Basel
Sybil MILTON, Washington
Jacques PICARD, Bern
Jakob TANNER, Zurich
Joseph VOYAME, St. Brais (Canton Jura)

[. . .]

Instructions to the Committee of Experts

The object of the inquiry shall comprise, in particular, the themes defined in Article 1, Paragraphs 1 and 2, of the Federal Act. Investigations shall also encompass the postwar period, notably subsequent government measures (Washington Accord, Registration Act of 1962, etc.) as well as the official historical evaluation of those events. The committee's work may also include the questioning of witnesses.

In conjunction with the field of inquiry defined by the Federal Act, the government wishes the following areas, in particular, to be investigated:

The importance of the gold trade and of foreign exchange transactions, the role of the Swiss National Bank, the role of the private banks, the importance of financial administration (with regard not only to victims of the Nazi regime but also to Germans and their collaborators). The state of knowledge of those involved regarding the provenance of assets. The conveying of fugitive funds via Switzerland to other countries. Dealings in works of art, jewelry, etc. The magnitude and importance of this trade in looted property, the state of knowledge regarding the provenance of such assets.

The role of Swiss armaments production, the acquisition of German businesses by Swiss concerns, notably within the context of Aryanization measures and the financing of export-import transactions.

Government measures and the legal bases of commercial and financial centers insofar as these are relevant to the inquiry. Relevant agreements between Switzerland and the Axis powers and the Allies. Official measures relating to foreign exchange control, bank supervision, political control of the Swiss National Bank, export and import controls, control of the trade in war materials.

The significance of refugee policy in connection with Switzerland's commercial and financial relations with the Axis powers and the Allies.

Measures for identification and control. Restitution of looted property and fugitive funds, treatment of dormant assets, treatment of assets deriving from the Axis powers. Measures for the restitution of looted assets to their owners or the descendants/heirs thereof, definition of legitimate claims.

Authorities' reports on their activities. Official historical evaluations, reactions to the publication of sources abroad.

The government may, either at the committee's request or on its own initiative, adjust the object of the inquiry to accord with fresh information or with the work of other investigative committees.

Notes

Introduction

1. Peter Bichsel, *Die Zeit* (Hamburg), October 11, 1996.
2. Peter Grose, *Gentleman Spy: The Life of Allen Dulles* (London, 1994), p. 148 ff.
3. Robert Urs Vogler, *Die Wirtschaftsverhandlungen zwischen der Schweiz und Deutschland 1940–1941*, Swiss National Bank (Zurich, 1983).
4. Hans Ulrich Jost, "Menace et repliement," in *Nouvelle histoire de la Suisse et des Suisses,* vol. III (Lausanne, 1983), p. 90 ff.
5. Jost, quoted in "Dossier: Die Mythen im Schliessfach Schweiz," *Die Zeit* (Hamburg), October 11, 1996.
6. See also Denis de Rougemont, *Ecrits sur l'Europe,* vol. II (Paris, 1994).
7. Daniel Keel, ed., *Herkules und Atlas, Lobreden und andere Versuche über Friedrich Dürrenmatt* (Zurich, 1990), p. 14.
8. Heinrich Götz, *Dürrenmatt* (Reinbek, 1993), p. 24.
9. Edgar Bronfman in *Die Neue Zürcher Zeitung,* October 25, 1996.
10. *Revue Juive* (Geneva), January 24, 1997; see also *Le Nouveau Quotidien* (Lausanne), January 9, 1997.
11. For a detailed account see *International Herald Tribune,* October 10, 1996; *The Times* (London), October 23, 1996; *Frankfurter Allgemeine Zeitung* October 24, 1996.

Part One: Hitler's Swiss Fences

1. There were exceptions: in Ethiopia and Somalia British troops fought the Italian colonial army; Gaullist troops attacked the Vichy government's garrisons in Gabon, the French Cameroons, Dakar, and Madagascar. (I refer here only to Black Africa. The whole of North Africa above of the Sahara was involved in the war.)

2. This view is espoused by British historians in particular, for example B. W. N. Medlicott, *The Economic Blockade*, vols. I and II (London, 1978).

3. Willi A. Boelcke, *Die deutsche Wirtschaft, 1930–1945, Interna aus dem Reichswirtschaftsministerium* (Düsseldorf, 1983).

4. The memorandum is reproduced in Wilhelm Vocke, *Memoiren* (Stuttgart, 1973).

5. Boelcke, op. cit., p. 219 ff.

6. Ibid., p. 239 f.

7. Hannah Arendt, *Eichmann in Jerusalem: A Report on the Banality of Evil* (New York, 1963).

8. Boelcke. op. cit. p. 249.

9. Guido Knopp, *Hitlers Helfer* (Munich, 1996), p. 71 ff.

10. *Politisches Archiv des Auswärtigen Amtes* (Bonn), vol. III, "Staatssekretär Schweiz 1943" file (Clodius Memorandum). Hereafter cited as Clodius Memorandum.

11. Niklaus Meienberg, *Reportages en Suisse: l'exécution du traître de la patrie Ernst S.* (Geneva, 1977).

12. Roland Buetikofer, *Le refus de la modernité: la ligue vaudoise et la Suisse 1919–1945* (Lausanne, 1996); see also Hans Ulrich Jost, *Les avantgardes réactionnaires* (Lausanne, 1992).

13. Alfred Häsler, *Das Boot ist voll* (Zurich, 1992), p. 85 f.

14. For reproductions of these radio messages see Klaus Urner, *Il faut encore avaler la Suisse. Les plans d'invasion d'Hitler* (Geneva, 1996). Accounts of the operations described are also taken from this volume.

15. Ibid., p. 86.

16. The text appears in Victor Monnier, *William E. Rappard, Défenseur des libertés, Serviteur de son pays et de la communauté internationale* (Geneva, 1995), p. 525.

17. Erich Schmid, ed., *Abschied von Peter Surava, Eine Dokumentation* (Zurich, 1996). (Erich Schmid has also made a film about Surava.)

18. See Frédéric Gonseth, "Esclaves de guerre pour entreprises suisses," *L'Hebdo* (Lausanne), September 19, 1996.

19. Willi Gautschi, *Henri Guisan* (Zurich, 1994).

20. Pierre Bourdieu and J. C. Passeron, *La reproduction, éléments pour une théologie du système d'enseignement* (Paris, 1970), p. 18; see also Bourdieu, "Le marché des biens symboliques," *Revue année sociologique* (Paris), 1971.

21. By rights, Switzerland's wartime press censorship deserves a chapter to itself. Its effects were disastrous, not only because it gagged critical comment from a normally diverse and lively Swiss press and thus deprived the public of vital information, but also because it promoted reports on the Third Reich, some of which were enthusiastic to a degree that now defies comprehension.

    An example: on February 18, 1943, Goebbels delivered his notorious "total war" speech at the Sportpalast in Berlin. On February 21 he noted in his diary: "The neutral press is publishing positively fantastic articles about me personally and about my kind of propaganda. The comments one reads in the Bern, Basel, and Zurich papers, for instance, could not have been couched in warmer or more sympathetic language in the German press itself. All in all, it may be said that the speech has achieved its purpose a hundred percent. I'm entitled to feel exceptionally happy about this propaganda coup. If the fight against Bolshevism had to have a spiritual foundation, it has now acquired one."

    I obtained Goebbels' diary extract from Iring Fetscher, who is preparing a critical edition of this speech by Goebbels.

22. Thomas Müntzer, leader of the Anabáptists, was beheaded in 1525; see Ernst Bloch, *Thomas Müntzer als Theologe der Revolution,* Suhrkamp complete edition, vol. 2 (Frankfurt, 1969).

23. Werner Rings, *L'or des Nazis. La Suisse un relais discret* (Lausanne, 1985); German ed., *Raubgold aus Deutschland, die Golddrehscheibe Schweiz im Zweiten Weltkrieg* (Zurich, 1985).

24. For a detailed account of these transactions see Marlise Simons, "The Ghost of Nazi Gold Returns to Haunt Lisbon," *International Herald Tribune* (Zurich), January 11–12, 1997.

25. The French version of this document appeared in *Le Nouveau Quotidien* (Lausanne), January 29, 1997.

26. Harold James in conversation with Felix E. Müller, *Die Weltwoche* (Zurich), November 14, 1996.

27. Michel Fior is the discoverer of the Rossy Plan. For his dissertation, "La Banque nationale suisse et l'or allemand 1939–1945," Fior researched 20,000 pages of National Bank board minutes. See Michel Fior, *Mémoire de licence,* unpublished dissertation, Neuchâtel University, 1996.

28. Alfred Hirs became general manager in 1942.

29. Tobias Kästli, *Ernst Nobs: Vom Bürgerschreck zum Bundesrat: Ein politisches Leben* (Zurich, 1995).

30. Swiss National Bank archives, Document no. 0014.

31. Marco Durrer, "Die schweizerisch-amerikanischen Finanzbeziehungen im Zweiten Weltkrieg. Von der Blockierung der schweizerischen Guthaben in den USA über die Safe-Haven-Politik zum Washingtoner Abkommen 1941–1946," *Kollektion Bankwirtschaftliche Forschungen* (Bern and Stuttgart, 1984), p. 270 f.

32. On the antithetical and complementary aspects of Christian and Aryan anti-Semitism, see the conversations between Elie Wiesel and Jean-Marie Lustiger, Cardinal Archbishop of Paris, himself of Jewish-Polish descent, in Elie Wiesel, *Et la mer n'est pas remplie* (Paris, 1966), p. 242 ff.

33. Vogler, op. cit., p. 7.

34. My thanks to the Israeli historian Shraga Elam, who works in Zurich, for sending me archival copies of these two letters.

35. Emil Puhl's testimony against Walther Funk, taken from the transcripts of the major war criminals' trial at Nuremberg, appears in Vogler, op. cit., p. 11 f.

36. Clodius Memorandum, p. 4.

37. Franz Egle, Swiss Foreign Ministry spokesman, rejected American charges that Switzerland had remitted the "dormant" accounts of Polish Jews held by Swiss banks to Poland in 1949 solely to enable Warsaw to indemnify dispossessed Swiss citizens in foreign currency.

Having branded those charges a gross untruth, Egle was compelled only four days later to retract his denial and acknowledge the existence of the clandestine transactions between Switzerland and Poland.

38. "Nazi Gold: Information from the British Archives," Foreign and Commonwealth Office, General Service Command, History Notes (London), no. 11, September 1996. Cited as Rifkind Report.

39. The first version of the Rifkind Report mistakenly spoke of 500 million *dollars.*

40. Linus von Castelmur, *Schweizerisch-Alliierte Finanzbeziehungen im Übergang vom Zweiten Weltkrieg zum Kalten Krieg. Die deutschen Guthaben in der Schweiz zwischen Zwangsliquidierung und Freigabe* (Zurich, 1992).

41. Elie Wiesel, *Les juifs du silence* (Paris, 1976).

42. The Helvetic Republic founded this archive in 1798, at the instigation of Napoleon I.

43. Christoph Graf in *L'Hebdo* (Lausanne), October 31, 1994, p. 4. I am also grateful to the archivists Daniel Bourgeois and Andreas Kellerhals for their valuable information.

44. Important documents relating to the Interhandel affair were kindly supplied me by Shraga Elam.

45. Robert Urs Vogler, *Der Goldverkehr der Schweizerischen Nationalbank mit der Deutschen Reichsbank 1939/1945.* (Zurich, 1983), p. 8.

Part Two: The Murderers

1. Rings, op. cit.

2. Pierre Arnoult, *Les finances de la France et l'occupation allemande (1940–1944)* (Paris, 1951); P. Kauch, "Le vol de l'or de la Banque Nationale par les Nazis (1940–1943)," *Revue de la Banque Nationale de Belgique* (Brussels, 1956); see also Peter Utz, "Goldfingers merkwürdige Machenschaften," *Tagesanzeiger-Magazin* (Zurich), no. 16, 1980.

3. Henri Michel, *La Seconde Guerre mondiale, Septembre 1939–Janvier 1943*, vol. I (Paris, 1968), p. 204.

4. Ibid., p. 454 ff.

5. Rings, op. cit., p. 35.

6. "Secrets of the Swiss," special report in *Newsweek,* June 24, 1996.

7. Quoted in Beat Balzli, *Treuhänder des Reiches* (Zurich, 1947), p. 139.

8. Rifkind Report, op. cit., p. 2.

9. Gideon Hausner, *Die Vernichtung der Juden* (Munich, 1979), p. 235 ff.

10. *Le Nouvel Observateur* (Paris), November 14, 1996.

11. This volume of documents may be inspected at the FCO Historians Library and Records Department, Clive House, London SW1 9HD; see also the analysis of the radio messages in *Der Spiegel* (Hamburg), no. 47, 1996; *Le Nouveau Quotidien* (Lausanne), October 31, 1996.

12. Bendet Hershkovits, quoted by Hersch Fischler in *Die Weltwoche* (Zurich), November 14, 1996.

13. Christopher R. Browning, *Ordinary Men—Reserve Police Battalion 101 and the Final Solution in Poland* (London and New York, 1992).

14. Jacques Picard, *Die Schweiz und die Juden, 1933–1945* (Zurich, 1994), pp. 387–461.

Part Three: Economic Warfare

1. Hans Ulrich Jost, *Nouvelle histoire de la Suisse et des Suisses,* vol. 3, p. 161.

2. Jakob Tanner, *Bundeshaushalt, Währung und Kriegswirtschaft* (Zurich, 1986).

3. Jean-Claude Favez, in the foreword to Klaus Urner, op. cit., 129 ff.

4. Ibid.

5. Jost, *Nouvelle histoire de la Suisse et des Suisses,* p. 160.

6. André Marty, "Die Bührle-Holding bleibt stumm," *Die Sonntagszeitung* (Zurich), May 5, 1996.

7. Niklaus Meienberg, *Es ist kalt in Brandenburg. Ein Hitler-Attentat* (Zurich, 1980). I quote from the French edition, *Maurice Bavaud a voulu tuer Hitler* (Geneva, 1982), p. 191 f. My thanks to Adrien Bavaud, Maurice's brother, for access to his valuable documentation.

8. Sebastian Speich, "Der gedemütigte Riese," *Cash* (Zurich), January 17, 1997.

9. Gautschi, op. cit., p. 522.

10. Details of the contract quoted in *Journal de Genève,* October 21, 1996.

11. Hans Mommsen and Manfred Grieger, *Volkswagen und seine Arbeiter unter dem Dritten Reich* (Düsseldorf, 1996).

12. For an account of their working methods, see *Der Spiegel* (Hamburg), no. 47, 1996; see also the interview with Peter Hilton in *Le Nouveau Quotidien* (Lausanne) October 1996.

13. Rifkind Report, p. 5.

14. Switzerland also represented the United States and Great Britain in several countries.

15. Michael Hirsh, Mark Frankel, and Christopher Dickey, "The Secrets of the Swiss," *Newsweek,* June 24, 1996.

16. A full list appears in Oswald Inglin, *Der stille Krieg. Der Wirtschaftskrieg zwischen Grossbritannien under der Schweiz im Zweiten Weltkrieg* (Zurich, 1991).

17. Sebastian Speich, "Freie Fahrt für die Nazis gegen Kohle und Eisen," *Cash* (Zurich), January 17, 1997.

18. Ibid.

19. Michel, op. cit., vol. II, p. 314.

20. Ibid., p. 303.

21. Woog, Peter, "Rapport concernant les fonds 'secrets' du nazisme," JUNA archive of the Swiss Federation of Jewish Communities; documents housed in the modern history archive of the Federal University of Technology, Zurich.

22. "Himmler Pounds Go Round and Round," *Daily Mail* (London), June 5, 1950.

23. Jorge Camarasa, *Odessa del Sur. La Argentina como refugio de Nazis y criminales de guerra* (Buenos Aires, 1995).

24. Ronald C. Newton, *The Nazi Menace in Argentina 1931–1947* (Stanford University Press, 1992).

25. Wilfried von Owen, in *El Sol* (Madrid), February 12, 1992.

26. Michael Bloch's comprehensive biography *Ribbentrop* (Paris, 1996) is instructive in this connection.

27. For details see *Newsweek,* June 24, 1996.

28. Edgar Bonjour, *Geschichte der schweizerischen Neutralität* (Basel and Stuttgart, 1970), vol. VI, p. 134 ff.

29. Ibid., p. 144.

30. Franz Blankart, "Der Neutralitätsbegriff aus logischer Sicht," *Discordia concors,* a tribute to Edgar Bonjour (Basel, 1968), p. 607 ff.

31. André Gorz, quoted in J. Halliday, "Svizzera, l'eldorado borghese," *Quaderni Piacentini,* no. 39, November 1969, p. 206.

32. Max Petitpierre quoted in Jacques Freymond, "Neutralité et neutralism," *Revue des travaux de l'Académie des sciences morales et politiques* (Paris, 1966), p. 98.

33. Blankart, op. cit., p. 617.

Part Four: Vanquishing the Victors

1. Castelmur, op. cit.

2. Quoted in *Das Israelitische Wochenblatt* (Zurich), October 11, 1996.

3. Monnier, op. cit.

4. Walter Stucki, *Von Pétain zur Vierten Republik* (Vichy, 1944; Bern, 1947).

5. For details of the settlement, see Castelmur, op. cit., p. 354 ff.

6. Ernst Nobs, the first Social Democrat to become a government minister, was coopted by the bourgeois parties when the tide of war had turned.

7. Kästli, op. cit., p. 247.

8. Daniel Frei, "Das Washingtoner Abkommen von 1946," *Schweizerische Zeitschrift für Geschichte* (Zurich), Yr. 19, p. 571.

9. Seymour J. Rubin in conversation with Felix E. Müller, *Die Weltwoche* (Zurich), November 7, 1996.

10. Stenographic bulletin of the Federal Assembly, extraordinary session, June 1946.

11. Paul J. Jolles in *Die Neue Zürcher Zeitung,* October 30, 1996.

12. See especially Durrer, op. cit.; Walter Spahni, *Der Ausbruch der Schweiz aus der Isolation nach dem Zweiten Weltkrieg, untersucht anhand ihrer Aussenhandelspolitik 1944–1947* (Frauenfeld, 1977); Inglin, op. cit.; Gian Trepp, *Die Bank für Internationalen Zahlungsausgleich im Zweiten Weltkrieg. Bankgeschäfte mit dem feind. Von Hitlers Europa-Bank zum Instrument des Marshall-Planes* (Zurich, 1993); Nicolas Kaloy, *SOS Banques Suisses. Leur responsabilité, leurs abus* (Geneva, 1996); Georg Kreis, "Der umstrittene Sieg über die Sieger," *Die Neue Zürcher Zeitung,* May 25, 1996.

13. Federal Archive. Document obtained from Shraga Elam.

14. Ibid.

15. Quoted in Frei, op. cit., p. 590.

16. Ibid.

17. Both quotations come from Monnier, op. cit.

18. Trepp, op. cit., p. 97 f.

19. Wilfred G. Burchett, *Der kalte Krieg in Deutschland* (Berlin, 1950), p. 216.

Part Five: The Holocaust Haul

1. See the interpretation of the Rheingold myth in Louis Janover, *Nuit et brouillard du révisionisme* (Paris, 1996), p. 9 f.

2. In the original: "Ces communautés que la nuit avait englouties pour les recracher vers un ciel en flammes." Wiesel, *Et la mer n'est pas remplie,* vol. II, p. 530.

3. Hannah Arendt, *Origins of Totalitarianism* (New York, 1951).

4. Yves Fricker, *Helvetia au miroir* (Geneva, 1996), p. 67.

5. Häsler, op. cit., p. 338.

6. Picard, op. cit., p. 368.

7. Schmid, op. cit., p. 203 f.

8. Christoph Graf, "Die Schweiz und die Flüchtlinge 1933–1945," *Studien und Quellen* (periodical of the Swiss Federal Archive, Bern), no. 22, 1996.

9. Stefan Mächler, "Ein Abgrund zwischen zwei Welten," ibid., p. 137.

10. See especially Saul Friedländer, *L'antisémitisme nazi* (Paris, 1971), and *Pie XII et le IIIe Reich* (Paris, 1964).

11. Saul Friedländer, *Quand vient le souvenir* (Paris, 1978), p. 86 ff.

12. Ibid.

13. Ibid.

14. Häsler, op. cit. I quote here from the revised edition (Zurich, 1992), in which he reproduces an article by Hermann Böschenstein, editor of the *Nationalzeitung* (Basel), August 24, 1942.

15. Guido Koller, "Entscheidungen über Leben und Tod. Die behördliche Praxis in der schweizerischen Flüchtlingspolitik während des Zweiten Weltkrieges," in Graf, "Die Schweiz und die Flüchtlinge," p. 19 ff.

16. Mächler, op. cit., p. 140 ff.

17. Ibid., p. 173.

18. In November 1938 Herschel Grynszpan, a seventeen-year-old Jewish youth, murdered Ernst vom Rath, a German diplomat at the Paris embassy, having mistaken him for the ambassador. The Nazis took advantage of this incident to launch a pogrom, the infamous *Kristallnacht,* on November 9.

19. Bonjour, op. cit., vol. III, p. 41.

20. Christoph Graf, "Die politische Haltung der Schweiz 1938–1939," lecture delivered at the international symposium "Der Weg in den Zweiten Weltkrieg," Bern University, June 25, 1988.

21. From the log of the Grenzackerstrasse (Riehen) frontier post. Quoted in Koller, op. cit., p. 59.

22. Gerhart Riegner, "Die Führung der jüdischen Gemeinschaft in der Schweiz während des Zweiten Weltkriegs," *Das Neue Israel* (Zurich), September 1985, p. 37.

23. Tanner, op. cit.; Philippe Marguerat, *La Suisse face au IIIe Reich* (Lausanne, 1991).

24. Häsler, op. cit., p. 48.

25. The introduction of compulsory visas for Austrian Jews was tantamount to closing the frontier.

26. Heinz Roschewski, "Heinrich Rothmund in seinen persönlichen Akten. Zur Frage des Antisemitismus in der schweizerischen Flüchtlingspolitik 1939–1945," in Graf, op. cit., p. 107 ff.

27. Ibid., p. 122.

28. Ibid.

29. Ibid.

30. Ibid.

31. Alfred Cattani, in *Die Neue Zürcher Zeitung,* March 15–16, 1986, quoted in Roschewski, p. 124.

32. Picard, op. cit., p. 407.

33. Jean-Claude Favez, *Warum schwieg das Rote Kreuz? Eine Internationale Organisation und das Dritte Reich* (Munich, 1994), p. 226.

34. Stefan Keller, *Délit d'humanité, l'affaire Grüninger* (Lausanne, 1994).

35. *L'Hebdo* (Lausanne), September 19, 1996.

36. Quoted in Anne-Frédérique Widmann, "Fonds juifs: Le Crédit Suisse ouvre une brêche dans cinquante ans de silence," *Le Nouveau Quotidien* (Lausanne), October 10, 1996; see also Oliver Schumacher, "Der lange Schatten des Holocaust," *Die Zeit* (Hamburg), September 13, 1996.

37. Quoted by Johannes von Dohnanyi, "Der heilige Zorn der alten Dame schreckt die Gnomen," *Die Weltwoche* (Zurich), October 31, 1996.

38. Roger de Weck in *Der Tagesanzeiger* (Zurich), October 26–27, 1996.

39. Federal Law Relating to Banks and Savings Banks, Art. 47. Maurice Aubert's comments on the law and regularly updated analyses of the administration of justice can be found in *Fiches juridiques* (Geneva).

40. Hans Ulrich Kellerhals in conversation with Beat Kappeler, *Die Weltwoche* (Zurich), October 24, 1996.

41. In major banks, two board members are always apprised of the real identity of holders of numbered accounts. This rule exists to combat temptation.

42. Picard produced this expert opinion at the request of Lawrence Lever of the BBC, London, in January 1993.

43. The Third Reich's outstanding debts exceeded 1.2 billion Swiss francs.

44. Picard, op. cit., p. 10.

45. Ibid., p. 11.

46. The law comprised sixteen articles. The maximum fine for violations was set at 10,000 Swiss francs.
47. Picard, op. cit., p. 33.
48. Quoted by Michaël von Orsouw, in "Herrenlose Vermögen: Die Juden wollen Gerechtigkeit," *Revue Facts* (Zurich) no. 45, 1996.
49. Jean Halpérin, in conversation with Jean-Christoph Aeschlimann, *Der Tagesanzeiger* (Zurich), December 12, 1996.
50. Gerhart Riegner, in conversation with Hubert Moser, *Die Sonntagszeitung* (Zurich), October 27, 1996.
51. Roger de Weck in *Der Tagesanzeiger* (Zurich), January 11–12, 1997.

Epilogue: Hope

1. Herbert Lüthy, quoted by Felix Müller in *Die Weltwoche* (Zurich), December 26, 1996.
2. All who acted contrary to the Swiss government's monstrous directives were penalized.
3. Tanner, op. cit, p. 16.
4. Jean-François Bergier, in conversation with Urs Zurlinden and Daniel Dunkel in *Revue Facts* (Zurich), January 9, 1997.

Afterword

1. Frank A. Meyer, "Jude, mach dass Du wegkommst!" *Der Sonntagsblick* (Zurich), No. 28, July 13, 1997.
2. Hans Ulrich Jost in *Der Bund* (Bern), June 11, 1997.
3. *Cash* (Zurich), September 26, 1997.
4. *Der Blick* (Zurich), June 20, 1997.
5. Ibid.
6. See especially "Führerbefehl: Schont die Schweiz!" *Cash* (Zurich), August 8, 1997, and "Und sie rollen doch," September 26, 1997 (and the accompanying extensive documentation).
7. Willi A. Boelcke in *Cash* (Zurich), August 8, 1997.

8. Alan G. Hevesi in *Die Sonntagszeitung* (Zurich), October 11–12, 1997.

9. *Neue Zürcher Zeitung* (Zurich), October 7, 1997.

10. The matter was raised by National Councilor Helmut Hubacher on October 8, 1997.

Acknowledgments

Raoul Ouédraogo and Arnaud Frauenfelder, assistants at Geneva University, helped to sift, classify, and check the extensive documentation underlying this book. Juan Gasparini provided me with important documents relating to Nazi exports of capital to South America.

Catherine Lorenz produced fair copies of the successive versions of the manuscript with great personal commitment and professional competence.

Daniel Bourgeois of the Swiss Federal Archive afforded me the benefit of his outstanding expert knowledge and friendly assistance. I could not have completed my research without the practical advice and bibliographic recommendations of other, internationally recognized historians who have researched Switzerland's relations with the Third Reich. Foremost among these are Jean-Claude Favez, Philippe Burrin, Shraga Elam, and Hans Ulrich Jost.

Valuable explanations of problems specific to banking techniques were given me by Renaud Gautier of Geneva, himself a private banker.

I obtained inside information about governmental and bank activities, as well as many confidential documents, some of vital importance, from persons who do not, for obvious reasons, wish their names to be mentioned. Their manifold contributions to the writing of this book sprang from deep personal conviction.

Erica Deuber-Pauli submitted the various versions of the manuscript to critical scrutiny and offered me sound advice.

Karl Heinz Bittel, my editor, rendered me valuable assistance in every way.

I owe a debt of gratitude to all the above.

Jean Ziegler

Index